AFRICAN LEGAL SINGULARITIES

Africa's Pioneering Contribution to Law and Practice

Translated from French by

Philip Akudugu ABUGRI

Alioune SALL

AFRICAN LEGAL SINGULARITIES

Africa's Pioneering Contribution to Law and Practice

Translated from French by

Philip Akudugu ABUGRI

Sénégal
L'Harmattan

By the same author

Singularités juridiques africaines. Ce que l'Afrique apporte au droit, 2023
L'émotion et la raison. L'Afrique face à la justice internationale, 2020
Disputes on human rights violation before the ecowas court of justice, 2019
Le contentieux de la violation des droits de l'homme devant la cour de justice de la CEDEAO, 2019
La justice de l'intégration. Réflexions sur les institutions judiciaires de la CEDEAO et de l'UEMOA - DEUXIÈME ÉDITION REVUE, CORRIGÉE ET AUGMENTÉE, 2018
Les relations extérieures de la CEDEAO, 2016
L'affaire Hissène Habré. Aspects judiciaires nationaux et internationaux, 2013
Les mutations de l'intégration des Etats en Afrique de l'Ouest
Une approche institutionnelle, 2007

10 VDN, Sicap Amitié 3, Lotissement Cité Police, DAKAR

senharmattan@gmail.com
senlibrairie@gmail.com

ISBN : 978-2-336-50388-2
EAN : 9782336503882

Since we have acknowledged that the humanity of all nations is the heritage of all humanity, if African traditions are not collected in time and recorded in writing, they will one day be missing from the universal archives of humanity.

Amadou Hampaté Ba

TABLE OF CONTENTS

Chapter 1 -- **13**
Hospitality clauses: dialogue before the letter of the law ----------- **13**
I. The formulation of hospitality clauses ---------------------------- 16
A. Consistency of Choice-- 16
B. The virtues of choice --- 21
II. interpretation of hospitality clauses ------------------------------ 33
A. A basis of jurisdiction -- 33
B. A centre for disseminating reference standards -------------- 37

Chapter 2 -- **41**
The fabulous destiny of the public authorities' regulatory body-- **41**
I. In the beginning was a "constitutional council"------------------ 43
A. Restraint as a choice -- 44
B. Abiding Bias-- 50
II. The African Inversion -- 54
A. The letter of the law-- 55
B. In the case law -- 58

Chapter 3 -- **73**
Tamed sovereignty -- **73**
I. IN AFRICA: THE DISMANTLING OF SOVEREIGNTY------- 75
A. Constitutional formulae and their interpretation-------------- 75
B. Theoretical Justification -- 83
II. IN EUROPE AND AMERICA: QUALMS ABOUT SOVEREIGNTY -- 87
A. Difficulty of articulating the relinquishment of sovereignty --- 87
B. The difficulty of ceding sovereignty ----------------------------- 94

Chapter 4 --103
The usages of a people or the dialectic of diversity and unity..103I
. TOPICAL ASPECTS OF THE BREAK ------------------------------105
A. Of Polysemy and Bias--106
B. Direct rather than indirect protection ------------------------110
of the people--110
II. Strategic aspects of the break--125
A. Addressing ethnic and minority issues-----------------------126
B. Containing the risk of secession--------------------------------131

Chapter 5 --137
ALTERNATIVE JUSTICE: SWAYING THE HOLD OF THE DICTATOR'S SWORD---137
I. Internally: a rediscovery of the ambiguity of justice------------141
A. On the question of legitimacy---------------------------------142
B. In terms of efficiency---150
II. externally: the international community's vacillations --------155
A. Exaltation--155
B. Doubt --158

Chapter 6: Two West African Bright Spots: Constitutional Treaty and Global Citizenship --169
I. On Constitutionality ---171
A. The Actual Constitutional Underpinnings of the ECOWAS --172
Protocol ---172
B. The Ambiguities of the "European Constitution"-----------179
II. On Citizenship --189
A. Precedence of the ECOWAS Protocol-------------------------190
B. The ECOWAS Protocol: Room for Improvement -----------192

Chapiter 7: The Imperative of Impartiality or the Flawed Concept of Electoral Law --195
I. The shortcomings of traditional methods of regulating elections ---197

A. The Governmental Model--198
B. The Political and Judicial Model----------------------------------205
II. The African path to impartiality------------------------------------211
A. A homegrown creation ---211
B. Ambitious mechanisms ---213

Chapter 8: An Unidentified Legal Object: The OHADA common court of justice and arbitration---221
I. a substantive revolution ---222
B. Qualitative aspects ---224
II. A procedural revolution ---228
A. From the appellate standpoint------------------------------------228
B. From the point of view of the classical principles -----------237
of international litigation---237

Chapter 9: Reforming Democracy : Building New Spaces for Dialogue ---247
I. The Crises of Democracy --248
A. Challenging established power-------------------------------------249
B. In quest of the lost power: re-discovering the "people" and the "citizen" --255
II. TWO AFRICAN RESPONSES --------------------------------------260
A. The National Conferences--260
B. The Forum for Democratic Debate --------------------------------269

Chapter 10: The right of intervention of the African Union--------277
I. A break from the celebration of state sovereignty --------------278
A. On general international law---------------------------------------279
B. On 'regional' law--282
II. a shift in the contemporary challenges to state sovereignty--286
A. On the notion of sovereignty--------------------------------------287
B. On the Attempt to 'Moralise' the Practice of Protection ----297

CHAPTER 1

HOSPITALITY CLAUSES: DIALOGUE BEFORE THE LETTER OF THE LAW

"The narrative capitalisation of law... is now rivalled by a geographical capitalisation of the law ".

J Allard and A Garapon,
Judges in globalisation. The new legal revolution.

A remarkable phenomenon that has captured the attention of legal scholars and publicists almost everywhere in the world in recent years has been the formation of a kind of collective consciousness, an intellectual and transnational solidarity between judicial actors from different countries or legal systems.

Globalisation, which has not left the law untouched, has of course played its part in this. The shrinking of the world and of objective solidarities, the similarity or analogy of the issues dealt with by a judiciary whose rising prominence is another sign of the times, the iterative or cyclical nature of the debates around these issues, themselves driven by the rapid spread of information, are all factors that have contributed to what is known as the " Judicial dialogue".

The protection of human rights is a prime example of this type of exchange of case law and mutual attention between national and international judicial authorities. While it is not the only one, it is undoubtedly the sector in which transnational judicial awareness has been most vigorously expressed, thereby delivering another victory to the *ius-naturale* doctrine of human rights, which defends precisely the idea that these rights, necessarily detached from the contingencies of time and place, and escaping any national determination, find their roots and their justification in what is best shared between humans: their humanity.

The Judicial dialogue - a concept that is provisionally taken for granted here, but around which so many questions could, in our view, be raised - is the result of the way the world moves and of the dynamic of rapprochement brought about by this phenomenon: rapprochement between people, rapprochement between economic, political, and judicial systems. It applies to everyone, and it does not spare legal norms and their application or interpretation. But what is being presented as "the new legal revolution"[1] has a specific African flavour to it. Even before the phenomenon took hold, as we have just emphasised, it had been anticipated, so to speak. The African Charter on Human and Peoples' Rights (ACHPR), around which the African human and peoples' rights protection mechanism is built, contains provisions that have no equivalent in any other protection mechanism. These provisions organise, codify, and systematise cooperation between judicial authorities, authorising protection bodies to draw inspiration from rules and practices devised in other protection frameworks. The ACHPR is therefore unique in that it provides a framework for receiving external sources. In so doing, the African document highlights its forward-looking, prophetic dimension, as what is known today as the Judicial dialogue has been enshrined or sealed since 1981, when it was adopted. In fact, in no other international human rights protection mechanism is there such a clear and

---

[1] Sub-title of the publication by J. Allard and A. Garapon cited in italics.

deliberate openness to standards from elsewhere, to use the words of the French professor Jean Carbonnier.

These provisions, which we have chosen to refer to here as the "hospitality clauses", are Articles 60 and 61 of the ACHPR. They read as follows:

> Article 60:
>
> "The Commission shall be guided by international law relating to human and peoples' rights, in particular the provisions of the various African instruments relating to human and peoples' rights, the provisions of the United Nations Charter, the Charter of the Organisation of African Unity, the Universal Declaration of Human Rights, the provisions of other instruments adopted by the United Nations and by African countries in the field of human and peoples' rights as well as the provisions of various instruments adopted within specialised agencies of the United Nations of which the parties to the present Charter are members".
>
> Article 61:
>
> "The Commission shall also take into consideration, as auxiliary means of determining the rules of law, other international conventions, be they general or special, establishing rules expressly recognised by the Member States of the Organisation of African Unity, African practices in accordance with international norms relating to human and peoples' rights, customs generally accepted as being the law, the general principles of law recognised by African nations as well as case law and doctrine".

These two provisions, which in fact apply to the two protection bodies currently in existence, the Commission and the Court, the omission of the latter from the text being explained by the fact that it did not exist at the time the Charter was drafted, are unprecedented in international human rights law. They formalise and even encourage borrowing from other systems. Their very wording should not be trivialised, because beyond the permission in principle that it carries, it embodies a subtle approach to safeguarding human rights. The wording of the two articles is, therefore, an initial source of interest (I). But the complex formed by these provisions has also provided the basis for a bolder approach to interpreting the permission granted, a kind of launching pad for interpretative adventurism by the organs of protection. This has, in fact, enabled these bodies not only to draw on it for jurisdictional authority, but also to use it as a pretext for expanding the body of rules to which they refer when dispensing justice (II).

I. The formulation of hospitality clauses

To understand the singular nature of the choice made by the African human rights protection mechanism, it is necessary to consider the very content of the option (A) and its innovative nature (B).

A. Consistency of Choice

A rapid exegesis of the two provisions mentioned above reveals that African States have opened at least three «windows» to the outside world. The first are texts adopted within the framework of the United Nations and its specialised agencies. That is quite a lot. The conventions concluded within the framework of the UN alone form an impressive group, to which must be added the others that have been adopted within WHO, ILO, UNESCO, FAO and so on. Moreover, nothing suggests that the borrowings likely to be made are limited to treaties or conventions. Legal instruments that are intrinsically non-binding could perfectly well be drawn upon by African protection bodies, as the terms of Article 60 are quite broad.

In fact, the African Commission on Human and Peoples' Rights has often referred to "soft law" instruments. Secondly, the text refers to "international law on human and peoples' rights". Here too, it goes without saying that this refers to both "formal" international law, consisting of texts, and "informal" law, especially case law. But the latter is dealt with even more specifically in Article 61 of the ACHPR. There is no doubt, as pointed out by Maurice Kamto[2] that case law, which is the main vehicle for borrowing, covers decisions by courts with universal jurisdiction as well as regional courts, and by specialised tribunals as well as tribunals with broad or general jurisdiction.

Moreover, in the codification of the borrowings envisaged by the ACHPR, articles 60 and 61 are not the only relevant references, although they are most often cited. A provision such as article 45 is more "discreet", and therefore less often brandished, but there is no doubt that in the general debate on hospitality clauses, it remains relevant. This article states that the mission of the African Commission on Human and Peoples' Rights is to "cooperate with other African or international institutions concerned with the promotion and protection of human and peoples' rights. While "Cooperate " with others may imply borrowing, it does not in any way circumscribe such cooperation to formal bilateral and diplomatic relations.

In addition to the range of usable sources, it is worth looking at the actual wording of the provisions in question. What emerges is, as noted by Emmanuel Decaux, the subtlety of the dialectic, " rich in promise "[3], he writes, between the universal and the regional. More precisely: between the regional and the universal because the African singularity consists precisely in using the regional as

---

[2] Kamto M., Commentaire de l'article 61, in Kamto M. (dir.), *La Charte africaine des droits de l'homme et des peuples et le Protocole portant création de la Cour africaine des droits de l'homme. Commentaire article par article,* Bruylant, 2011, p.1129.

[3] Decaux E., Commentaire de l'article 60, in Kamto M., (dir.), op cit., p. 1116.

leverage to reach the universal, starting from the particular to reach the general. In this way, the option that has been chosen is locally rooted, which is the whole point of the recurring " African references". However, putting down roots paves the way for openness: it is not an inward-looking process, but a prologue to hospitality or a prelude to the journey.

It is therefore important to understand that in the approach of African states, the universal and the regional are not opposed to each other, in principle. On the contrary, the latter can birth the former; it can birth the universal. This is because the universal is not a given, but a construct, the work of the States themselves. The dialogue between the universal and the regional must therefore be approached from a perspective that is both dynamic and commercial, in the sense that trade means exchange. The universal is not a singular, it is a plural, or more precisely: a synthesis of pluralities, the balanced and symbiotic form of diversity, not a monolithic magma but a melting pot. From this point of view, the universal is not imposed on States, but it is the States that conceive of it, inform it, and give it substance. Article 60 of the African Charter reflects this subtle dialectic: it is in self-affirmation that openness to others is nested, and self-awareness opens onto the awareness of others.

In this hospitable predisposition, in this openness to the universal, the reference to the Universal Declaration of Human Rights must be taken seriously[4]. This legal instrument is the only one to be expressly cited in Article 60, and it has a specific feature: it has a degree of universality that very few human rights instruments have. At least, three reasons account for this.

Firstly, the Declaration is the consensual instrument par excellence, given the historical context in which it was adopted. In 1948, the world was in the middle of the Cold War and getting the

---

[4] Ibid.

two opposing political blocs to come to an agreement was no mean feat. Yet it was against this backdrop that this document was drawn up. The vote that sealed its adoption says it all: forty-three countries in favour, five abstentions[5] and five refusals to participate[6]. The text is based on a transactional spirit, which explains, for example, why it does not include the right to private property, which is not acceptable to communist countries. The African states, which did not exist when the Declaration was drafted, are nevertheless aware of the symbolic and historical importance of this text. In a way, they are re-appropriating it, revealing a form of generosity and open-mindedness. This is the second element that needs to be highlighted. It should come as no surprise, then, that the African Court on Human and Peoples' Rights, established only in 2006, has helped to affirm the customary crystallisation of the Declaration, after the fashion of the International Court of Justice in the case of " Diplomatic and Consular Staff of the United States in Tehran"[7]. In a judgment handed down on 22 March 2018, in " Anudo Ochieng Anudo vs Republic of Tanzania", the African Court held that the Universal Declaration of Human Rights of 9 January 1948 was "an integral part of international customary law"[8].

It should also be noted that the tropism of the Declaration is not confined to the African human rights protection mechanism. It exists across the entire African Union system (it should be remembered that the ACHPR, which refers to the Universal Declaration, was adopted within the framework of the OAU). The Declaration is the only instrument referred to in the Constitutive

---

[5] Saudi Arabia, Byelorussia, Poland, Czechoslovakia, and Ukraine.

[6] Honduras, South Africa (apartheid regime), USSR, Yemen, and Yugoslavia.

[7] ICJ, Judgement of 24 May 1980, p. 42: The arbitrary deprivation of their liberty and the use of severe physical restraint are manifestly incompatible with the principles of the Charter of the United Nations and the fundamental rights set out in the Universal Declaration of Human Rights. ».

[8] §76 of the judgment

Act of the African Union adopted on 11 July 2000, and there is no other textual reference in this treaty. It therefore holds a real attraction for African bodies, an attraction explained precisely by its universal content.

The third and final point that needs to be emphasised regarding the special place given to the Declaration by the ACHPR is the existence, on this specific point, of an African originality. Indeed, the other regional legal instruments for the protection of human rights acknowledge this UN General Assembly resolution and refer to it, but in ways that differ from the approach of the African Charter. In the American and European conventions on human rights, the Declaration is placed among the symbolic accessories. It is referred to very sparingly, so to speak, since it is the preambles to both texts that refer to it, without more. At best, it can be said that they claim its symbolic heritage, follow in its historical wake, and proclaim a form of continuity with it. But nothing else. More precisely, the Declaration has not been turned into an operational litigation instrument. In the African system, it has this decisive property: it is a tool at the service of the interpreter or the judge; it is a legal instrument available and endowed with immediate contentious effectiveness.

The proof is to be found both in the textual statements and in the case law. With regard to the wording of the regional conventions, we note that the Declaration is referred to in the preamble to the American and European texts, respectively, in the following non-committal terms: " Considering that these principles have been enshrined in the Charter of the Organization of American States, in the American Declaration of the Rights and Duties of Man, in the Universal Declaration of Human Rights, and that they have been reaffirmed and developed in other international instruments...", "Reiterating that, in accordance with the Universal Declaration of Human Rights, the ideal of a free man (...) can only be achieved through the promotion and protection of human rights and fundamental freedoms.) can only be achieved by creating conditions under which everyone may enjoy their rights", and «Whereas the Universal Declaration of Human Rights, proclaimed by the General Assembly of the United Nations on 10 December 1948, aims at achieving the universal and effective recognition and observance of the rights set forth therein...". As we can see, the proclamation is solemn, but it goes no further than a " petition of principle" in these American and European statements. In the African Charter, the reference is found in the body of the treaty, and above all, it is explicitly stipulated that the supervisory body is «inspired" by it. The statements are, therefore, not quite the same. The 1948 Declaration represents a kind of quintessence of universalism, which is why it occupies a special place in the architecture of the ACHPR and in subsequent case law.

B. The virtues of choice

The choice that African states have made through hospitality clauses is praiseworthy in several respects.

Academic writers are unanimous in emphasising the innovative nature of these clauses. Emmanuel Decaux notes that it is the result of a "much more ambitious approach" than that of other human rights protection mechanisms, insofar as it tends "to combine the regional guarantee of human and peoples' rights, in all their specifically African dimensions, while taking account of the major reforms of international human rights law"[9]. L. Hennebel and H. Tigroudja note that "the African situation is exceptional, and no other human rights treaty contains such referral clauses"[10]. In other regional protection frameworks, reference to external sources "is always the result of free interpretation by the bodies themselves "[11].

---

[9] Decaux E., op cit., p 1108.

[10] Hennebel L. and Tigroudja H., *Traité de droit international des droits de l'homme,* Paris, Pédone,2016, p. 150.

[11] Ibid.

Maurice Kamto also notes that "Articles 60 and 61 are specific to the African Charter on Human and Peoples' Rights"[12]. Laurence Burgorgue-Larsen also describes the choice made in noteworthy terms. After underscoring the distinctive African feature of "faithful de-compartmentalisation" whereas other systems practise "rebellious de-compartmentalisation" for, being far removed from the texts[13], she observes, " the African system of protection gives pride of place to sources " from elsewhere". It gives uncommon freedom to the interpreters of the law when the need to clarify the meaning of the rights and duties of men and peoples enshrined in the Banjul Charter arises. It confers exceptional substantive jurisdiction on the Arusha Court, enabling it to be both an African regional judge and a universal judge "[14]. The choice that has been made has a prophetic, predictive resonance because, continues the author, "whereas the law was for a long time a closed system, a system delimited - not to say cloistered - by self-sufficient rules steeped in verticality and hierarchy, those days are gone. The law is now open to the world, to its metamorphoses, now destabilising, now reassuring, as they take shape within societies"[15].

Hospitality clauses are not only remarkable because they are unique and unparalleled in terms of the world's systems. They are also remarkable because there is something prophetic and visionary about them. In 1981, who could have predicted the interactions and reciprocal influences of case law that we are witnessing today, and which form the substance of the Judicial dialogue, a phenomenon whose name may be debatable, but whose very reality no one would dream of contesting, if we consider it to consist in the circulation and borrowing of case law?

---

[12] Kamto M., op cit, p.1118.

[13] Burgorgue-Larsen L., *Les 3 Cours régionales des droits de l'homme in Context. La justice qui n'allait pas de soi,* Paris, Pédone, 2020, pp. 249, 256.

[14] Burgorgue-Larsen L., op cit, pp. 244-245.

[15] Ibid.

Articles 60 and 61 of the African Charter are the very adumbration of dialogue and, from this point of view, their inclusion is a true stroke of genius. They also bear witness to an unabashed openness, a form of generosity that should be highlighted. "Hospitality", a word that has somewhat fallen out of fashion, is the virtue to which they resolutely aspire.

The African distinctiveness is undeniable from another point of view. In other parts of the world, judges have also been able to open their minds to outside sources and incorporate them into their reasoning and judgement. Most of the time, this has been done based on what Emmanuel Decaux calls the " most favoured freedom clause"[16] and Laurence Burgorgue-Larsen "the imperative of non-regression"[17]. The idea is to maintain the level of protection of rights at a minimum, to exclude any reasoning, approach or reference that would result in lowering this level of preservation. In the American and European systems, the two provisions that perform this qualitative stabilisation function are articles 29 and 53. Their wording is almost identical:

> Article 29 of the American Convention on Human Rights:
>
> " No provision of this Convention shall be interpreted as:
>
> a) Permitting any State Party, group, or person to suppress the enjoyment or exercise of the rights and freedoms recognized in this Convention or to restrict them to a greater extent than is provided for herein.
>
> b) Restricting the enjoyment or exercise of any right or freedom recognized by virtue of the laws of

---

[16] Decaux E., op cit., p. 1106.

[17] Burgorgue-Larsen, op cit., p. 249.

any State Party or by virtue of another convention to which one of the said states is a party;

c) Precluding other rights or guarantees that are inherent to the human persona or derived from representative democracy as a form of government;

d) Abolishing or limiting the effect that the American Declaration of the Rights and Duties of Man and other international acts of the same nature may have".

Article 53 of the European Convention on Human Rights:

" Nothing in this Convention shall be construed as limiting or derogating from any of the human rights and fundamental freedoms which may be recognised under the laws of any High Contracting Party or under any other agreement to which it is a party".

Such provisions deal with the relationship that the American and European conventions are likely to have with external sources. But it will be agreed that they do not follow the same approach as articles 60 and 61 of the ACHPR. An in-depth examination of these texts reveals that the way in which they apprehend the Other is not entirely the same. It is not certain, in our view, that the American and European provisions, in themselves, are dedicated to a philosophy of openness. They stipulate that no provision of these instruments can or should be interpreted as "degrading" a recognised right. The question then is whether these directives should be understood as hospitality clauses. Nothing is less certain, even if, it must be reiterated, the afore-mentioned articles may have been used to import sources. There is room for doubt because *the referenced provisions speak less of others than of themselves.* The evocation of the Other could be no more than a pretext for positioning oneself, for casting oneself into the limelight. We talk about the Other to better talk about ourselves, to better highlight our own value. It is not " the Other like myself", to paraphrase José Saramago, but first and foremost "concern for oneself", to quote Michel Foucauld.

There has perhaps been a tendency to analyse articles 29 and 53 as containing not only the question of inter-subjectivity (relationship with other norms), but also that of hospitality (reception and promotion of other norms). While inter-subjectivity is not a problem here (because the articles in question do refer to the question of their relationship with others), hospitality is certainly less obvious. Indeed, when I state that I am inherently and absolutely incapable of being an obstacle to the fulfilment of the Other - that is, of a right stipulated by the Other - it is perhaps myself that I value more than that Other. Openness is then only hinted at and does not necessarily lead to acceptance and hospitality. At the extreme, the "most favoured freedom clause" could be a means of manipulation of the Other insofar as it veils self-celebration, insofar as evoking the Other becomes the best way of talking about oneself.

In terms of a predisposition to hospitality, then, there is no common ground between the African statement and the others. This is the difference between the positive affirmation of a willingness to welcome external sources and the proclamation of a determination never to be an obstacle to these sources being considered because we cannot, by definition, constitute such an obstacle. A friendship pact in one case, a non-aggression pact in the other.

But there is something else. The ACHPR does not contain a provision equivalent to that of articles 29 and 53 analysed above. Yet the non-regression clause is common in human rights conventions. It is found, for example, in the International Covenant on Civil and Political Rights[18]and in the Arab Charter on Human Rights[19]. The question then is whether this provision was omitted precisely because, for the drafters of the African Charter, articles 60 and 61 completely made up for it. In other words, these two provisions would be the only ones to govern the question of external sources; they would form the Charter's ministry of external relations, they would be self-sufficient and they would have clearly taken the decision to envisage their relationship with other international conventions differently, in terms of " inspiration" or taking into account, rather than in veiled antagonistic terms of "the instrument offering the best deal", to borrow the words of Emmanuel Decaux[20]. All this calls for reflection and further analysis, but if this possibility were to be confirmed, it would mean that the difference between the African approach and the others would be even more fundamental, would refer to choices of principle and would effectively lead to two quite different conceptions of the relationship with the Other. If true, such an opposition would reinforce some of the observations made earlier about the difference between the two approaches.

In any case, the virtues inherent in the choice of principle expressed in articles 60 and 61 of the CADHP are numerous. In short, they are the same as those that are extolled today when we talk about the "Judicial dialogue".

First and foremost, there is an interest in looking at the Other, and this is the thesis that this book seeks to uphold, since certain African legal experiences, while undeniably rich and innovative, have not, in our view, received the attention they deserve. Mental or intellectual disorientation is first and foremost a test of rationality. Openness to the Other is a measure of self. It is an act of

---

[18] Article 46 of the ICCPR

[19] Article 43 of the Arab Charter.

[20] Decaux E., op cit., p.1106.

generosity that cannot be taken for granted, were it only because it is not necessarily the natural inclination of people or institutions. If organicism exists - this tendency to develop by closing itself off - if the natural movement of any organ is to extend the tentacles of its jurisdiction, if jurisdictions are therefore naturally driven by an expansionist ambition, and if, on the other hand, judging is an act of sovereignty a matter of an attribute defined by its exclusivity, then we must agree that there is a mystery or a paradox of judicial hospitality. J. Allard and A. Garapon are left to wonder: " what are the forces that lead judges to take standards from elsewhere so seriously that they sometimes confer on them more prestige and effectiveness than their own legal arrangement"[21].

Venturing outside oneself, far from one's comfort zone as we say today, is both advantageous and adventurous. Judges have not suddenly become altruistic or philanthropic, but they do so out of self-interest: the interest in supporting their arguments, grounding their judgments, and presenting them as meeting some sort of international or even universal jurisprudential standard. Thus, we cite others, we flex our intellectual muscles against those of others, as Montaigne would say, to show that we are "within the norm", thus protecting oneself against adverse critique.

But you never travel with impunity. By integrating external data, by virtually making it, a criterion for the validity of our own judgement, we run the risk, precisely, of seeing the limits of that judgement exposed. This is the test of rationality inherent in any comparative approach. There is a risk of self-questioning, an exposure to doubt, when we deliberately draw on external sources. Such an approach, which was deliberately adopted by the Africans in the design of their human rights protection mechanism, necessarily involves a process of moderating perspective. The exercise is healthy, in that it encourages the subversion of

---

[21] Allard J. et Garapon A., op cit., p 58.

prejudices and other hardwired ideas. As Allard and Garapon further state « a truth that is deemed universal because it is based on an anthropological discourse suddenly discovers its cultural singularity[22], and "the diversion through other legal cultures enables a critical, and perhaps more rational, reading of one's own. For it is not only the values common to the various legal cultures that are thus revealed and assessed, but also the differences and possibly the contradictions between them", the two authors further posit[23].

Sovereigns are averse to sharing. Exclusive according to the law itself, they have a natural tendency to close themselves off. They develop in the muffled comfort of self-containment, and the openness shown by hospitality clauses is a danger to them. It is well known that when the Supreme Court of the United States, in its ruling in Lawrence vs. Texas, 26 June 2003, drew inspiration from a solution developed by the European Court of Human Rights. This borrowing sparked off a firestorm in Congress. One member of Congress, Tom Feeney, thought it appropriate to remind the Court that "the meaning of the laws of the United States should not be based on judgments, laws, or acts emanating from foreign institutions, unless they inform an understanding of the original meaning of the Constitution "[24]. The United States Supreme Court, at least at certain times in its history, has built up a solid reputation for hostility to outside sources and for holding to an extreme judicial nationalism[25].

In a remarkable article devoted to "The subversive function of comparative law", Horatia Muir Watt highlighted the dissolving

---

[22] Allard J et Garapon A., op cit., p.61.

[23] Ibid.

[24] Cited by Allard J and Garapon A, op cit., p.13.

[25] Tushnet M., « The possibilities of Comparative constitutional Law », *Yale Law Journal,* 1999, pp.1225 et s. Cited by Muir Watt H., « La fonction subversive du droit comparé », *Revue internationale de droit comparé*, 2000, p. 518.

effect that the comparative approach has on "ethnocentrism, i.e., the widespread conviction (regardless of the country) that national categories and concepts are the only ones conceivable"[26]. The beneficial effect of taking an interest in the Other produces a mirror effect described by the author in the following terms:

> " It is first and foremost self-awareness that is fostered by looking at the Other. If the comparativist takes on the appearance of Janus, it is first because the gaze he casts on the other reveals realities not perceived from within the system under observation (...). Secondly, because having seen and understood the other, the comparatist's perception of himself, or of his own rights, is altered. One of the most important advances in contemporary comparative thought consists precisely in the attention given to this critical perception of one's own legal reality informed by a view of the other "[27].

What is ultimately criticised is " the characteristic rationality of Western thought », which « rests on one pillar, the univocal meaning of law "[28]. It goes without saying that essentialist views, those based on the idea that there is *one* meaning of law, necessarily produce monopolistic thinking, that of a *monopoly* over the law, which is in itself a negation, albeit covert, of the legal inventiveness of other societies.

There is also a premonitory, prophetic dimension to the choice of principle made by the ACHPR in 1981. At a time when, as has already been said, no one was yet talking about jurisprudential interaction or Judicial dialogue, the decision was taken to open to

---

[26] Miur Watt H.,op cit., p. 515.

[27] Muir Watt H., op cit, p.518.

[28] Muir Watt H., op cit., p. 517.

external sources. Subsequent history has shown that the drafters of the ACHPR had a brilliant vision, in the truest sense of the word, a pioneering, forward-looking vision. For not only is the global judicial world a reality, but human rights are the breeding ground for these exchanges. Perhaps this was to be expected. Fundamentally *ius naturale,* i.e., universalist, human rights law is, in its very principle, driven by an equalising process. The universality of human rights is a matter of ontology, it cannot be a thing, which of course does not mean that this universality is without nuances - nuances of a cultural nature in particular - or that it is immune to any questioning.

Hospitality clauses are not just about hospitality, their function is not limited to welcoming external norms, they also induce an inter-subjectivity, an existential collusion, which leads to an interlocution. To welcome is to meet, and to meet is to engage in dialogue. What is at stake in this face-to-face dialogue is intelligence, in the original sense of the word. As Robert teaches us, the faculty of knowing, of understanding, or the quality of the mind that understands and adapts easily. Encountering others therefore requires pedagogy, since it is a question of making yourself understood by them too. The clauses of hospitality are not therefore exhausted in the reception, welcome or accommodation phases. By receiving another person, you reveal yourself to them, and from this initial contact comes the exchange, the dialogue in which the aim is to make yourself understood. Hospitality clauses therefore call for pedagogy, all the more so, as Chaïm Perelman points out, since the address in question could well spread well beyond a restricted circle, and reach out to everyone, touching a universal audience.

This pedagogical requirement in the act of judging is at the heart of several contemporary issues of a Legislative and judicial nature. For the legislator, it naturally means drafting legislation at a human level, legislation that is comprehensible and intelligible, as the judges of the Constitution would say, even in Africa. From now on, this intelligibility, which also implies 'accessibility-', both material and intellectual, yielding clarity, becomes a criterion of the 'quality' and ultimately the validity of legal rules. The new educational requirement also demands clarity from judges. Judicial acts must be clear; the law must be as comprehensible as possible.

The. question of the reasoning of judgments and rulings is therefore at stake, since such reasoning may seem abstruse and esoteric, and deciphering it a science for the initiate. The trend of jurisprudence based on the real and intellectual connections between judges, which has its roots in openings such as the African hospitality clauses, can no longer be reconciled with the solitary and casual exercise of the judicial function. Exercised under the watchful eye of others, it becomes subject to their judgments and is obliged, at least factually, to submit to a form of standardisation, of "normalisation", that is to say, subjection to a normative frame of reference. As F. Malhière:

> "As the judge's normative power is no longer in doubt, the judge must assume it and legitimise it through the exercise of his guiding mission in the development of the law. They can no longer afford to take a back seat in the dialogue between legal players, limiting themselves to drawing up a line of case law without specifying its sources or the consequences thereof. The increasing power of judges requires them to maintain a more explicit dialogue with the legislature and with other judges, which will make it possible to enlighten litigants, practitioners, scholars and citizens"[29].

Ultimately, it is justice - whether national or international - that consents to being subjected to the scrutiny of evaluation, not just by

[29] Malhière F., *La brièveté des décisions de justice (Conseil constitutionnel, Conseil d'État, Cour de cassation). Contribution à l'étude des représentations de la justice*, Paris, Dalloz, 2013, p. 563.

insiders but by everyone. Because in this new configuration, the judgement passed on justice ceases to be exclusively expert, exclusively technical. The act of judging takes on a dimension that goes beyond the technical or mechanical aspects of the law; it has cultural, social, and axiological implications. Justice is no longer the preserve of lawyers; it has become a matter for society. It is no exaggeration to suggest that what is at stake, and what instruments such as hospitality clauses have in store, is quite simply a form of "secularisation" of legal institutions, which are thus ' humanised' again.

In more direct and systematic terms, this is called democracy. Openness eventually gives rise to democracy, the democratisation of justice. This democratisation can be understood in two ways. Justice, exercised under public scrutiny, becomes subject to public judgement, and the judge, concerned about the repercussions of what he says, strives to make himself clearly understood, and tries to be pedagogical. F. Malhière writes in this regard that: " the importance of providing the grounds of their rulings is not only technical, but also democratic. The corollary of power is accountability, which is exercised through the reasons advanced for decisions taken by the authorities. By giving reasons for their decisions, judges give an account of the exercise of their power, by expressing it rather than hiding it. As their decisions are addressed to an increasingly wider audience, they need to be drafted in a way that is more explicit, transparent and pedagogical "[30].

Articles 60 and 61 of the ACHPR, the hospitality clauses, thus trigger a virtuous spiral. Being acts of openness, they are also acts of convergence or collusion, which do not place the recipient in a passive position. The interpretation given to them by the African Commission and Court is in keeping with this. It was an ambitious interpretation, which quickly transcended the relatively cautious

---

[30] Malhière F., op cit., p. 571

frame of their wording. The provisions in question very quickly became the impetus for a bold jurisprudential policy, as we shall see.

II. INTERPRETATION OF HOSPITALITY CLAUSES

Articles 60 and 61 are the springboards for a particularly bold interpretative undertaking. The protection bodies took advantage of a relatively innocuous statement to widen their room for manoeuvre, and even to upset the balance established by the ACHPR. Drawing on external sources, they have asserted their jurisdiction over matters not specifically covered by the African Charter. This is a somewhat audacious move, since it relates to jurisdiction itself, a sensitive issue if ever there was one, since it is a matter of public order (A). But the boldness does not stop there. By virtue of the hospitality clauses, the Commission and the Court have in a way freed themselves from the strictures of the Charter, by finding other reference standards and ruling by virtue of other texts. We are no longer really dealing with the permission granted by the provisions in question (which speak of « drawing inspiration from " or "taking into consideration "), but rather with the undermining of textual limits, with the systematic extension of the judge's powers (B).

A. A basis of jurisdiction

The hospitality offered by Articles 60 and 61 goes a long way. The African human rights bodies, the Commission, and the Court, do not refer to them only insofar as they allow external standards to be "inspired" or "taken into consideration". Case law shows that these two bodies go much further. They derive from these two provisions a kind of shelter to seek the basis of their jurisdiction elsewhere. In short, to free themselves from their reference text - the African Charter - to assert their ability to hear a case. The approach is certainly surprising, audacious, and those given to orthodoxy would certainly find fault with it. On a question as crucial as determining jurisdiction, the Charter could have remained the relevant text, on a par with no other. It and it alone gives the measure of the sacrifices of sovereignty that States have willingly accepted; it cannot be any other legal instrument. It should therefore be the judge's compass in this case. Practice, however, reveals deviations from this standard of conduct.

Thus, in *Anudo Ochieng Anudo vs. Republic of Tanzania* (judgement delivered on 22 March 2018), the Court " notes that neither the African Charter on Human and Peoples' Rights nor the International Covenant on Civil and Political Rights contains an article dealing specifically with the right to nationality. On the other hand, the Universal Declaration of Human Rights, which is recognised as a part and parcel of international customary law, provides in Article 15 that "No one shall be arbitrarily deprived of his nationality". The Court therefore considered that it was cloaked with jurisdiction to deal with the issue. In other words, the basis of its jurisdiction is not the African Charter, but the Universal Declaration of Human Rights, the jurisprudential « sneak attack» represented by this circumvention being based on the customary nature of the Declaration. This approach is doubly adventurous: on the one hand, it relies on a " foreign " legal instrument, while, on the other hand, it bases its jurisdiction on an international custom.

In *Media Rights Agenda vs Nigeria* (6 November 2000), which resulted from a communication submitted on 25 May 1998 by a Nigerian NGO, the issue was the failure to respect the rights of defence and an allegedly unfair conviction. As in the *Anudo* case decided by the Court, the Commission made a finding of failure to respect the right to a public trial. The Court points out that " neither the African Charter nor the Commission's Resolution on the right to due process and a fair trial contains any specific provision on the right to a public hearing". The Court remained unfazed, however, declaring immediately afterwards that "this notwithstanding, the

Commission is empowered by Articles 60 and 61 of the African Charter to draw inspiration from international legislation in the field of human and peoples' rights and to take into consideration subsidiary norms other than general and special international conventions, customs generally accepted as law, general principles of law recognised by African States as well as case law and publicist"[31].

Having said that, the Court will look to external sources to establish its jurisdiction. It finds it in Comment 13 of the UN Human Rights Committee on the right to a fair trial, as well as in the « fundamental principles relating to the independence of the judiciary » (drafted within the UN) as well as the Commentary on Article 14 of the ICCPR by the UN Human Rights Committee [32]. As in the *Anudo* judgement, therefore, the basis of the organ's jurisdiction is derived from an instrument other than the African Charter itself. In the operative part of its judgment, the Commission found that some provisions of the ACHPR had been violated, as well as the following Principle 5 of the fundamental principles on the independence of the judiciary. This brings us full circle: starting from an external source to establish its competence to hear the case, the Commission also concludes that there has been a breach of foreign legal instruments.

Sections 60 and 61 of the ACHPR are, therefore, far, very far-reaching. In addition to the boldness of their formal inclusion - an African exception - one must add the boldness of their interpretation. In the two cases referred to above, which gave rise to decisions by judicial and quasi-judicial bodies, it is not simply a question of drawing inspiration from (article 60) or taking into consideration (article 61). These expressions suggest that external sources should be considered laterally that intervention should be

---

[31] Case 224/98, « Media Rights Agenda c Nigeria », §51.

[32] §65 on the ruling.

supplementary, ancillary, subsidiary and not primary, which should remain the prerogative of the ACHPR, the official reference standard.

However, this support function conferred on external sources is thwarted here, since these sources are promoted to an important rank, they play a principal and not a secondary role insofar as they sometimes constitute the very basis of the body's competence. They are therefore elevated to the status of reference standards. On a question as central as that of the statutory capacity to hear a case, on a debate as essential as that of jurisdiction (a question of public policy, we are told), African bodies are free to seek the basis for their intervention outside the established text. We are no longer, to tell the truth, in the orthodoxy of inspiration and consideration suggested by the hospitality clauses. Clearly, these clauses are being used as part of a strategy to go beyond the Charter and circumvent its limits, in a quest for jurisdiction or a desire for jurisdictional authority.

Be that as it may, we can see where, in the African system for the protection of human rights, the codification of appeal to external sources and the institution of hospitality clauses are leading. Moreover, the behaviour of protection bodies has not failed to « rub off » on that of litigants, particularly applicants. Taking note, so to speak, of these bodies' willingness to make room for external sources, applicants will construct arguments referring to these sources, thus provoking a fundamental debate on the subject. The objective result of this trend has not been long in coming. By virtue of Articles 60 and 61, the protection bodies no longer hesitate to refer to external texts when they rule, not on their competence, but on the very merits of the referrals, based on the claims presented to them.

B. A centre for disseminating reference standards

If external standards can constitute a basis for the Court's jurisdiction, this means that applicants are free to refer to such standards on the merits, i.e., in support of their claims. Articles 60 and 61 thus form a kind of epicentre, a focal point for the dissemination of external rules, both upstream (basis for jurisdiction) and downstream (basis for the claims expressed by the applicants). In such circumstances, it is not absurd to wonder whether these hospitality clauses, as they have been interpreted, do not lead to a form of devaluation of the African Charter itself, in the sense that it would be equivalent to these external sources, or would have the same value as them.

In any event, the applicants to the protection bodies do not seem to have been mistaken, since they are "firing on all cylinders", i.e., they do not hesitate to invoke provisions external to the Charter in support of their applications. The litigants have been instructed by the courts themselves: seeing that the judges were basing their decisions on other legal instruments, the claimants have acquired the habit of drawing on other texts to support their claims, the habit of claiming rights based on international conventions other than the ACHPR.

A look at the Court's case law is revealing in this respect. Over the period 2006-2016, for example, it appears that applicants invoked the American Convention on Human Rights in at least four cases, the European Convention on Human Rights in two cases, Protocol No. 1 thereto in one case, the International Covenant on Civil and Political Rights four times before the Commission and twenty-five times before the Court and, finally, the Universal Declaration of Human Rights in twenty cases[33].

---

[33] *Law report of the court,* vol 1 (2006—2016), « Legal Instruments cited », p.XXVII et s.

Some cases have made rather bold use of external sources. The case of "Tangayika Law Society, *The Legal and Human Rights Centre and Reverend Christopher Mtikila vs Tanzania*" led to the African Court's judgment of 14 June 2013. It challenged the right to participate in public affairs. The judges ruled in favour of the applicant, as this right had been violated by the Tanzanian authorities. The solution reached is recommended by the Commission's quasi-jurisprudence, but it is careful to recall the provisions of Article 60 of the ACHPR and, on this basis, relies on the American Convention on Human Rights[34], the ILC's Draft Articles on State Responsibility[35], the ICCPR, Article 25 of which is presented as " reflecting the spirit of Article 13 of the African Charter on Human and Peoples' Rights"[36].

In the judgment of 5 June 2015 in the case of " The successors in title to the late Norbert Zongo, Abdoulaye Nikiam aka Ablasse, Ernest Zongo and Blaise Ilboudo and Mouvement burkinabe des droits de l'homme et des peuples vs Burkina Faso ", the Court again referred to external sources, either textual sources (American Convention on Human Rights)[37] or case law (European Court on Human Rights)[38]. In the same case, the judgment of 28 March 2014 refers to the ECOWAS Treaty[39], the Universal Declaration of Human Rights[40] and the ICCPR[41].

Finally, in *Lohé Issa Konaté v Burkina Faso* of 5 December 2014, which deals with sanctions imposed on a journalist, the African Court again refers to the ECOWAS treaty and to a General

---

[34] §106.

[35] §108.

[36] §107.

[37] Note 26.

[38] Note 25

[39] §180.

[40] §117

[41] §116.

Comment of the UN Human Rights Committee on defamation laws, as well as to the case law of the same Committee and of the European and Inter-American Courts of Human Rights[42].

The drafters of the African Charter on Human and Peoples' Rights doubtless had no idea that Articles 60 and 61, in which they made room for external sources in the interpretative work of the Commission and the Court, would have such far-reaching repercussions. These provisions have had unexpected consequences. Original in terms of the arrangements for the external relations of international human rights conventions, and remarkable for its mere existence, its interpretation and utilization have led to a proliferation of sources that can be invoked before the two protection bodies. The choice made by the designers of the ACHPR ultimately proved to be premonitory, as the reality of contemporary jurisprudential interactions attests. Hospitality clauses are not only unique in their wording, but they are at the heart of major issues in human rights law and justice today.

---

[42] §§160 and 161 of the judgment.

CHAPTER 2

THE FABULOUS DESTINY OF THE PUBLIC AUTHORITIES' REGULATORY BODY

Dialectical suppression means: To suppress while preserving the suppressed, which is sublimated in and by this preserving suppression.

Alexandre Kojève, *Introduction to Reading Hegel*

The birth and establishment in France of a Constitutional Council responsible for reviewing the constitutionality of laws under conditions hitherto unknown in France was a major event in that country's political and constitutional history. As heirs to the French legal and judicial tradition, many African states did not fail, many years later, and in particular because of the political transitions towards pluralism in the 1990s, to adopt a constitutional review model close to that of the former coloniser. Both the name and the very tasks of the new constitutional courts were based on the French model. Subsequent case law also reveals borrowings from the Constitutional Council, imports that are regularly cited, to the extent that we tend to forget that in this same field, African judges have built up a body of case law that is often innovative.

We would like to focus on one of these innovations, which has scarcely attracted the attention of publicists to date.

It revolves around the notion of 'regulation' as understood by the judges of the Constitution. More precisely, it revolves around the concept, developed by the French judge in his famous ruling of 6 November 1962, of a body regulating the activity of the public authorities. It was by attributing such an identity to itself that the Council refused to review the disputed referendum law, which had been adopted pursuant to Article 11 of the 1958 Constitution inspired by General de Gaulle. It is well known that most publicists considered recourse to this provision to be irrelevant, and advocated the use of Article 89, which is specifically devoted to the « review» of the Constitution. No decision has ever been so controversial and scholars so divided, so much so that one of the Council's ex officio members, former French President Vincent Auriol, saw it as an additional reason to distance himself from an institution that some people were quick to see as a threat to the very existence of the Constitution, that some were quick to regard as the creature and instrument of the executive.

This concept of " body regulating the activities of the arms of government», advanced to somewhat justify the refusal to censure the initiative taken by General de Gaulle was, therefore, at the core of the decision. It certainly had a precise meaning and function. However, the same notion, used in Africa, was to take on a completely different meaning, even one opposed to that of the French judge.

The scope of the conceptual reappropriation by African judges must be assessed from two viewpoints. On the one hand, African constitutional judges are going to rely on what Herbert Hart calls the "open texture" of the concept itself– the concept of regulation – o make it play a role opposite to that which the French judge defended, a diversion of meaning which is also the manifestation of a power of interpretation that is assumed and certainly bolder than that of the French judge. On the other hand, African constitutional judges have relied on the notion of regulation to act in highly political areas and in circumstances that it is no exaggeration to describe as perilous. In the African context, the debate therefore goes beyond mere semantic opposition.

The contribution of African constitutional courts has consisted in making the status of "regulatory body" the instrument of an unvarnished intrusion into the functioning of the State, particularly when that functioning runs the risk of being interrupted or paralysed. The distance that separates the French model from the African model is clear. Variations on the notion of regulation have led to two very different understandings of the concept and, subsequently, of the function of the judicial body responsible for applying it. This difference can only be appreciated if we look back at the historical circumstances under which the concept emerged (I). On the other hand, it is important to dispel an impression that the foregoing developments are perhaps likely to create: the impression that only case law has brought about the reversal of the perspectives in question. In fact, the shift that has occurred on the African continent can be found both in the texts, i.e., the Constitutions, and in the case law. In this respect, the break with the French point of view may well be described as total (II).

I. IN THE BEGINNING WAS A « CONSTITUTIONAL COUNCIL »

It is well known that, from the outset, the French constitutional court was intended to play a relatively limited role.

Several factors bear this out. The judgment of 6 November 1962 is precisely in this restrictive sense (A). A lot of water has undoubtedly gone under the bridge since then, with certain developments in the history of this Council and its remit tending, if not to revise, at least to moderate this point of view. These developments, of which the advent of the Preliminary Constitutional Question (2008 constitutional review) is the most recent, have been presented as sealing a kind of emancipation of the French body. However, a closer look at the reality of the situation casts doubts on this, to the extent that the initial position, that of a « modest » council, does not seem to have completely disappeared (B).

A. Restraint as a choice

We shall not repeat here the entire history of the introduction of the review of the constitutionality of laws in France under the Fifth Republic. The desire is to restrict the new body, to keep the spectre of a « rule of judges » at bay as far as possible, and to confine their function to, essentially, mediator, consisting of preventing or arbitrating territorial disputes between the executive and the legislature. In other words, a body high above political society, perched on the pinnacles of the State, and therefore the counterpart of the "organs of the State" in any case somewhat inaccessible to the subjects of the law, i.e., private individuals, since in principle it is not intended to enter the somewhat humdrum field of freedoms. Under these conditions, of course, it is advisable to avoid describing it as "jurisdictional", as such an attribute smacks of the sulphur of contestation and paves the way to sanctions against the authorities.

It all began in 1962, when the President of the Senate, Gaston Monnerville, referred the matter to the Council based on article 61 paragraph 2 of the French Constitution, with a view to assessing the constitutionality of the law that had just been adopted by referendum and that amended the method of electing the President of the Republic. The Council declared that it had no jurisdiction to hear the case. The reasons it gave were essentially as follows: "The jurisdiction of the Constitutional Council is strictly delineated by the Constitution and by the provisions of the Organic Law of 7 November 1958 on the Constitutional Council...the Council cannot therefore be called upon to rule on cases other than those exhaustively provided for by these texts"[43]. Furthermore, " it follows from the spirit of the Constitution, which has made the Constitutional Council *a body that regulates the activity of the public authorities* that the laws that the Constitution intended to refer to in Article 61 are only those passed by Parliament and not those which, adopted by the people following a referendum, constitute the direct expression of national sovereignty"[44]. The French Constitutional Council invokes other considerations, linked in particular to the text of the Constitution and to constitutional review in France, but it is around this mandate that the Council believes it has been assigned that the debate here takes place.

The central notion of a "body regulating the activity of public authorities", based on which the Council declines its jurisdiction, must be linked, more generally, to the very idea that the drafters of the Constitution of the Fifth Republic had in mind regarding the review of constitutionality and of the body responsible for carrying it out. Such a body must remain confined to a limited role, and the review must not unduly upset the political players in general, and the lawmakers, in particular.

There are a few indications, statements and positions that clearly confirm this bias.

First, the assurances given by the leading politicians who inspired the French Constitution, namely General de Gaulle himself and his right-hand man Michel Debré. On 13 June 1958, the Prime Minister replied to René Cassin, who was concerned about the introduction of a genuine review of the constitutionality of laws in France, that such a method of circumscribing political power " was not on the

[43] §1 of ruling n°62-20 DC of 6 November 1962.

[44] § 2 of the ruling.

agenda"[45]. It also seems that the same point of view was expressed to justify Michel Debré's rejection, during the preparatory work on the Constitution, of any procedure whereby the Council would review the constitutionality of laws on referral from the Court of Cassation or the *Conseil d'Etat*.[46] Not only was the very principle of a genuine review of the constitutionality of laws precluded, but the prospect of the Council extending its review to respect for the rights and freedoms set out in the Constitution was promptly rejected, given the subversive potential of such an extension and what the framers of the constitution then considered to be a risk of "rule of the judges . Government Commissioner Raymond Janot even went so far as to assure his audiences that, in principle, the constitutional preamble, which contains such rights and freedoms, " has no legal value".

The limitations of the new body's role are reflected in its name. Neither really a political body, nor frankly a jurisdictional institution, the new body is caught up in a form of nominal indeterminacy, which explains why it is even called a "Council", a relatively neutral concept, a kind of nominal compromise that has the virtue of appeasing the most sceptical. In a lecture given at the *Constitutional Council* itself, Elisabeth Zoller noted that "the Constitutional Council was not originally created as a court. Its main mission was to oversee the separation between law and regulation (...). The Constitutional Council was thus not a court between civil society and the State, but a council with decision-making powers between the four constitutional public authorities entitled to refer matters to it. It came face to face with the

---

[45] Cited by Rousseau D., Gahdoun P.H., Bonnet J. (dir.), *Droit du contentieux constitutionnel*, Paris, LGDJ, 2020, p.29.

[46] Ibid.

consequences of this in 1962 when it had to rule on the constitutional review sought by General de Gaulle"[47]. Michel Debré, again, confirms: "it is neither in the spirit of the parliamentary system, nor in French tradition, to give the courts, i.e., every person who can sue and be sued, the right to examine the value of the law. The project has therefore devised *a special institution* that can be seized by only four authorities: the President of the Republic, the Prime Minister, the two Presidents of the Assemblies, and so on."[48].

The concept of " body regulating the activities of public authorities " is based on this limited area of intervention. When the *Constitutional Council* introduced this concept in its 1962 decision, there was no doubt that it was referring to the narrowness of its own wriggle room and the relative weakness of its powers. In this sense, a regulatory body is distinct from or contrasts with a judicial body. By defining itself as such, the Council signals its agreement with those who conceived it, that it is anything but a jurisdiction. From this perspective, and in concrete terms, the control exercised by the Council essentially consists of monitoring the dividing line between the areas of competence of the Executive and the Legislature and preventing or resolving turf disputes within the State. Publicists have identified three areas in which the Constitutional Court intervenes in this respect. The first relates to what might be called bringing Parliament into line: these are articles 37 (definition of a specific material power), 40 (limitation of the power of parliamentary initiative in the name of financial imperatives) and 41 (reiteration of the principle of the delimitation of powers between the Executive and the Legislature). The second area targeted is the review of the constitutionality of organic laws

---

[47] Zoller E., « Le constitutionnalisme français », lecture delivered at the Constitutional Council on 19 October 2018 (directly accessible on internet).

[48] Ibid. Italics mine.

and the Rules of Procedure of the Assemblies; one will be agreed that its philosophy is also linked to the undertaking to " rationalise parliamentarism ", i.e., to weaken Parliament. Ensuring that international commitments are compatible with the Constitution (Article 54) is the last area in which the Council intervenes[49].

The Council's role is essentially that of a standard-setter, operating in the sphere of standards and overseeing the production of standards. It is in this sense that legal doctrine has no doubt felt entitled to add the qualifier « normative » to « the activity of public authorities » to which the Council refers. There has been a shift in terminology, from case law to doctrine: while the Constitutional Council refers in its decision to its role as "regulator of the activities of the public authorities", doctrine - in the words of Louis Favoreu in particular - is more concerned with "the regulation of the *normative* activities of the public authorities".[50] – thus, slightly modifying the expression. The two expressions are not quite the same, but the addition is no doubt conceivable since, in the Council's mind, a regulatory body is essentially active in the field of standards and not in that of freedoms in particular.

The modifier " normative " is self-evident if we remain within the logic of the Council itself. From the minimalist perspective of this body, the control exercised by the Constitutional Court can only be confined to the supervision of normative activity and, in particular, to the supervision of the territorial limits of the Executive and the Legislature. This is therefore a deliberately abstract form of review because it concerns a dispute over standards. Detached from both individuals, who are concrete subjects of law, and political actors, who are involved in issues of power, the Council adopts an Olympian stance, moving in the

---

[49] Rousseau D et al (dir.), op cit, p.34.

[50] Favoreu L., « Le Conseil constitutionnel, régulateur de l'activité normative des pouvoirs publics », *Revue de droit public*, 1967, pp. 13 et s.

ethereal world of abstract principles: not a rectifier of wrongs, but a stakeholder in the smooth running of the State, not a judge but a regulator[51]. It seems that by restricting the Council's role to the control of normative activity, Louis Favoreu has revealed the reality of its function. The strictly legal nature of the control of regularity entrusted to it, he writes, "confines it within fairly narrow limits (...). As to its purpose, the regulatory function is related to objective and abstract controls " given that "the Council does not have the power to assess the necessity or merits of the regulation referred to it in the light of extra-legal criteria "[52].

Does such a viewpoint align with the notion of regulation? A word will be said later about the ambiguity of this term, but it is clear that the French Constitutional Council's understanding of the concept is in line with that of a number of authors - not all, of course. For G. Marcou, for example, regulation refers to the " Description of a global system and the function that maintains and reproduces the order of such system"[53]. Terms such as "description", " maintenance", " reproduction", undoubtedly suggest the neutrality of the regulator and fit squarely with the French constitutional court's idea of regulation. In any event, from the very first years of its operation, the French judge has clearly indicated that he had no intention of setting himself up as a " judge", either of the public authorities or of individuals.

Can we say that things have changed today? It is common practice, when tracing the history of the establishment of the French Constitutional Council as a court, to cite three significant dates: 1971 (the "Freedom of Association" ruling, which paved the way for litigation concerning the violation of rights and freedoms), 1974

---

[51] Zoller E., op cit.

[52] Favoreu L. op cit, pp.46-47.

[53] Marcou G., « La notion juridique de régulation », *Annuaire Juridique droit administratif* 2006, p.46.

(constitutional reform opening up the possibility for political minorities to bring cases before the Council) and 2008 (the advent of constitutional review by way of exception through the Question Prioritaire de Constitutionnalité, QPC (by which litigants challenge the constitutionality of a given provision in the law). Since then, it seems that the Council's march towards " jurisdictionnalisation " is on. Objectivity dictates, however, that we state that although the restrictive conception of 1962 is no longer entirely appropriate, and although the days of the body regulating the activities of the public authorities seem to be over, the bias towards restraint is still alive and well. This means that consensus on the role and mandates of the French body is far from absolute. Has the Council remained more or less the same since 1962?

B. Abiding Bias

Although the French Constitutional Council has evolved, particularly towards " jurisdictionnalisation ", it is not certain today that it perfectly meets the criteria of a court of law. In support of this view, three types of argument may be put forward: they relate to the declarations of the politicians who are heirs to the framers of the Constitution - and of the Constitutional Council -, to the case law of the Council itself and to the development of the last major reform of the judicial system, which is the QPC, precisely presented as an important milestone in the " jurisdictionnalisation" process.

In 2009, when the QPC reform came into force, French President Nicolas Sarkozy said: " In our Republic, the Constitutional Council is the guardian of the separation of powers (...). I do not believe that its purpose is to become a supreme court that oversees all the courts and establishes a judicial counter-power that competes with the legislature and the executive. That would be contrary to the spirit of the reform and to our Constitution. Our democracy would have nothing to gain from a perpetual conflict between the various arms of government and the different authorities through which it finds expression"[54]. Such a statement is at variance with the argument that the Council is a judicial body. It is not irrelevant that it was made by a Gaullist politician, or above all by a sitting President of the Republic who initiated the QPC. The opinion expressed by President Sarkozy shows that the debate on the very identity of the Council is not over, even though, of course, one can still argue that the essential thing is not what the Constitutional Council is, but what it does - but that is a different kettle of fish.

The Council's own case law lends some credence to President Sarkozy's opinion. Two years after this statement, the Council issued this landmark opinion: " Whereas the Constitutional Council is one of the *constitutional public authorities*, and that by adopting the afore-mentioned provisions, the legislature has disregarded the scope of its own competence...". This judgement on the Social Security Financing Act for 2012, handed down on 15 December 2011,[55] further clouds the Council's perception of its own self. A « constitutional public authority » is, without doubt, not a " jurisdiction ". Commenting on this verdict, Elisabeth Zoller rightly points out that " the foremost reason for the existence of the Constitutional Council is therefore not to defend an individual whose rights have been infringed upon, not least because the victim cannot bring the matter directly before it. The Council's primary *raison d'être* is to show the way for the majority not to be tyrannical, and while it is true that the institution of the QPC gives rise, on the initiative of the litigant, to a confrontation between the law and constitutionally guaranteed rights and freedoms, it is not the rights of the litigant that justify the possible unconstitutionality of the law, but the defects of the law in the protection it is supposed to give them."[56].

---

[54] Cited by Zoller E, op cit.

[55] Judg 2011-242 of 15 December 2011, « Law on social security financing for 2012 ».

[56] Zoller E, op cit.

Having made this observation about a given decision, it seems that the whole development of the QPC bears it out. Yet the QPC has been presented as crowning the entry of the individual into the constitutional arena and thus marking an essential stage in the " jurisdictionalisation " of the Council, if by this we mean not only the possibility open to individuals for initiating litigation, but also the existence of a number of principles governing judicial procedure, such as the adversarial nature of proceedings and debates, the exchange of documents, equality of arms between parties, etc. The QPC is therefore merely the tree that hides the forest of the removal of the citizen from the constitutional arena, better still: it would be a smokescreen, a sort of subterfuge designed to give the illusion of access to constitutional justice when, in fact, everything about this litigation procedure reveals a profound intention to keep the individual out of the constitutional sphere.

The idea that the QPC, which is supposed to bring constitutional issues closer to the litigant, on the contrary distances him from them, has been defended by a significant section of legal scholars. It turns out that the development of this review by way of exception reveals less a desire to do justice to an aggrieved individual than to clean up a legal order, less a subjective dispute than an objective, normative dispute. P. Egéa, for example, has clearly highlighted how this type of litigation eclipses subjective data, veils the litigant and removes him from the trial stage. Both at the stage of initiating the proceedings - which remains the responsibility of the high courts, which are the only ones able to judge the relevance of the constitutional arguments raised by the applicant, through their power to make or refuse a referral to the constitutional court - and at the stage of planning the effects of a ruling of invalidity - where considerations of expediency take precedence over considerations of legality - the private individual is kept out of the debate. The judgment on this new legal route is therefore incisive: « the author of the QPC is ultimately no more than the instrument, rendered invisible in the course of the procedure, of a system in which he plays the necessary and limited role of initiator of a process that goes beyond him. He is the invisible hand of the institution of *a post facto review*... Without knowing it, he will have played the role of a public prosecutor for the constitutionality of laws... The French-style review of the constitutionality of laws has no litigants but only " initiating agents" who serve a public interest: respect for the rights and freedoms guaranteed by the Constitution "[57].

The QPC would thus be the most striking proof of what might be called the constitutional isolation of the citizen, thereby casting doubt on the " jurisdictional" nature of the French Constitutional Council. But if we concede that this body is not jurisdictional in nature, can we nevertheless continue to maintain that it has remained a " body regulating the activity of public authorities "? The fact that the Council has not become a court does not mean that it has remained a regulatory body. Two points can be made in this regard. The first is that it is precisely possible to stop being a 'regulator' without getting to the level of a ' Court'. By this we mean that those who deny the jurisdictional nature of the institution can concede that it is no longer a simple regulatory body. In other words, and schematically speaking, we could say that the French Constitutional Council is at an intermediate stage, between the minimalism of the regulatory function and the maximalism of the jurisdictional mandate, understood as the individualised defence of citizens' rights and freedoms. Such a hypothesis can be sustained, at least, because the QPC, despite its technical imperfections regarding the jurisdictional function, has clearly and

---

[57] Egéa P., « L'efficience de la garantie des droits par le Conseil Constitutionnel », in Mouton St., *Le régime représentatif à l'épreuve de la justice constitutionnelle*, Colloque de Toulouse, Paris, LGDJ, 2016. V aussi dans le même ouvrage les contributions de Dubois J.P., « L'émergence d'une nouvelle citoyenneté constitutionnelle dans le procès constitutionnel ? » ; Hummel J. ? « Portait du juge constitutionnel en acteur politique. Sur le rôle institutionnel de la « délicatesse », et Vidal-Naquet A. ? « La justice constitutionnelle, est-elle le nouveau canal de participation, d'opposition et/ou de contrôle du peuple au pouvoir ? ».

systematically conferred on the Council the right to intervene where individual freedoms are concerned, and thus to go beyond the mere separation of powers, which is in fact what the regulatory function boils down to.

A second argument is that the French Constitutional Council itself has never used the term "regulatory organ", since 1962. It may well be that, in its own mind, it has ceased to be one. Or, more precisely, that it no longer performs that function alone, but that it does something else as well.

There is therefore a great deal of evidence to suggest that the French constitutional court has ceased to do nothing but regulate. But we must return to our problem. The important thing to remember about this is that, in the Council's mind as well as in the scholarly literature, a " body regulating the activities of public authorities"is a body which, on the whole, imposes limits on itself in the exercise of its office, a body which, by vocation, practises self-restraint, i.e., judicial restraint. It is on this point of principle that many African judges will take issue. The concept of the regulatory body is taken up again, but from a perspective that is the exact opposite of that of the French Council. What has been achieved is an inversion of perspective, a conceptual reappropriation worthy of Hegelian "Aufhebung": capturing a notion in order to transform it, sublimate it or, if we wish to remain faithful to the philosopher's rhetoric: suppressing it by conserving it, conserving it by suppressing it.

II. THE AFRICAN INVERSION

The break with the perspective of the French constitutional model, which has nonetheless inspired many African states in several respects, is not simply the result of a praetorian process of re-appropriation (B). It is more deliberate and more systematic since the constituent state itself used it in drafting its text (B). This amounted to « enhancing » the regulatory function, in contrast to the French viewpoint.

A. The letter of the law

The break with the French perspective here lies in the fact that the regulatory function is quite simply not envisaged as consisting solely in delimiting areas of jurisdiction. In the 1962 decision of the French Constitutional Council, it is in this arbitration and adjudication function that the regulatory mission is exhausted. It was pointed out above that if the addition of the adjective "normative" to the "activity of the public authorities" has been readily accepted, it is precisely because regulation represents the most modest level of the judge's intervention, which is that of the division of jurisdiction between constitutional bodies.

The difference with the African point of view lies precisely in the fact that, in the name of regulation itself, it will go beyond the task of adjudication and incorporate the function of reparation, i.e., include in the remit of the judge-regulator the area of individual rights and freedoms. This is clearly a different approach. This is further demonstrated by the fact that when the French Constitutional Council handed down its decision in 1971 " Freedom of Association" - which now makes him a judge of liberties - was seen as a breach of the regulator's argument. In a nutshell, regulation and the defence of liberties have not been compatible in the logic that has emerged since 1962. On the contrary, many African constitutions make the two compatible. The following wording, taken from current or recently repealed African Constitutions, is ample proof of this.

Article 99 of the Constitution of Togo of 27 September 1992:

> " The Constitutional Court is the highest jurisdiction of the State in constitutional matters. It rules on the constitutionality of the law and guarantees fundamental human rights and public liberties. It is the regulatory

body for the functioning of institutions and the activities of public authorities".

Article 114 of the Constitution of Benin:

" The Constitutional Court is the highest court of the State in constitutional matters. It judges the constitutionality of the law and guarantees fundamental human rights and civil liberties. It regulates the functioning of institutions and the activities of public authorities".

Article 83 of the Gabonese Constitution of 26 March 1991:

" The Constitutional Court is the highest court of the State in constitutional matters. It judges the constitutionality of laws and the validity of elections. It guarantees fundamental human rights and civil liberties. It regulates the functioning of institutions and the activities of public authorities ".

Article 75 of the Constitution of Djibouti of 4 September 1992: "The Constitutional Council ensures that constitutional principles are adhered to. It reviews the constitutionality of laws. It guarantees fundamental human rights and public freedoms. It regulates the functioning of institutions and the activities of public authorities ".

Article 85 of the Malian Constitution of 25 February 1992:

" The Constitutional Court rules on the constitutionality of laws and guarantees fundamental human rights and civil liberties. It is the regulatory body for the functioning of institutions and the activities of public authorities".

Other examples could be cited[58]. These texts establish a kind of expansion of the concept of regulation. Regulation extends not only to rights and freedoms, but also to " the workings of institutions". In practice, it is difficult to distinguish between the activity of public authorities and the workings of institutions, as the two can easily be confused. The addition that exists in African texts may, in some respects, not be very clear-cut.

From our comparative perspective, however, we cannot but recognise that the workings of institutions can generate two added values, which set it apart from the concept of the French judge. The first is that it is undoubtedly appropriate to African jurisprudence, as we shall see, since in almost all the cases identified, the aim was to remedy a functional defect, or more precisely, to ensure continuity in the functioning of the institutions and thus avoid a gridlock or a crisis. Clearly, this is more a case of the workings of institutions than of the less appropriate concept of activities of public authorities. Secondly, the very principle of such an addition is likely to corroborate the idea that, based on the expressions used on both sides, African judges would be less constrained than the French judge since their regulation is likely to have two objects, whereas there is only one for the Constitutional Council of France. To sum up, two differences may be noted in the understanding of the concept of regulatory body, which are products of the very texts, and which stem from the fact that the African bodies are not limited to regulating the activity of public authorities but extend to the operation of the institutions and the guarantee of freedoms. The material scope of regulation is therefore broader in Africa.

But this is not the only point of departure. Dissent from the French model has also manifested itself in case law. What needs to be emphasised here is that the regulatory function has been

---

[58] For example, article 93 of the Guinean Transitional Charter, article 166 of the Chadian Constitution of 31 March 1996.

invoked by judges not only to go beyond the timid arbitral vision of the French judge, but as a lever to intervene in situations of peril, of absolute constitutional urgency because the very functioning of the State was compromised. It is in their capacity as regulators that African judges have virtually delivered solutions to constitutional crises. Regulation has therefore been seen in a more than ambitious light. The judge entered the State and its functioning, unlike the French Constitutional Council, not as a neutral regulator of a mechanism in which he admitted playing a marginal role, but as an asset, as a crisis resolution body, proving that the regulator can be an influential player[59].

B. In the case law

Here again, reference should be made to a number of decisions handed down by African constitutional courts. Here we find a conception of regulation that is completely opposed to that of the French judge. Whereas in 1962 this notion justified the self-limitation of the jurisdictional function, on the African continent it provides the basis for bold activism. An examination of the relevant case law reveals that the regulatory function has been invoked in two series of cases: those in which it was needed to overcome one-off crises, to resolve political contradictions between different parties - particularly in the context of the functioning of parliament - and those which, more decisively concerning the functioning of the State, led the constitutional court to virtually rewrite the Constitution, thus exercising a genuine constituent power.

Judgements handed down by the Constitutional Courts of Benin, Togo and Madagascar fall into the first category. The ruling of 12 May 2003[60] delivered by the Beninese judge bordered on the composition of the leadership of the National Assembly. The

---

[59] V. Nicaise M. « La fonction de régulation des juridictions constitutionnelles en Afrique francophone », *Annuaire international de justice constitutionnelle* XXIII, 2007.

[60] Judg DDC 03-077 of 12 May 2003, « Orou sego Orou Gabé », *LR* 2003, p.311.

parliamentary majority had brought the matter before the Court because it considered the measures advocated or taken by the oldest member of the National Assembly's Bureau to be unconstitutional, since they were seen as favouring the opposition and therefore hurting the parliamentary majority. The divergent views led to a stalemate in the running of the Bureau. The matter was referred to the Constitutional Court by some MPs, and the Court, in its capacity as the body that regulates the functioning of the institutions, relied on a very " general" provision of the Constitution to carry out its responsibility, which is Article 35, which states that "citizens entrusted with a public function or elected to a public office have a duty to perform it with conscience, competence, probity, dedication and loyalty in the interest of, and with respect for the common good ". In a subsequent decision, the Court held that " the oldest member must convene the National Assembly as of the date of this ruling and continue without interruption, i.e., during the same sitting, with the election of the other officers"[61]. Finally, it orders that the officers of the Assembly be sworn in « no later than midnight on Wednesday 14 May 2003 »[62]. Two facts are likely to show that we are a long way from the French conception of the regulatory body: the very "broad" and " permissive" provision cited by the Court – article 35 of the Constitution – and the exercise of a power of injunction by the judge, a fact one would hardly imagine in the performance of a simple task of determining jurisdiction. The second case law from Benin is somewhat similar to the one just mentioned. It concerned the composition of another institution, the Independent National Electoral Commission. That ruling was delivered on 12 January 2001, the " Bio Bigou Bani Léon"[63] case, which also ended up censuring the composition of the National Assembly. After

---

[61] Judg DCC 03-078, *LR* 2003, p. 323.

[62] Ibid.

[63] Ruling DCC 01-011 of 12 January 2001, *Report* 2001, p. 59.

recalling that it acts as a "regulatory body for the functioning of institutions and the activity of public authorities", the Court proceeds to declare that "the composition of the Independent National Electoral Commission as decided by the National Assembly, leads to a confiscation of this institution by certain parliamentary groups in violation of the rule of equality laid down by Article 26 of the Constitution and is therefore not likely to ensure the transparency and fairness of elections as required by the rule of law and pluralist democracy". It rules that "the two posts unduly allocated to the " Consensus National " and "PRD" caucuses should be allocated to the « Nation et développement » and " Solidarité et progrès " caucuses, respectively"[64]. This ruling by Benin's Constitutional Court, like its predecessor, remedies an injustice and corrects a legislative error. It is about "equality", a concept whose contours are difficult to define in some cases. By taking on the task of bringing it to life, the judge is certainly no longer in the position of a "neutral" regulator.

Like its counterpart in Benin, the Togolese constitutional court is a " a body regulating the functioning of institutions and the activities of public authorities". It is in this capacity that it delivered its judgement of 22 March, 2017[65]. The matter at issue related to the consequences of a constitutional bill tabled a few months earlier by the opposition. The parliamentary majority considered that the debate on this proposal was inappropriate insofar as prior to it there should have been a " consensus", a condition laid down in another context by the Truth, Justice and Reconciliation Commission. As previous work had shown that no such consensus existed, it was pointless to debate the draft.

For their part, the sponsors of the text considered that deliberation on the text was a requirement of the 2006 "Global

---

[64] *LR* op cit., p. 68.

[65] Constitutional court of Togo, Judg n° C-001/17 of 22 March 2017.

Political Agreement " of 2006. In the end, the Court ruled as follows: "Considering that the request of the MPs of the *Alliance nationale pour le changement* (ANC) seeks to remedy a situation that prevents the regular functioning of the National Assembly; considering that Article 99 *in fine* of the Constitution provides that the Court is " the regulatory body for the functioning of the institutions and the activity of public authorities", that it is therefore more a question of the functioning of a State institution". Then, after referring to certain provisions of the National Assembly's Standing Orders, the Court stated that "The Legal Committee must adopt its Rules of Procedure and place them on the desk of the National Assembly for submission at the plenary session; failing which, the Speaker of the National Assembly, in his capacity as such, is obliged to ensure that the committees function properly"[66].

The intervention of the Malagasy judge as a regulatory body occurs in a slightly different context. In 1996, the Court was called upon to declare that the President of the Republic was "permanently prevented from holding office" at the petition of a group of MPs. Seeing that the qualified majority vote that would have allowed the declaration of definitive disqualification could not be achieved, the deputies decided to opt for another route: the declaration of disqualification by the Court (article 50 of the Constitution). The Constitutional Court of Madagascar upheld the application, ruling that:

> " there has been a breach of the Constitution in that the President of the Republic has not promulgated a certain number of laws in accordance with the conditions laid down in Article 57; that, in addition, placing the Inspectorate General of State under the Presidency is in breach of Article 62 (...); that it is therefore necessary to declare that the President of the Republic is permanently

---

[66] Ibid.

precluded from holding office in accordance with Article 50 of the Constitution"[67].

All these examples highlight a relatively audacious understanding of the regulatory function, certainly in contrast to the minimalist construction of the French Constitutional Council.

But the regulatory function has been taken a step further. It has been invoked in support of genuine judicial undertakings to rewrite the Constitution, in the service of the judicial exercise of a genuine constituent power. No doubt the seriousness of the issues at stake had something to do with it. In these cases, the very functioning of the State was compromised. To avoid paralysis, the Constitutional Court conceived of its role as a regulatory body in particularly broad terms. It has become a genuine State power, rubbing shoulders with the others, but from a different perspective to that of the French judge when he describes himself as a " constitutional public authority » in the afore-mentioned ruling of 15 December 2011. He is not a behaved and discreet guest at the State banquet, somewhat embarrassed around the edges, like the French judge, almost apologising for being there and careful, of course, not to disturb the peace of the premises by exercising a power that is too intrusive or injunctive. In the African context, the regulatory judge is, on the contrary, a directive judge, an arbitration body that has fully integrated the dynamic dimension of its office. This is borne out almost spectacularly by two judgments: the "Gabonese" and " Madagascan" judgments.

The ruling handed down by Gabon's Constitutional Court dates from 14 November 2018. It relates to a request made by the Prime Minister for an interpretation of the provisions of Articles 13 and 16 of the Constitution. The question was how to deal with urgent and crucial matters that can only be discussed by Cabinet, a body that only the President of the Republic can chair, in the event of

---

[67] Constitutional Court of Madagascar, Judgment n°7, MCC/D3 of 4 September 1996.

temporary incapacity of the President of the Republic. There are certainly constitutional provisions relating to the incapacity of the Head of State, but they only cover " vacancy of power" and "permanent incapacity", matters that were not at issue. In answering the question posed, the Court recalled that it has " the power to interpret the Constitution and other texts of constitutional value case of doubt or lacuna". It further observed that Article 13 " contains a loophole *that should be filled by adding another paragraph worded as follows*: "In the event of the temporary incapacity of the President of the Republic for any reason whatsoever, certain functions vested in the latter, with the exception of those provided for in articles 18, 19 and 109 clause1, may be exercised, as the case may be, either by the Vice-President of the Republic or by the Prime Minister, with the special authorisation of the Constitutional Court to which the matter has been referred by the Prime Minister or one tenth of the members of the Government, whenever necessary."[68].

The Court saw fit to specify that " beyond the request for interpretation, the Prime Minister also raised the problem of the regular functioning of the Government in one of its regalian mandates which is the holding of Cabinet meetings" and that finally, "the Constitutional Court, in its capacity as regulatory body, authorises the Vice President to convene and preside over a Cabinet meeting which will deal exclusively with the agenda attached to the Prime Minister's request". If there remained any doubt as to the boldness of the judge's approach, it should be added that he was careful to note, in the operative part of his ruling, that he "decides" that "Article 13 of the Constitution contains a loophole that should be plugged by adding another paragraph worded as follows (…)"[69].

---

[68] Italics mine.

[69] Constitutional court of Gabon, Judgment n°219/CC of 14 November 2018.

This case law is remarkable for at least three reasons. First of all, it comes into play in a context of risk of disruption to the workings of the State, since it relates to the functioning of the Government and Cabinet. It shows that the regulatory function is a crisis function. Secondly, the regulatory judge is unabashedly rewriting the Constitution. It is customary for a judge to censure an act and suggest that it be rewritten, but when it is the judge himself who, in a consultative capacity that does not imply any alteration to the constitutional provisions, takes it upon himself to make such an alteration, thereby exercising, in fact if not in law, a genuine constituent power, the potential for a government of judges concealed in the regulatory function becomes apparent. There is one final reason to question the ruling of the Gabonese Court. In it, the judge does not observe the traditional reverence of the judiciary towards the political authorities of the State. He does not restrain himself from a foray into the inner workings of the State, so to speak. The Gabonese regulatory judge interferes in the workings of the Executive by determining, without, in any way, elaborating on the reasons for his choice, the authority that should chair Cabinet meetings: it will be the vice-president, not the prime minister.

The similarities here with the ruling of 25 May 2018[70] by the Constitutional Court of Madagascar is striking. In this case, the High Constitutional Court was asked to declare that the President of the Republic, Hery Rajaonarimampianina, had failed to establish the High Court of Justice, in defiance of the provisions of the Constitution. The court was asked to find that the Head of State had "failed to act" in accordance with article 167 of the Constitution, which stipulates that the President must appoint the members of the High Court of Justice within twelve months of the President's investiture. The fifty-three Members of Parliament also criticised the Head of State for delaying in appointing members to the two

---

[70] Constitutional court of Madagascar, Judgment n°186HCC of 25 May 2018.

other institutions of the Republic, the Independent National Commission for Human Rights (CNIDH) and the High Council for the Defence of Democracy and the Rule of Law (HCDDED). The High Court came to the conclusion that "there is reason to note that this delay marks a clear desire not to proceed with the installation of the HCJ (...), that the President of the Republic has thus not honoured his obligations " to set up the HCJ despite the injunction made by the High Constitutional Court to complete the process, and that the High Court is sovereign in its assessment of the nature of the sanctions" that should therefore be imposed. Finally, the Malagasy judge considered " that the President of the Republic should be stripped of his mandate by the High Constitutional Court pursuant to article 167 of the Fundamental Law".

This whole construction is built around the regulatory function assigned to the constitutional court. The High Court is careful to make this clear:

> "Whereas the High Constitutional Court recalls that, in accordance with the spirit of the Constitution, it is the body that regulates the functioning of the institutions and the activity of the public authorities, particularly when the latter are impeded in the exercise of the powers conferred on them by the Constitution due to the effects of a political crisis, such as the situation that prevails at present; whereas, however, this regulatory function, carried out in exceptional circumstances, is analysed as a remedy in the interest of the Constitution and is dictated by the need to ensure respect for the spirit of the Constitution; that such a regulatory function for public authorities is currently established and recognised by neighbouring constitutional courts or institutions in countries in the African zone, such as those in Gabon and Benin, and that the High Constitutional Court of Madagascar is a member of and adheres to the principles

> of the various Associations of neighbouring constitutional courts or institutions throughout the world... ".

The Malagasy constitutional judge then defines his own mission, which is, he says, «to assume the minimum obligation of ensuring respect for the principle of non-regression of constitutional values and the principle of " no-return to the legal acquis' of the democratic rule of law".

These developments warrant a few comments. Firstly, they illustrate what might be called the possible excesses of regulatory power. Indeed, in the name of such a power, the Malagasy judge has gone very far, even though nowhere in the Constitution in force is there any mention of such an empowerment. In other words, the assignment of the regulatory function is the result of a purely prejudicial approach, which is not backed by any law; it is the means by which the judge arrogates powers to himself. Hence the evasive, and certainly questionable, nature of the reasons given for the judgment: to justify this self-proclamation, the High Court of Madagascar relies on such « volatile » elements as its inclusion in the concert of international constitutional jurisdictions or its membership of " Associations". And when it claims that the regulatory function is "recognised and settled", it cites no more than two examples - in which the said function is expressly provided for in the Constitution - and has some difficulty in making this empowerment appear to be widely shared.

It is also curious that the High Constitutional Court should assert, again by virtue of its power to regulate, that it « sovereignly assesses the nature of the sanctions » that it may impose in the event the Head of State fails to act. Article 167 of the Constitution does refer to sanctions, but this is simply to specify that the High Court may impose them under the same conditions as the High Court of Justice to be established. So, this is not really a matter of discretionary power on the part of the constitutional judge. This raises a real question of principle, bearing in mind that determination of the legality crimes and offences, as well as the related penalties, is an individual right and an element of fair trial. In these circumstances, it is astonishing that the High Constitutional Court, as a judge of human rights, should disregard this.

There are other aspects of the decision that show that the power to regulate allows many things to happen. The references to " spirit of the Constitution" first. This happened at least, twice. Nothing is more "elastic" than the " spirit" of a text, especially a constitutional text, whose elusive brevity is a well-known characteristic. Then there is the question of the "interests of the Constitution", of which the High Court makes itself the only judge, or so it seems. Finally, the exercise of a genuine power of injunction - observed in the case law cited above - is not trivial. The judge indicates to the political authorities the course of action to take, defines a political agenda and outlines a precise transitional plan, a plan of which the operative part of the decision gives an idea. Moreover, this genuine transitional programme, following the disqualification of the President of the Republic and specified at the end of the judgment, is drafted in a formally normative manner, with « articles », numbering about fifteen.

It seems that the Malagasy regulatory judge realised the somewhat heretical nature of his approach, since he gives the impression of justifying it after the fact: the power to regulate, which is not provided for in the constitutional text, would be exercised in troubled times, times of "crisis", of "exceptional circumstances", the judge goes on to say. Such circumstances, the ruling continues, are likely to "impede" the functioning of the institutions. And the rules on which his saving intervention is based would be principles that are in some way superior, such as those referred to in the ruling: "the foundations of a democratic Republican order", " the decisive imperative of responsibility» or the « value system". Clearly, following the slope of regulation leads to the frontiers of extra- or supra-constitutionality.

But there is one point on which the judge in Madagascar is saying the same thing as the other regulatory judges in Africa: regulation means ensuring that institutions continue to function and that the activities of public authorities are perpetuated and do not grind to a halt. The African judge-regulator is a mechanic for the public authorities, a tugboat for the State, enabling government machinery to get moving again. It must be said again that we are a long way from the concept of the Constitutional Council in France. African practice is typical of a conceptual reappropriation, a conceptual hijacking. The notion of "regulatory body" is seized upon and transformed, adopted, and reshaped. In itself, its African destiny attests to the fact that the judge exercises a creative power, and those imported institutions are like writings that fall into the public domain: no one knows what will become of them tomorrow; their meaning, as Paul Ricoeur would say, lies ahead of them and not behind them. Above all, this destiny demonstrates that we are witnessing an African singularity.

If the same concept - regulation - has led to such different and opposing outcomes, it is undoubtedly because it conceals a certain ambiguity. And indeed, the feeling produced by attempts to specify it is one of perplexity or scepticism. An author such as G Marcou proposes a definition that would be closer to the French version of regulation - we are talking about the conception of the French constitutional judge-. For him, regulation refers to "the description of a global system and the function that maintains and reproduces the order of such a system"[71]. Insofar as such a definition emphasises the conservatory or stabilising dimension of regulation, it might well be thought that it is similar to the approach taken by the French Constitutional Council in its 1962 decision. It is

[71] Marcou G., op cit.

in this sense that the same author was able to write that "regulation is an attractive word because it evokes the ability to establish order or rationality"[72]. This view is far from shared, however. There is, in fact, a body of doctrine which considers that the concept of regulation remains substantially vague, eluding thus, a perfectly clear definition.

Other approaches go even further. At the exact opposite end of the spectrum to the above definitions, they emphasise the freedom offered by the power of regulation, and the capacity for subversion rather than conservation that it suggests.

In respect of the first position, one may think of Jean Gicquel who, for example posits that "expression is as suggestive as it is imprecise"[73]. Similarly, N. Barbaroussis refers to a "vague and general notion...susceptible to a subjective approach...a notion influenced by the practice of political institutions..." [74]. G. Timsit's view is not much different when he points out: "According to some, nothing is regulated", whereas for others, who hold a "perfectly antithetical position", regulation must be "recognised"[75]. And when other authors try to define regulation "positively", there is always a halo of uncertainty in its contours: Michel Verpeaux, for example, states that "regulation is halfway between advice and a general, abstract decision "[76]. One may well wonder whether it was not the convenience and elasticity of the concept of regulation that led the Constitutional Council to use it. It should be remembered

---

[72] Marcou G., « Régulation et service public. Les enseignements du droit comparé », in *Droit de la régulation et service public...*, cited on p.11.

[73] Gicquel J., préface à Barbaroussis N. , *La fonction régulatrice du président de la République hellénique »,* Paris, LGDJ 2000, p.IX.

[74] Barbaroussis N., op cit., p 257.

[75] Timsit G., « Régulation et théorie du droit », in *Droit de la régulation, service public et intégration régionale. Comparaisons et commentaires*, Tome 1, Paris, L'Harmattan, p 249.

[76] Cited by Mborantsuo M.M., *La contribution des cours constitutionnelles à l'Etat de droit en Afrique,* Paris, Economica, 2007, p.239.

that nowhere in the French Constitution is there any mention of a regulatory body. It is the Constitutional Council that has proclaimed itself as such, but without dwelling on the meaning of the word, even if we can guess that in its mind it is intended to suggest the modesty of an office.

The appeal to the " Spirit of the Constitution", which is also found in the 1962 decision, is equally perplexing. While one might well defend the idea that the 1958 Constitution has a spirit which is not to establish a strong constitutional court, the fact that, based on this same Constitution, it was possible to extend jurisdiction to rights and freedoms in 1971 puts into perspective the constraint that this spirit might constitute. In other words, there is no such thing as the "spirit of the Constitution" that would impede the interpretative developments that the courts would like to promote. The spirit of a constitution is never a given, but almost always a construct. From the point of view of both the "Spirit of the Constitution", the Constitutional Council has therefore chosen to frame the debate in very relative terms; the truths of the 1962 decision are not the gospel and the notion of regulation remains malleable.

It is undoubtedly because it is open to very different interpretations that, going further and taking the exact opposite view to the "regulation – conservation" theory, Some authors uphold a third thesis: that the regulatory function enables us to go : "well beyond the primary function" of the judge, and that it includes "the discretionary power to choose between two or more equally legal actions"[77], the wielder of regulatory power always has "a margin of manoeuvre"[78]. This approach is clearly the one that best reflects the African jurisprudential conception, the African constitutional judges' understanding of regulation.

[77] Manessis A., cited by Barbaroussis N., op cit., p 245.

[78] Mborantsuo M.M., op cit, p. 47.

In any event, the comparative use of the notion of regulation ultimately reveals two faces of the constitutional court: a rather timid one – the French Constitutional Council of 1962 – and a more activist face – the African constitutional judges -. Confined to the role of neutral regulator of a mechanism of separation of powers, the French judge would be more the embodiment of an arbitral archetype of the jurisdictional function - after the fashion of a match referee, who, by definition, does not partake in the game. -: a person fundamentally imbued with restraint and neutrality, acting only to punish deviations, in charge of detecting misdemeanours and reminding people of the rules of the game. In contrast, the African judge would be more akin to a coach, according to the threefold principle set out by François Ost [79] : it sets out the rules of the game, of course, but it also has a supplementary role to play, and does not hesitate to lay down rules where they do not exist and where failure to do so could be perilous.

All in all, this is a familiar dichotomy, as Riccardo Guastini recently pointed out : the doctrine of "judicial restraint" emphasises the importance of deference to the democratic legislature: judges, especially constitutional judges, who lack any : democratic legitimacy, since they are not bodies elected by the people, must not encroach on legislative power; a law must be declared unconstitutional only when it is clearly contrary to the Constitution (...). The doctrine of (…) Judicial activism (…) suggests to judges an interpretation that is fundamentally free of any textual constraints: it fosters free creation of constitutional law by judges, with a view to adapting constitutional values to real life needs (…). The result of judicial activism is a constitutional law that is fundamentally complete, without lacunae: in the sense that constitutional principles are supposed to regulate every possible

[79] The triad is as follows: judge - peacemaker, judge - referee, judge – coach. V. Ost F., in Gérard Ph., Ost F., Van de Kerhove M., *Fonction de juger et pouvoir judiciaire*, Bruxelles, Publications of saint Louis University faculties, 1983, pp 1-70.

matter, so that there is no vacuum of constitutional law, no *Rechtsleererraum* [80].

Faced with the potential of crises, whether minor or major, African constitutional judges have taken the initiative to fill scabrous gaps, to make up for perilous shortcomings, by virtue of their understanding of the notion of regulatory body for the functioning of institutions or the activity of public authorities.

In so doing, they have achieved a twofold feat: they have reappropriated a concept based on their own needs, thereby taking a step back from the model that may have inspired them, and they have laid the foundations for an adventurous interpretative strategy in a political and social context that is not always favourable.

---

[80] Guastini R., « L'interprétation de la Constitution », in Troper M. et Chagnollaud D., *Traité international de droit constitutionnel. Théorie de la Constitution, T.1* », Paris, Dalloz, 2012, pp.484-485.

CHAPTER 3

TAMED SOVEREIGNTY

The idea of sovereignty must be radically eliminated.
This is the great cultural change we need
Hans Kelsen

Jean Bodin, known as one of the pioneering and incisive theorists of State sovereignty, asserts in *The Six Books of the Commonwealth* that sovereign majesty loses its lustre if it is subject to encroachment on any of its parts . His contemporary, Cardin Le Bret, equally intent on asserting the authority and independence of the State, added that sovereignty, is no divisible than a point in geometry. The sixteenth century in Europe undoubtedly remains the century of the affirmation of State sovereignty. Our times still bear the scars of this raging exaltation of the Sovereign. While the imperative to co-exist peacefully and the inter-dependence of States have forced them to relax their perception of this essential attribute, the predicted extinction of sovereignty, announced in some quarters, is still some way off. We live in an age of co-operation, but we also live in an age of stiffening sovereignty. Those who view with suspicion or reluctance the growth, natural or provoked, of solidarities that imply renunciations, savour a kind of revenge at the sight of these resistances to the strengthening of the international order and are quick to celebrate the "awakening of nations".

In the more specific context of the establishment of large groupings under the banner of "integration" which is seen as one of the pathways to economic and social development, an area in which the reduction of state sovereignty can be observed at its best, the African continent stands out. Indeed, its relationship with sovereignty is rather peculiar. Eager to assert their sovereignty - an understandable propensity for communities that have been subjugated by foreign domination for so long - these nations, somewhat curiously, agree to "give up", their individual freedom as part of the process of building African "Unity". For the sake of coming together, a promising prospect, a mythical and rallying utopia, these States agree to relinquish substantial prerogatives, even their very existence, as they are so keen to assert their right to self-determination.

This fact must be borne in mind when we compare this reality with the situation in other parts of the world. The alluring sirens of integration have sounded in other parts of the world. Europe, like America, has seen such a unifying project. There is a "Pan European" movement just as there is a "Pan-American" ideology. The desire for unity, with its harmony, persistence, and theorists, has crossed the three continents of Africa, Europe, and America in one fell swoop.

But the distinctiveness of African legal systems has been that, faced with the dissolving dynamics of sovereignty that such a project necessarily entails, they have anticipated, accepted, and organised the "disarmament" of their Sates. Meanwhile, nowhere is the violence inflicted upon states by this process self-evident, nowhere is integration a long, still river, and in Africa itself, state resistance to such a process is not only real but has taken on a disturbing dimension.

There is no angelism or Manichaeism here, of course. The fact is, however, that on the specific question of the legal possibility of the evanescence of sovereignty, African states have developed mechanisms - essentially constitutional in nature - to "devitalise" these sovereignties and make the tension between freedom and subjugation less virulent. In Europe and America, not only has membership of the Community project been less 'fervent' in its expression, but its realisation has willingly given rise to sometimes lengthy, complex, and occasionally controversial legal restructurings. Over and above these prerequisites, and in terms of substance, one might say that the level of sacrifice of sovereignty that States agree to, and their commitment to reducing it, is not the same, far from it. It is therefore the intensity of the commitment expressed by the States that is a second factor differentiating the approaches.

A contrast therefore emerges when, in relation to the imperatives of regional grouping, we look at the approach to the question of sovereignty in Africa on the one hand (I) and in Europe and America on the other (II).

I. IN AFRICA: THE DISMANTLING SOVEREIGNTY

This work of defusing sovereignty is primarily the result of constitutional statements, which have, for the most part, been the subject of an amended jurisprudence (A). In theory, there seems to be nothing to stand in the way of such a flexible approach to state sovereignty (B).

A. Constitutional formulae and their interpretation

As soon as they acceded to international sovereignty, i.e., to life itself, the African states included the question of their unity in their political agenda, expressed in the very wordings of their respective Constitutions, a position of principle regarding their integration.

These declarations of principle, set out in fundamental laws, have given rise to interpretations in case law when treaties involving sacrifices of sovereignty are examined.

These constitutional expressions are characterised by the fact that the question of regionalism, i.e., continental grouping, is not only formulated in terms of adherence, of subscription to a principle, but its consequences are also clearly assumed. More precisely, the States not only express their willingness to commit themselves to such a process, but they also indicate the purpose of such a commitment through, on the one hand, the reference to a federative political unit and, on the other, the idea of the total dissolution of their sovereignty.

A Constitution such as that of Burkina Faso, which not only proclaims the need for *" economic and political integration"*, but also aims for a *"federative unity of Africa"*[81] before indicating that the country may enter into agreements implying a *" total surrender of sovereignty"*[82], falls into this category. The Constitutions of Niger, Mali and Senegal also fall into this category, all three providing for *" total ...surrender of sovereignty to realise African Unity"*[83].

Other States merely indicate their willingness, or even the need - in the strong sense of the term - to achieve regional or sub-regional unity. This doctrinal position sometimes refers to *"awareness"*, *"dedication"*, or even *" commitment"* to achieving this unity, and sometimes to the possibility of *"signing agreements"* in furtherance of same. A significant number of Constitutions adopt this stance insofar as they do not dwell on the political consequences of

---

[81] Preamble to the revised Constitution of Burkina Faso of 1991. The notion of an African federation is repeated in article 147.

[82] Article 146 of the Burkina Faso Constitution.

[83] Article 172 of the Constitution of Niger, article 117 of the Malian Constitution and 96 of the Senegalese Constitution.

African integration. This is the case for states such as Benin[84], Guinea[85], Togo[86], Cameroon[87] and Chad[88]. Other States, albeit in a minority, adopt a more reserved stance, resulting either in the mention of a relatively modest degree of integration - in fact, mere "cooperation"[89] - or total silence on the matter[90].

The fact is, however, that even in states that have not explicitly stated their willingness to " relinquish" their sovereignty, precedent relating to these provisions has tended to favour processes involving substantial transfers of competence from States to organisations tasked with the business of integration in general, whether this involves legal integration - legal sector harmonisation projects - or economic or political integration. There are several major decisions - that could fairly be described as "rulings of principle" - on the debate concerning the concessions of sovereignty implied by regionalism. These decisions were handed down by the constitutional judges of Senegal, Benin, the Democratic Republic of Congo (DRC), The Republic of Congo,

---

[84] Preamble to the Constitution of Benin: "Proclaim our commitment to the cause of African Unity and undertake to do our utmost to achieve sub-regional and regional integration.».

[85] Preamble to the Guinean Constitution of 2010: talks of *« commitment to the cause of African Unity and the sub-regional and regional integration of the continent »*. Article 123 adds, under the title « duties of the State », that the latter shall *« promote the unity of the nation and of Africa »*.

[86] Preamble to the Togolese Constitution: *« We resolutely commit to defending the cause of national unity, of African Unity, and to work towards the realisation of sub-regional and regional integration»*

[87] Preamble to the Constitution of Cameroon: the people of Cameroon, *« "convinced that the salvation of Africa lies in the achievement of ever closer solidarity between the peoples of Africa, affirms its determination to work towards building a united and free Africa »*.

[88] Preamble to the Constitution of Chad (revised version, 2004): *« Proclaim our attachment to the cause of African Unity and our commitment to do our utmost to achieve regional and sub-regional integration »*.

[89] This is the case of Côte d'Ivoire, whose Constitution merely alludes to agreements *« on coordination and free cooperation »*, or Morocco which refers to « relations of cooperation ».

[90] One may here mention the case of Gabon, Algeria, Madagascar, and Tunisia.

Burkina Faso and Côte d'Ivoire, and relate in particular to the treaty of the Organisation for the Harmonisation of Business Law in Africa (OHADA), signed in 1993 and, to a lesser extent, to the constitutive treaty of the pan-African organisation itself, the African Union (AU), which in the year 2000 replaced the Organisation of African Unity (OAU), established in 1963.

In the case of Senegal, as in that of Benin, Côte d'Ivoire, and the Democratic Republic of Congo (DRC), the assessment of the constitutional validity of international commitments has given rise to a body of positive jurisprudence that is often bold, yet always mindful of the letter of the Constitution. Two other decisions should be linked to this stance in favour of ceding State powers to international organisation: those handed down by the judges of Côte d'Ivoire and Burkina Faso when determining whether the Constitutive Treaty of the AU was in conformity with the Constitution. In the case of the Republic of Congo, on the other hand (OHADA treaty), the constitutional court was less open to sacrifices of sovereignty on the part of States, save in a specific context to which we shall return.

About the OHADA Treaty - which, it should be remembered, transfers to an international court the power of cassation hitherto exercised by national supreme courts - it was the Constitutional Council of Senegal that first handed down Judgment no. 3/C/93 dated 16 December 1993. Asked to rule on the specific issue of whether relinquishing the power of cassation of the Supreme Court of Senegal[91] was in consonance with the Constitution, the Constitutional Council would immediately reason from the point of view of State sovereignty, of which the power to judge is undoubtedly understood to be an essential component. The judge's position is clear: not only can the transfer of the power to judge be

---

[91] Articles 14, 15 and 16 of the OHADA Treaty.

analysed only as a *"limitation of competence"*[92], but although the articles in question had instituted *"a real relinquishment of sovereignty, they would not be unconstitutional"* for the reason that such a relinquishment was permitted by paragraph 3 of the Preamble to the Constitution of the time, which stated in principle that *" The people of Senegal, desirous of preparing for the unity of the States of Africa and of ensuring the prospects that this unity entails ; mindful of the need for political, cultural, economic and social unity, which is indispensable for the affirmation of the African personality; mindful of the historical, moral and material imperatives which unite the States of West Africa, DECIDE that the Republic of Senegal will spare no effort at achieving African unity"*[93].

The Constitutional Court of Benin, seized to rule on the same question - the conformity of the OHADA treaty with the national Constitution - would demonstrate the same liberalism, the same benevolence towards regionalist needs. In its decision of 30 June 1994[94], the Beninese judge relies both on general considerations and on the requirements of integration, itself : *" a partial surrender of sovereignty under a treaty cannot constitute a violation of the Constitution, insofar as Article 144 of the Constitution provides that the President of the Republic shall negotiate and ratify international treaties and agreements, and the said treaty is also justified by the need for regional or sub-regional integration, as reaffirmed in the Preamble and Article 149 of the Constitution".*

In Côte d'Ivoire, consideration of the OHADA Treaty led to the decision of 23 December 1994. In a particularly blunt manner,[95] the constitutional council opined that *"notwithstanding certain provisions*

---

[92] Considering n°8 of the ruling.

[93] Considering n° 9 of the afore-mentioned ruling of 16 December 1993.

[94] Ruling DDC 19-94 of 30 June 1994 delivered by the constitutional Court of Benin.

[95] Publicists have referred to a « *model of judicial restraint* » See V. DJEDJRO M. *Les grands arrêts de la jurisprudence constitutionnelle ivoirienne*, Abidjan, CNAT, GIZ, 2012, p. 96, for a critique of this.

which may entail changes in national legislation, the said Treaty does not contain any provisions contrary to the Constitution. " and concludes that the treaty is in consonance with the Constitution, giving the impression that the most important thing for the Court is to issue a certificate of conformity in principle with the international treaty referred to it. Any " *changes in national law*" that may occur are relegated to a secondary position.

Similarly, in a 2010 ruling, the Supreme Court of Justice, acting as the transitional constitutional court in the DRC, welcomed this founding treaty of OHADA in so far as the provisions submitted to it, in its view, constituted *"clauses transferring jurisdiction and limiting the sovereignty of Member States to OHADA, which may be adopted pursuant to Article 217 of the Constitution, which states that "The Democratic Republic of Congo may conclude association or community treaties or agreements involving a partial surrender of sovereignty with a view to promoting African unity"*[96].

The Constitutional Court of Burkina Faso also accepted that the national authorities could perfectly well transfer State powers affecting the sovereignty of the State, in relation not to the OHADA treaty, but to the Constitutive Act of the African Union. It reasoned based on Article 146 of the Constitution, which states that the country may " *conclude agreements with any African State, association or community involving a total or partial ceding of sovereignty; consequently, the Constitutive Act of the African Union, adopted in Lomé on 11 July 2000, is therefore in conformity with the Constitution of 2 June 1991"*[97].

Finally, on the same Constitution, the Ivorian courts handed down a judgment on 27 February 2001. This was judgment no. 15-2001, handed down by the Constitutional Chamber of the Supreme

---

[96] Supreme Court of justice, Judgment on R.Const.112/TSR, 5 Feb 2010.

[97] Supreme Court of Burkina Faso, constitutional chamber, Legal Opinion n°11 CS/CC on the Constitutive Act of the African Union, 8 June 2001.

Court, which at the time acted as the Constitutional Court. Focusing on Article 13 of the said Act, which refers to the possibility for the ministerial organ of the AU - the Executive Council - to draw up common policies in a range of areas, including that of nationality, the Ivorian judge considered that the founding treaty of the AU " *may be declared to be in keeping with the Constitution insofar as the afore-mentioned Article 13 is not conceived as conferring on the Executive Council the power to supplant constitutional bodies deriving from national representation and to interfere in the day-to-day management of the question of nationality in each Member State.*"[98].

The case law in favour of sacrifices of sovereignty, which has only been contradicted on one occasion in the sample selected[99], may be justified on several scores.

From the point of view of exegesis alone, it can be based on the existence of the clause " *total or partial relinquishment of sovereignty*". The decisions handed down by judges in Burkina Faso, the DRC and, to a lesser extent, Benin explicitly refer to this clause. The

---

[98] Ruling n°15-2001 of 27 February 2001 of the Supreme Court, *in* DJEDJRO M., op cit., pp. 341-342.

[99] In this concert of rulings in favour of regional or sub-regional integration, there is a voice of discord. This stems from the opinion issued by the supreme court of Congo (Brazzaville) on 1st October 1998[99], asserting that by dispossessing the national jurisdiction of some of its competence (of cassation especially), the OHADA treaty is, partially, contrary to the Fundamental Act of 24 October 1997. This Act was then playing the role of a constitution during a transition period, pending the adoption of a new Constitution.

The significance of this Opinion should not, however, be exaggerated in our view. There is a simple reason for this: at the time the case was referred to it, the judge had no reference standard, no normative compass. It should be remembered that this Opinion was issued under the influence of a « Transition Charter », a provisional legal instrument as its name suggests, and which, no doubt for this reason, contained no provisions relating to the international commitments of the Congolese State, unlike the Constitution which it replaced [99]. In such a context, which is not the only distinctive feature of this Legal Opinion [99], the national court, lacking a lifeline, concluded as it did. Was this inevitable or, in other words, could a different opinion have been envisaged? The resources of interpretative activity are numerous, and there is nothing to rule out this possibility.

existence of such a clear provision in the text of the Constitution makes the judge's work easier in a way.

In the case of Senegal and Benin, however, this clause did not really come into play, as it did not exist in the Senegalese Constitution at the time (the revised 1963 Constitution) and was only very partially invoked by the Beninese judge, who based his ruling, as we have seen, on the fact, very briefly mentioned, that the President had the power to « negotiate and ratify » treaties. The Senegalese judge also relied on general considerations relating to the country's adherence to the ideals of Pan-Africanism. There is some reason, we believe, to see in these "bold" interpretations[100] a form of militancy by the judge, a striking manifestation of " judicial activism». The Ivorian judge also used this stealth technique in the two judgments he delivered: that of 23 December 1994 on OHADA and that of 27 February 2001 on the Constitutive Act of the AU.

It would seem to us that all this case law, which is based on a flexible conception of the principle of sovereignty, should be approved. Aside from the commitments formulated in national Constitutions, it is the mere prospect of international cooperation, the stringent requirements of coexistence and the pooling of projects and undertakings between States that justify the very relative perception of sovereignty demonstrated by case law. The dangers of the concept of state sovereignty as a rigid dogma of international relations have long been highlighted. Pushed to its extreme limits, the notion of State sovereignty is likely to lead to the

---

[100] The same adjective is used by KIENOU S.M., « L'incidence du droit régional africain sur le droit constitutionnel des États francophones d'Afrique de l'Ouest », *Revue française de droit constitutionnel*, 2017/2, p.419; for a similar but slightly different opinion, see RAYNAL J-J, « Intégration et souveraineté : le problème de la constitutionnalité du traité OHADA », *Penant,* n°832, janvier- avril 2000, p.18. SALL A. in « Note sous la décision 3/C/93 du conseil constitutionnel du Sénégal », *Penant* n°827, mai-août 1998, pp.232 et s., Provides some commentary on the ruling of the Constitutional Council.

very negation of international law, as Charles Chaumont[101]. already thought. But without going as far as the eminent scholar, it seems to us that it is possible to justify the African positions by remaining within the purely constitutional framework within which the limitation or dissolution of sovereignty was expressed.

B. Theoretical Justification

The question of the sacrifices of sovereignty involved in a project of regional integration has aroused the interest of publicists and spawned numerous scholarly studies. In sooth, this debate has been burdened by two assumptions: it has been conducted from an essentially European prism, and it has been considered almost exclusively from the perspective of the exercise of secondary constituent power, i.e., in terms of constitutional revision. Of course, these two determinants are not necessarily relevant to African states.

Another feature of the debate is that it has tended to be framed in terms of the "continuous degradation" of sovereignty. Subsequently, the problem came down to locating the critical level of sacrifice, i.e., the level below which the state would cease to exist. A substantialist prejudice - the substance of the State - therefore dominated the academic debates that ensued.

Remaining solely within the constitutional framework of European states, some academic writers have concluded that it is impossible to maintain statehood once a certain number of sacrifices of sovereignty have been made. This is the meaning of the question posed by the author J. Combacau:

---

[101] CHAUMONT Ch., « Recherche du contenu irréductible du concept de souveraineté de l'État », *Mélanges Basdevant,* 1960, p.114. Jules Basdevant referred to sovereignty as *« dangerous mystic »* (RCADI 1936, t.IV, p ;377) and, elsewhere, Georges SCELLE thought of it as a *« fiction »* or even *« a logical impossibility»* (*Précis de droit des gens,* Sirey, 1932, T.1, p.13).

" Are there (...) unavailable freedoms in international law, and can the State indefinitely reduce the sphere of its individual liberties? There is no doubt that it can validly annihilate itself as a State, for example by merging with others into a new federal entity or, as the GDR did, by merging into an existing State; but the answer is perhaps not as obvious to the following question, which is quite different: can it renounce any of its competences and constrain its powers, whatever they may be, and nevertheless persist in its status as a State within the meaning of international law, of which sovereignty is a statutory element? "[102].

This scepticism, which seems to be expressed in absolute terms - although it is well known that it is European integration that is in view - has also been expressed regarding the framework of the constitutions of the EEC/EU Member States. As they were - and almost all of them remain - they do not seem to leave room for any substantial erosion of state sovereignty. Th de Berranger writes that "if one day the initial federal purpose of the Community project were to be realised in the « United States of Europe", this would not be permitted by any of the national Constitutions in their current state. A simple revision of these would not suffice. It would be requisite to accept a veritable constitutional *hara-kiri* at the national level"[103]. For J.Ph. Derosier too, « constitutionalizing the European Union is a legal impossibility if it is understood as the establishment of a form of " United Sates of Europe" i.e a sovereign state comprising all the current Member States as non-sovereign

[102] Combacau J., « Pas une puissance, une liberté », *Pouvoirs* n°67, 1993, p.57.

[103] De Berranger Th., *Constitutions nationales et construction communautaire. Essai d'approche comparative sur certains aspects constitutionnels nationaux de l'intégration européenne,* Paris, LGDJ, 1995, p.5

federated entities[104]. Finally, remaining more specifically on the question of constitutional review, O. Beaud notes that "a constitution cannot itself rule that it authorises its own destruction and abolition by any constitutional review"[105], a proposition confirmed by the Italian Constitutional Court[106].

In fact, the preservation of this " Constitutional Grail", the idea that there is a world inaccessible to secondary constituent power, that constitutional revisions cannot do everything, cannot afford to do just anything, is developed by so many authors, and ultimately refers to the following thesis: the dissolution of the State into a federal whole, the : "scuttling" of the sovereign State can only be achieved by a total break with the legal order in force, by *fiat*, a spectacular *break* with the legal order, which is a major political act. It is therefore a political decision that brings about the death of the sovereign State. Such a killing, such a *hara-kiri* is only conceivable if one abandons the legal order in force. An eminently political act of dissolution has no place in the existing legal order. We are indeed in a situation beyond the constitution if the Constitution has not envisaged the possibility of such a suicide. But if it has clearly envisaged it, as in the African Constitutions, not only is it not necessary to "leave" the Constitution (since it "contains" the act of interruption), but this break can, from a psychological point of view, be envisaged with less apprehension, less fear of the unknown, less widespread terror.

We should agree, therefore, that it is at a political level, ultimately affecting the very freedom of States, that the question is resolved. Freedom - that is to say, sovereignty - also serves to bind, and freedom can impede freedom by adhering to an agreed

---

[104] Derosier J.Ph., *Les limites constitutionnelles à l'intégration européennes. Étude comparée : Allemagne, France, Italie*, Thèse, Paris I, 2010, summary of thesis.

[105] Beaud O., « La souveraineté de l'État, le pouvoir constituant et le traité de Maastricht », *Revue française de droit administratif*, 1993, pp.1050-1051.

[106] Cited by de Berranger Th., op cit. p. 309.

discipline. The judicial body of the League of Nations taught us this many years ago in its very first ruling: "The power to enter into international obligations is precisely an attribute of the sovereignty of the State (...) a restriction on the exercise of its rights of sovereignty which a State has accepted by treaty cannot be regarded as a violation of sovereignty"[107]. What is important to retain from this passage is only this positive or appeased dimension of sovereignty, which is precisely the dimension emphasised in African positions.

It must therefore be acknowledged that the decision to dissolve the State is taken at a higher political level, a freedom that no one would question. Puzzled by the capacity of positive constitutional law to "absorb" the dilution of the State, legal scholars are forced to concede this original and substantial freedom of States: " the problem is no longer truly legal, but fundamentally political" Th de Berranger[108] admits that in the end, "political will takes over from the law". It is the Member States that remain unanimous that are the masters of the game: they are free to amend the Treaties or not, and to make any constitutional changes that may be necessary, using not the power of revision but the original constituent power [109]. A state can decide, in the name of its own sovereignty, to "scuttle" itself, to cease to exist as such and lose itself in a whole. African states have politically accepted the principle of this *hara-kiri* and have not shied away from naming what will become of them in their national texts: the federal state or something similar, in any case, a new reality that will necessarily lead to their demise, a new legal being into which they will sink. This open acceptance of the unionist ideal and the adherence to a tamed sovereignty that it implies are not necessarily to be found in Europe and America.

---

[107] IPCJ, in the « Wimbledon » case, judg 17 about August1923, Series A, n°1, p.25.

[108] De Berranger Th., op cit., p.312, note 264.

[109] De Berranger Th. Op cit, p.5

II. IN EUROPE AND AMERICA: QUALMS ABOUT SOVEREIGNTY

The contrast with the way sovereignty has been treated on the African continent in the context of regional integration is twofold. In America, and especially in Europe, resistance from States has certainly been stronger. It is as if these states were plagued by a kind of sovereigntist nostalgia, which is reflected in the difficulty both of thinking about and defining the ceding of sovereignty (A) and of putting it into practice (B).

A. Difficulty of articulating the relinquishment of sovereignty

State reticence begins with words. While there is frank talk of the « dissolution» of the State in the African context, notably through the creation of federal groupings, European and American States do not go that far, evoking the concessions that integration requires but holding back from two points of view: using "vague" or euphemistic expressions on the one hand, and by the indeterminacy of the beneficiary of the transfers of sovereignty on the other. This two-fold impasse leads to a timid or watered-down expression of the commitment to ceding its powers, with misgivings about sovereignty leading people to be economical with language and to hold back their discourse.

This is remarkable in the European context[110]. The concessions that the State is prepared to make, when they are simply not linked to any purpose, are stated pithily, and remain linked to "distant", evanescent, "vaporous" goals. The concessions are linked to the needs of international organisations or international institutions in

[110] On the subject, see the work of De Berranger Th., cited above: *Constitutions nationales et construction communautaire.*

Germany[111], in Belgium[112], Luxemburg[113], The Netherlands[114], Denmark[115], Greece[116], Italy[117] and Spain[118]. It may also be in a bid to "promote cooperation and the international legal order" (Denmark)[119], the " need to organise and protect the peace" (France)[120], or linked to " an order ensuring peace and justice amongst nations" (Italy)[121]. In the end, it seems that only three states clearly identified the construction of Europe as the justification for ceding sovereignty. However, unlike African states, which had clearly « internalised » the Pan-Africanist perspective and its institutional implications, and expressed these in their very first Constitutions, these European references were inserted following ad hoc constitutional reviews, carried out with a view to ratifying specific treaties. This rewriting of the Constitution in response to changing circumstances can be seen in States such as France (rewriting of Article 88, particularly when the Maastricht Treaty came into force), Ireland (revision in 1972 prior to the country's entry into the EEC) and Portugal (which also revised Article C7 of the Constitution with a view to accession to the EEC).

A difference then arises between the processes of African and European integration. While the construction of Europe is certainly a long-standing undertaking, going back much farther than the formation of the nucleus from which, it was to develop (the 1957

---

111 Art. 24§1er of the Constitution.

112 Art 25 b of the Constitution, art. 34

113 Art 49 of the Constitution.

114 Art 92 of the Constitution.

115 Art 20§1 of the Constitution.

116 Art 28§2 of the Constitution.

117 Art 3 para.11 of the Constitution.

118 Art 93 of the Constitution.

119 Art 20

120 Para 15 preamble to the 1946 constitution.

121 Art 11.

Treaty of Rome), the designation of Europe as the beneficiary of transfers of competences or concessions of sovereignty has been slow in coming. Instead, it was achieved under the pressure of cyclical factors, linked to the ratification of the various treaties that marked out the process. This has not been the case in Africa.

As a result, the very identification of the eschatological figure - the end or purpose in view - i.e., the specification of the enterprise for which sacrifices were accepted, was earlier and more precise in Africa. Whereas on the European continent we had to deal with stale nations, slowly built up through adversity – Whether it was a desire for national affirmation in the face of " empires" or the papacy, endemic or sporadic conflicts with other sub-national entities - the enemy within - or multi-national entities - the enemy without - and which did not raise the question of their regrouping until long after they had established their existence, African states, at the very moment of their birth, i.e. their accession to international sovereignty, had to address the issue of their survival, an issue implied by their dilution into small groupings. There has been a curious phenomenon of self-dissolution by nascent subjects who, at the very moment they come to life, not only project their own death, but orchestrate the modalities thereunto. This is an essential constitutive fact of the history of African states: their anti-colonial struggle was at one with the exaltation of their unity, and their emancipation and development could not be thought of in isolation from their integration. It is therefore understandable that the legal instrument on which these States are founded - the Constitution - should dwell on the issue of their unity, and that provisions should be devoted to it. This is, first and foremost, a question of adherence to a creed, of the political affirmation of readiness to integrate into a larger whole or into larger entities.

As far as the Pan-American project is concerned, the differences that emerge are not so much to do with the identification of the eschatological figure as with the institutional precision of the integration project. By this we mean that the constitutional statements of the American states, while they do indeed evoke Pan-Americanism as a creed, or Latin America as a space, almost all fail to focus on the consistency of the undertaking, on its identity at the institutional level, on what precisely the states want to build[122].

On the one hand, the same timid expressions can be seen as those previously mentioned in relation to Europe. For example, Brazil is only "seeking" to foster Latin-American cooperation[123], Bolivia[124], Colombia[125], Ecuador[126] and Uruguay[127] want to "promote" or " encourage" same.

On the other hand, the terms or expressions associated with adherence to the Pan-American project in no way suggest ambitious forms of integration, except for the Constitution of Ecuador, which is not only fairly detailed in its definition of the content of Latin American integration - unification or harmonisation of numerous areas of legislation - but also refers to the prospect of "Latin American Citizenship"[128]. Apart from this, when they do venture to address the eschatological aspect, the texts are not very precise. The Argentine Constitution refers to the establishment of supra- national organisations[129], while the Paraguayan constitution refers to a supra-national legal order[130].

---

122 See Mora Burbano I. C's *Les constitutions sud- américaines...* cited above for a general reading on the subject matter

123 Art 4 of the Constitution.

124 Art 265 of the Constitution.

125 Art 150.

126 Art 423.

127 Art 6.

128 Art 423.

129 Art 75 Para 24

130 Art 145.

There is one final point which reveals a kind of intellectual difficulty in conceiving of major challenges to the sovereignty of the State.

This relates more specifically to the construction of Europe, and is reflected in the recurrent, almost cyclical nature of the debate on constitutional review. Despite formulations that might have been thought sufficiently open to withstand the dispossessions implied by the succession of European treaties[131], there is a kind of sceptical predisposition to admit that the slightest advances in integration can be cast in the mould of positive constitutional law. In other words, every time - or almost every time - a treaty is signed, it must be ratified by a revision of the State's Constitution. So, there is a kind of intellectual resistance, a latent reluctance to think about sacrificing sovereignty, a deeply cultural attachment to the independence of the State.

The debate has become somewhat thorny, even obsessive on occasion. It will be recalled that a State such as France has, since the opening of the Union phase (Maastricht Treaty of 1992), carried out at least six constitutional reviews, ranging from the implications of the new Union to the implementation of the principle of subsidiarity, the transfer of competences linked to the movement of persons, the European arrest warrant, the competences of the supra-national Parliament and the consultation of the French people in the event of an application by a State for accession to the EU.

In Germany, the adoption of each major European treaty has given rise either to lively doctrinal debates or to jurisprudence characterised by a certain reluctance to accept the sacrifices brought about by deeper integration. Already with the Maastricht Treaty, some legal scholars had expressed the view that the relevant provision (Article 24 (1) of the Constitution) was incapable of

---

[131] De Berranger Th., op cit., p. 109.

"containing" the changes that the treaty entails. The notorious jurisprudence "So lange I", delivered on 24 May 1974 emphasised that article 24 was not sufficient to shift what the Judge called the "the basic structure of the Constitution", which change seemed to be implied by the European Treaties. There were, however, judges within the jurisdiction - a minority - who thought the opposite: that the provision in question was perfectly sufficient to form the basis for the new transfers of competence[132]. On the very subject of the Treaty on European Union, the German judge was categorical: " the principle of democracy places limits on the expansion of the tasks and powers of the European Communities", he wrote in his judgment of 12 October 1993. Later, as we shall see, it was the weapon of "national constitutional identity" that was to be used as a buffer against the advance of European integration.

Ireland is also a country with a strong revisionist streak. Its very entry into the EEC gave rise to an initial revision of its Constitution: in 1972, Article 29 of the Constitution was revised. (European Communities Act), with a view to acceding to the Community, and in 1987, the Constitutional Court also addressed the question of the constitutional implications of the Single European Act in two rulings. A judgment of 9 April 1987, in the ("Crotty" case), held that a constitutional review was necessary, but here too a minority of judges took the view that an amendment to the Basic Law was superfluous.

The same discussions had taken place in Belgium when the very first European institutions were being set up. As early as 1952, the government, supported by some legal experts, took the view that the Treaty establishing the European Coal and Steel Community (ECSC) and then the European Defence Community (1952) required changes to the Constitution. However, not only was there a body of scholarly work supporting the view that constitutional

---

[132] De Berranger Th. Op cit, p 299.

review was unnecessary, but the country's own authorities had shortly before taken the view that positive law authorised the transfers of powers required by the treaties. In fact, after two attempts, the revision was carried out in 1970[133].

All in all, at the beginning of the 90s - which corresponded to an overheating of the European machine-, that only two States seem to have been less sensitive to the temptations of revisionism, considering that the provisions of their fundamental laws were sufficient to « bear » the changes brought about by integration. These are Denmark and the Netherlands. In the case of Denmark, Article 20, which establishes the principle of delegation of national powers, has been considered sufficient. It seems that the 1983 Constitution conceived in sufficiently broad terms the powers that could be entrusted or vested in international institutions[134]. The relatively recent members Spain, Greece and Portugal took care to include specific provisions in their Constitutions in anticipation of their accession.

The relative hesitancy by European and American states in conferring a precise and above all ambitious institutional form, when they express their adherence to the regionalist creed, contrasts with the verve of the African option, which bears witness to a de-dramatised vision of state sovereignty. Behind the cautious rhetoric and the silence on the ultimate aims, behind the revisionist temptation that arises every time the demand for integration that knocks on the doors of States, we can guess a form of intellectual prevention in admitting the surrender of sovereignty, in considering that it requires special texts and procedures to be undone. But this reluctance to conceive, to think about the surrender of sovereignty is not the only manifestation of the empire that sovereignty wields. At the stage, not of intellection on the

---

[133] De Berranger Th., op cit., p 92.

[134] De Berranger Th., p.96.

surrender of sovereignty, but of its practice, it is also possible to observe some facts or reasoning likely to confirm the difference in approach between the African continent and the European continent, chiefly.

B. The difficulty of ceding sovereignty

Having been chased out the door, sovereigntist resistance is coming back through the window. In the European context in particular, this comeback is taking place in two ways. On the one hand, even if they were to relinquish some of their competences to the supra-national entity, these States would justify their dispossession by the revocability of the latter, with the possibility of taking back what has been given even becoming the criterion for the legal admissibility of the sacrifice. To put it another way, the sacrifice of sovereignty only becomes legally conceivable when it is possible to go back on it, when it is affected by precariousness and revocability, when it is never definitive. Still about this sovereigntist nostalgia, it is necessary to assert that there is a constitutional core that is not subject to corrosive international dynamics, a residual sovereignty that is unattainable, a reserve of national competence that cannot be altered by the demands of the international or regional order.

Revocability as a condition for the legal validity of the ceding of sovereignty can be understood as a reactive construction to Europe's claim to a form of eternity. It should first be remembered that the 1957 Treaty of Rome itself clearly stipulated that it was "concluded for a limited period" (article 240). The case law of the Court of Justice has reinforced this clause, since according to the landmark Costa v Enel judgment of 1964, the EEC Treaty created " a community of *unlimited* duration (...) endued (...) with real powers deriving from a limitation of competence or a transfer of powers from the States to the Community, those States having "limited their sovereign rights". In the judgement in *Commission vs*

French Republic from 14 December 1971, the Court held that "the provisions of the treaty cannot be deemed to have elapsed".

Such decisions thus tend to confer a form of permanence on the EEC/EU. It was therefore in reaction to such a claim, and out of a principled attachment to the sovereignty of States, that the latter, as well as some academic writers, developed the thesis of the revocability of accession to the European treaties, and even made this essential precariousness a criterion for the validity of the concessions made by the Member States.

The possibility of renouncing treaties is first highlighted by the Luxembourg Constitution. Under the terms of Article 49a of the Constitution, the powers delegated to the European organisation are temporarily devolved to the Member States. As has been noted by legal experts, over and above the purely technical question, this was a matter of opposing a transfer of sovereign rights[135]. Consequently, when asked to give an opinion on the ratification of the Maastricht Treaty, Luxembourg's *Conseil d'Etat* reiterated the idea that, assuming that European treaties are in fact concluded for an unlimited period "renunciation is a matter of right"[136]. It was also based on the preservation of the power to say "no" that the minority judges of the Irish Supreme Court took the view that a constitutional review prior to the entry into force of the Single Act was not necessary, the sovereignty of the State being preserved by the simple right of the Member State to prevent it. The German Constitutional Court, in its Maastricht decision of 12 October 1993, also attached importance to the possibility of Germany renouncing the Treaty, as did the Polish Constitutional Court later, in a ruling of 24 November 2010[137]. In this respect, a " general tolerance for

---

[135] De Berranger Th., op cit, p 95.

[136] Opinion n°39-380 of 26 May 1992, cited by de Berranger Th., op cit, p. 96.

[137] See Matsumoto Couveinhes F. et Nollez-Goldbach R. (dir.), *la dénonciation des traités. Techniques et politiques,* Paris, Pédone, 2022, p.43.

unilateral renunciation", could be observed. A trend which shows that, contrary to what the "experts" on European law maintained based on the alleged intentions of the States, and the Luxemburg Court, the transfers of competence from the States to the Union had never been irreversible[138].

If there were still any doubt about the importance of the parameter of reversibility of transfers of powers as a criterion of their legal validity, we would add the major political statements that have settled the debate. The French Minister of Justice, Michel Vauzelle, for example, during the parliamentary debate on the Maastricht Treaty. Addressing the National Assembly on 28 April 1992, he stated that "it is impossible to alienate national sovereignty irreversibly... Neither a treaty nor a constitution can bind a people forever... "[139].

European practice itself proves that renunciation remains possible, despite assertions or insinuations to the contrary. Two referenda in the history of European integration have resulted in withdrawals: one took place in the early 1980s, resulting in the withdrawal of Greenland, a part of Denmark, which joined the EEC in 1973 (agreement of February 1983 between the Danish government and the EEC), and the other, in 2016, was the British referendum sealing Brexit. It is true that, in the case of the latter, the question of renunciation had in the meantime been explicitly settled by the insertion of Article 50 in the EU Treaty, thanks to the signing of the Lisbon Treaty, bringing to finality this long-standing debate.

The ability to renounce, the subsistence of the power to say no therefore tends to be a condition of validity for relinquishing sovereignty or transferring powers. This clearly testifies to a form of resistance on the part of the State, and thus contributes to the

---

[138] Ibid.

[139]Cited in de Berranger Th., op cit, p.20.

difficulty, mentioned earlier, of practising the relinquishment of sovereignty. There is another technique of retention, another concept that states use to stem the rising tide of transfer of powers to European institutions: the notion of national constitutional identity.

The emergence of this notion, or rather its expansion, can be traced back in time. Indeed, as early as the first "So lange" judgment of 29 May 1974, the German Constitutional Court literally evoked the notion of "identity" as a limit to European influence, but it was at the end of the Common Market, and on the eve of the qualitative jump spurred by the Maastricht Treaty, that the concept of national constitutional identity was invoked[140]. Even though its meaning may not be unequivocal[141], one must agree that the only thing that matters here is that it acts as a refusal, that it is a response to the European onslaught, that it responds to a need to "defend" ourselves. As A. Viala writes:

> "It is as if the nation states, mourning the loss of their own sovereignty by accepting the primacy of European law, were focusing their attention solely on what they could not renounce, through their own identity, without denying themselves. This gives rise to the feeling that the resistance of domestic legal orders can no longer be expressed in terms of power or state sovereignty but, more fundamentally, in terms of existence or cultural visibility."[142].

---

[140] Rousseau D., « L'identité constitutionnelle, bouclier de l'identité nationale ou branche de l'étoile européenne ? », in Burgorgue-Larsen L. (dir.), *L'identité constitutionnelle saisie par les juges en Europe,* Paris, Pédone, 2011, pp.90-91.

[141] Rousseau D., op cit, pp.96 et s. ; Burgorgue-Larsen, « L'identité constitutionnelle en question (s) », in Burgorgue –Larsen L., op cit, pp. 157 et s.

[142] Viala A., « Le concept d'identité constitutionnelle. Approche théorique », in Burgorgue-Larsen L., op cit, p. 8.

The concept of national constitutional identity can be found in the constitutional case law of many EU Member States. From «founding» members such as Germany, France, and Italy, to «new» members such as the Czech Republic, Latvia, Poland, and Spain,[143], judges are making use of it. In Germany, the concept made its debut with the "So lange" rulings of 1974 and 1986. The latter, dated 22 October, sets out in clear terms the function of national constitutional identity: "The power conferred by Article 24 (1) of the Basic Law is (...) not without constitutional limits. This provision does not authorise the identity of the constitutional order in force in the Federal Republic of Germany to be alienated through the granting of sovereign rights to inter-State institutions, by an intrusion into its fundamental features and the structures of which it is composed» of elements likely to alter it. In the case law relating to the Treaty of Lisbon, dating from 2009, the German courts refer more specifically to national constitutional identity: « the obligation imposed by Community law to respect the constituent power of the Member States as masters of the Treaties corresponds to a constitutional identity that is non-transferable and not subject to integration"[144], the obligation imposed by Community law to respect the constituent power of the Member States as masters of the Treaties corresponds to a constitutional identity that is non-transferable and not subject to integration, it states by way of principle.

In France, the concept appears for the first time in the decision of the Constitutional Council of 27 July 2006. According to the Council, "the domestication of a community directive is the result of a constitutional requirement; it is for the Community courts alone to ensure that the directive complies both with the powers defined by the Treaties and with the fundamental rights

[143] See the work of L. Burgorgue – Larsen cited above for all these national case laws on this idea of constitutional identity « as understood by the judges in Europe ».

[144] §235 of the judgment.

guaranteed by Article 6 of the Treaty on European Union... It could only be otherwise if the directive ran counter to a rule or principle inherent in France's constitutional identity".

In Spain, in an opinion handed down on 13 December 2004, the Constitutional Court laid down the principle that the constraints resulting from the supra-national European order must be « compatible with the fundamental principles of the social and democratic State based on the rule of law established by the national Constitution. The limits on transfers of competence to the European Union could be linked to "respect for the sovereignty of the State, for our basic constitutional structures and for the system of values and fundamental principles enshrined in our Constitution". It should be noted that the Spanish judge, on several occasions in this Opinion, refers to German case law.

Moreover, the notion of national constitutional identity has been codified, i.e., incorporated into a number of constitutions. Article 23 (1) of the German Basic Law, which is clearly devoted to the EU, postulates that the Europe of which Germany is a member " is committed to the principles of federalism, social cohesion, the rule of law and democracy, as well as to the principle of subsidiarity, and guarantees protection of fundamental rights comparable to that provided by this Basic Law". Moreover, the notion of national constitutional identity has been codified, i.e., incorporated into several constitutions. Article 23 (1) of the German Basic Law, which is clearly devoted to the EU, postulates that the Europe of which Germany is a member 'is committed to the principles of federalism, social cohesion, the rule of law and democracy, as well as to the principle of subsidiarity, and guarantees protection of fundamental rights comparable to that provided by this Basic Law'. These ideals may well constitute the hard core of Germany's constitutional identity. While the Swedish Constitution seems to place the cursor of constitutional identity on the preservation of fundamental rights regarding the 1950 European Convention (Article 5, Chapter X of the Constitution), the Portuguese Constitution refers to the "fundamental principles of the democratic state based on the rule of law" (articles 7§6 and 8§4).

These are not, of course, the only examples that could be cited of the enshrinement of the concept of national constitutional identity. Although the concept, as we have seen, began to flourish in the 1990s, when the construction of Economic and Monetary Union proper began, it is linked to a concept of sovereignty that is already familiar: that of seeing sovereignty as a substance that must not be degraded, as constitutionally inalienable. It is this substantialist conception that emerges from case law that goes back much further than that of national identity, case law in which the French Constitutional Council, for example, referred to the "essential conditions for the exercise of sovereignty". We have also seen that, as early as 1974, the German courts were erecting barriers to the progress of European integration. The theory of national constitutional identity therefore has its roots in a philosophy whose manifestations go back further than the shift towards union in the 1990s.

In the final analysis, all this case law is a veritable theory of the reserve of sovereignty. But the very idea of an inexhaustible supply of sovereignty is not so neutral. It is part of a form of mummification of sovereignty, a form of freezing that ends up being a celebration: the insistence on stressing the incompressible minimum of sovereignty ends up producing the feeling - true or false - that sovereignty itself that cannot be compressed, that an inalterable or metaphysical sovereignty could be a permanent sovereignty.

This is a far cry from the African position of 'partial or total ceding of sovereignty'. While it is not possible to deduce from these differences any kind of value judgement, given that they also stem from national histories that are irreducible to each other, we could limit ourselves to making a purely factual judgement: that the demystification of sovereignty, the seeds of which are to be found in African constitutions, is certainly more conducive to the development of an international law that necessarily draws its strength from the organised weakening of States.

CHAPTER 4

THE USAGES OF A PEOPLE OR THE DIALECTIC OF DIVERSITY AND UNITY

The rainbow owes its beauty to the varied shades of its colours

Amadou Hampaté Ba, *The Life and Teachings of Tierno Bocar, The Sage of Bandiagara*

The latest of the world's major human rights protection systems - the European and American models having preceded it by several years - the African mechanism for guaranteeing rights stems from the African Charter on Human and Peoples' Rights (ACHPR), adopted in 1981 in Nairobi (Kenya). This international treaty, which came into force in 1986, establishes a single supervisory body, a quasi-judicial body, the African Commission on Human and Peoples' Rights.

While the statement of "human duties", in the Charter is not in fact unique to Africa - the preamble to the French Constitution of 1795 and the American Declaration of Human Rights of 1948 both contain such statements - the codification of "peoples' rights" is certainly original. In this endorsement, one must first read a kind of homage to their own history: that of colonised peoples, subjected to foreign domination from which they have just freed themselves. From this point of view, the African Charter must be seen in relation to other major norms of international law, which reject the colonial phenomenon and affirm the right of peoples to self-determination.

But the presence of " peoples" in the "human" rights protection instrument is not merely symbolic or commemorative, essentially focused on the past. Peoples, as legal beings, did not cease to exist with the end of colonisation. They continue to assert themselves from at least two points of view.

On the one hand, as one author has written, "the right to self-determination cannot be reduced to the right to independence"[145]. Decolonisation is over, but the right to self-determination continues to apply. Support for this proposition can be found in the other rights enjoyed by peoples, which are set out in Articles 20 to 24 of the African Charter on Human and Peoples' Rights: the right to existence, the rights of colonised and oppressed people to free themselves from the bonds of domination by all means, the right to assistance in "the liberation struggle"[146], as well as the right to "freely dispose of their wealth and natural resources", the right to the legitimate recovery of stolen property, to the unimpeded use of their resources and wealth[147], and even the right to a satisfactory and global environment"[148]. In other words, the right to self-determination *stricto sensu* does not exhaust the rights of peoples; outside any context of foreign domination, such rights can be validly claimed.

On the other hand, and above all, the ingenuity of the African human rights protection mechanism has been that it has not confined the legal protection of peoples to human communities that

---

[145] Hébié M. Commentary on article 20 of the ACHPR, in Kamto M. (dir.), *La Charte africaine des droits de l'homme et des peuples et le Protocole portant création de la Cour africaine des droits de l'homme. Commentaire article par article,* Bruylant, 2011, p.469.

[146] All these rights appear in article 20 of the ACHPR.

[147] All these rights are contained in article 21.

[148] Article 24.

have been the victims of foreign domination, but has extended it to sub-national communities, thereby achieving a two-fold feat: conferring rights on human units that could not be taken into account as a matter of course, and resolving in a very pragmatic way the thorny issue of the legal preservation of minorities confronting international law. As a result, a pluralist and equivocal approach - in the literal sense of these terms - has been preferred in the understanding of the notion of people as rights-holders in the African mechanism. This interpretative creativity, which we owe to the quasi-judicial body - the African Commission on Human and Peoples' Rights - is an original achievement. It has had two benefits: it has provided direct and immediate legal protection for sub-national entities, thereby resolving topical issues (I) and, in a more forward-looking, if we may say so, more strategic way, it has taken up two challenges: that of taking account of the ethnic factor, which is too often presented as being ignored in African law, and preserving, despite everything, the imperative of the unity of States in the face of the risk of fragmentation that such an approach entails (II). There is an African singularity here, because the protection of peoples' in this continental system has no equivalent in either the European or the American human rights protection mechanisms. Adopted only in 1981, the legal system put in place and its quasi-jurisprudential interpretation can therefore be considered to represent a real break with the past.

I. TOPICAL ASPECTS OF THE BREAK

There are two aspects to the boldness of the African approach. Firstly, and starting from the positive law constituted by the ACHPR, the concept of "peoples" was given a polysemic quality, at least a dual content (A). From then on, the way was paved for direct, and not merely indirect, protection of the peoples in question. It is on this crucial point that Africa's originality lies, for such direct protection does not exist in any other system for safeguarding human rights. In Europe, as in America, the protection of human communities has been achieved at the cost of a travesty of human rights; the rights attached to peoples is "artificially" done, such rights being in principle recognised only for individuals (B).

A. Of Polysemy and Bias

From the outset, the question arose as to who was entitled to the rights stipulated in Articles 19 et seq. of the ACHPR. In other words, the African Commission on Human and Peoples' Rights, a quasi-judicial body, was asked to define what was meant by peoples. It answered the question quite boldly. Indeed, when human communities, sub-national entities, invoked before it the benefit of Article 19 - on the equality of peoples and the prohibition of any domination by one over another - the Commission in no way ruled out such a claim in principle. In other words, it intended that an ethnic group within a sovereign State could perfectly well rely on a provision whose wording might suggest that it concerned only peoples subject to foreign domination. The Commission therefore leaves open the possibility that a given human group within a State may be the victim of a violation of Article 19, i.e., that it may validly allege that it is "dominated". In other words: the *peoples* here referred to are not just peoples under colonial or foreign domination, but also any human entity in a State that suffers ostracism, bullying and massive violations of rights, transgressions perpetrated by the very Member State.

This is where the interpretative genius of the African body lies. It would have been conceivable that the right of a peoples not to be dominated was limited to colonialism. The Commission's opinion is that such domination is not limited to a coloniser, of a foreign power, and that it can be exercised by a Sovereign State. In several cases brought against the State of Mauritania in the 1990s, the Commission endorsed this point of view, the boldness of which has not escaped the scrutiny of legal scholars[149]. In one of these cases, for example, in which Article 19 was at issue, it stated: "The Commission must admit, however, that the information made available to it does not enable it to establish with certainty that the Charter has been violated in the manner alleged here. It has, however, identified and condemned the existence of discriminatory practices against sections of the Mauritanian population [150]. This kind of "reservation" regarding Article 19 - in the sense that the Commission has never formally excluded it - can be observed in several other decisions it has handed down. One example is a 1998 " communication " concerning Zambia. Therein, the Commission states that a people can be defined as "a group of Zambian citizens identifiable by common descent, ethnic origin, language or cultural habits"[151] . Such a definition of the concept of a people proves that in the African human rights protection mechanism, not only is the right of peoples not limited to the claim to independence (right to self-determination), but it can also be applied to identity-based groups within a sovereign State. Having thus clearly indicated its understanding of the holder of the rights set out in the ACHPR, the Commission takes sides, in systematic and definitive terms, on the question posed. Here is what it wrote in a decision handed down in 2009:

> There is a school of thought, however, which believes that the "right of a people" in Africa can be asserted only vis-à-vis external aggression, oppression, or colonization. The Commission holds a different view, that the African Charter was enacted by African States

[149] Bedjaoui and Ouguergouz F., Commentary on article 19 of the ACHPR, publication by Kamto M (dir.) cited above, pp. 447 and 448. See also Hébié M., op cit, p. 453, as well as Mubiala M., *Le système africain de protection des droits de l'homme,* Bruxelles, Bruylant, 2005, p. 36. The latter identifies, at least three possible meanings of the word « people ».

[150] Judg of 11 May 2000, cited by Bedjaoui M and Ouguergouz F., op cit., p. 448.

[151] Communication 211/98, « Legal Resources Foundation Vs Zambia », §73.

to protect human and people's rights of the African peoples, against both external and internal abuse[152].

If there subsisted any doubts as to the quasi-jurisprudential understanding of the concept "People" a deliberately polysemic word, one needs only refer to the conclusions of the report of the working group set up by the same Commission "on indigenous peoples /communities", published in 2005. It was in a quest to clarify the rights holders contemplated in articles 19 *et sequitur* that the Commission decided to set up an experts' Committee to examine the concept of «indigenous peoples» in Africa[153]. Now, the conclusion of the report fuses up the quasi-jurisprudential schools of thought identified, confirming thus the plurality of meanings that the word "peoples" entails. One reads in this reference document that "Africa has gone past the struggle against colonisation. The African Charter must therefore be construed and interpreted in light of current realities, chiefly characterised by the pressing need to promote and protect the human rights of *vulnerable groups and peoples within States*"[154].

It does seem that this quasi-jurisprudential orientation is rooted in the Universal Declaration of Human and Peoples' Rights, adopted on 4 July 1976 in Algiers, which traces the contours of the African conception of the matter, since considers that " *when a people constitute a minority within a State,* it is entitled to have its identity, traditions and language as well as its cultural heritage respected" (article 19). It is in this sense that one must construe the provisions on right " to culture" and "the preservation of cultural

---

[152] Communication n°279/03, 296/05, 27 May 2009, « Sudan Human Rights Organisation, Centre of Housing Rights and the Sudan Eviction », § 222.

[153] Resolution on the Rights of indigenous People/Communities in Africa, African Commission of Human and Peoples' Rights, 6 November 2000, 28th session, Benin, Fourteenth annual activities of the Commission, 2000-2001, OUA, Doc AHG 229 (XXXVIII).

[154] Report of the Experts working Group of the African Commission on Human and Peoples Rights on indigenous peoples/communities, p.4

identity" spelt out in the text (article 2, section IV). This is a far cry, as one can clearly see, from the reticence of the French constitutional judge who considers that the reference to a "Corsican people" in a law is "contrary to the Constitution, which only recognises the French people, comprising all French citizens, without distinction of origin, race or religion"[155]. The concept developed by the African body is therefore characterised by a certain de-dramatization, even a form of good will in pole opposite to the sort of dogmatism which could characterise a unitary, strict, ideologies, of the notion of people "people".

The pluralist approach taken by the African system has been critiqued based on considerations relating to international law itself. The liberty taken regarding the approach adopted by this general international law has been criticised to some extent; the "demagogical way the concept" "people" has been employed has been denounced, as well as its "very unfortunate" usage[156]. The critiques seem rather virulent to us, the words used a tad harsh. Firstly, because there is absolutely nothing preventing the African system from asserting a form of autonomy vis-à-vis the universal approach. There is no reason why small, regional legal systems, reflecting local solidarity, cannot, on given points, give free rein to their creative genius. This has been the case with American regional law on issues such as political asylum, and with European law on the relationship between the supra-national system and national legal systems. It is therefore quite conceivable that African states will develop an autonomous conception of the notion of "people". Moreover - and this is a second argument - we shall see that the subversive potential of the polysemic bias has been "brought under control", contained in practice through what is referred to below as the containment of the risk of secession. For if the international

---

[155] French Constitutional council, ruling n°91-290 of 9 May 1991, §13.

[156] Hébié M., op cit., p 459.

legal order stands out for its reluctance to enshrine the attribute of peoplehood, it is because it fears what passes for the quintessence of the rights of the people, which is the right to self-determination. However, the African experience reveals something else and tempers this apprehension. The perils of the African option should therefore be put into perspective.

Recognition of the plurality of the people is the prerequisite for the uniqueness of the African concept. This uniqueness consists in the direct, immediate legal protection of peoples, where other mechanisms for safeguarding human rights provide, at best, only indirect, oblique protection.

B. Direct rather than indirect protection of the people

The argument put forward here, which is corroborated by the relevant case law, is simple: whereas in the other two major systems for safeguarding human rights, the protection of peoples is not self-evident and is achieved by extrapolating the rights of individuals - i.e., in an indirect way - the African mechanism resulting from the ACHPR achieves direct - i.e., direct - protection of peoples.

Articles 19 to 24 of the ACHPR confer specific rights on peoples', not private individuals. These rights have been asserted in contentious proceedings by ethnic or identity-based groups in States party to the Charter, and the very principle of claiming the benefit of the provisions in question has never been challenged by the Commission itself. When the applicants' claims have been rejected, it has been based on insufficient evidence, but never because their legal grounds were flawed. In other words, the articles relating to the rights of peoples were perfectly appropriate to the disputes submitted to the African human rights bodies. In the African context, therefore, peoples are direct holders of rights; they do not need the veil of private individuals to exist or to enjoy given prerogatives.

The African Court on Human and Peoples' Rights itself, in the interesting case of "African Commission on Human and Peoples Rights Vs Republic of Kenya" (Judgment of 26 May 2017), declared that " nothing would prevent (the) rights of peoples, such as the right to development (Article 22), the right to peace and security (Article 23) or the right to a healthy environment (Article 24) from being recognised, where necessary, specifically, to the ethnic groups and communities making up the population of a State "[157]. This position of principle is illustrated in a plethora of cases.

It has already been noted that, regarding Article 19 on the right to equality of peoples, which excludes any domination exercised by one group against another, the African Commission has never rejected in principle the invocation of Article 19. The "Mauritanian cases" that came before the Commission in the 1990s bear this out. We have also seen how the group of experts appointed to examine the categories of "peoples " and "indigenous communities" has, in the report *supra,* considered that the right to equality and to non-discrimination of peoples went beyond the context of colonisation and foreign domination.

Article 20 of the ACHPR was invoked in the Katanga People's Congress Vs Zaire case. The case was a delicate one because what was really at stake was the very right to self-determination, a highly sensitive prerogative if ever there was one. We will come back to the unease that this referral aroused, but it should be noted at this stage that although the request was not successful, the Commission in a way downplayed the right in question by arguing that all peoples have a right to self – determination[158].

Other provisions recognising the rights of peoples have been confirmed. In the *Sudan Human Rights Organisation, Centre of Housing Rights and Evictions vs The Sudan* , the violation of Article 22

---

[157] § 199 of the judgment.

[158] Communication 75/92, « Congrès du peuple kantagais/DRC », §3.

of the ACHPR, was found, and expressed in the following terms: "Attacks and forced displacement of people in Darfur have denied them the opportunity to engage in economic, social and cultural activities. The displacement hinders their children's right to education and the pursuit of other activities. Instead of deploying its resources to address the marginalisation in Darfur that was the main cause of the conflict, the Respondent State instead launched a punitive military campaign that constituted a massive violation, not only of the economic, social, and cultural rights, but also of other individual rights of the people of Darfur. Based on this analysis of the nature and extent of the violations, the Commission finds the Respondent State in violation of Article 22 of the African Charter. "[159]. Article 22 concerns the right of peoples to economic, social, and cultural development. Earlier, the Commission took care to point out that the Charter " protects the rights of all individuals and of all peoples whatever their race, ethnic origin, religion or other social origin. Articles 2 and 19 of the Charter are very explicit in this respect (...). The Commission considers that the people of Darfur are «a people», in the terms of article 19, and do not deserve to be dominated by a people of another race in the same State. Their claim to equal treatment stems from their alleged underdevelopment and marginalisation (..)"[160].

Lastly, the violation of Articles 21 and 22 - among others - was found in relation to the "Ogiek people" in Kenya. In the aforementioned judgment of 26 May 2017, the African Court on Human and Peoples' Rights observed that the Kenyan government had also violated Article 21 of the Charter since the Ogiek had been deprived of the right to enjoy and freely dispose of the food wealth produced by their ancestral lands. [161]. The breach of Article 22

---

[159] §224 of the ruling.

[160] § 223 of the ruling.

[161] § 201 of the judgment.

results from the fact that 'the Ogiek were expelled from the Mau Forest by the defendant, without proper consultation[162].

Beyond the application of the Charter, the organs of the African human rights protection system have endeavoured to explain the reasons for the choice made to provide immediate protection for peoples. In the above-mentioned Communication on Darfur, the Commission states that by ensuring the legal protection of peoples, " it contributes to Africa's acceptance of its diversity"[163]. Deliberately adopting a pedagogical stance, the Commission goes on to argue that "it is regrettable that Africa tends to deny the existence of the concept of "people" because of its tragic history of racial and ethnic sectarianism. The Commission believes that racial and ethnic diversity contributes to a rich culture that should be celebrated. Diversity should not be seen as a source of conflict"[164].

A final singularity of the African approach needs to be highlighted. This is the impact of the openness to external sources resulting from Articles 60 and 61 of the Charter. These provisions, as shown in a special chapter in this book, open up the possibility for the supervisory bodies of the regional human rights protection mechanism to "draw inspiration » from other norms and practices to apply the ACHPR. In the specific case of the legal protection of peoples, this possibility has been rather boldly interpreted, another illustration of African particularity. Firstly, on the part of the judicial body itself. In the Ogiek case, for example, the Court argued that "Article 22 of the Charter should be read in the light of Article 23 of the United Nations Declaration of Human Rights (...)"[165]. The Court proceeds in the same way in delineating a definition of the

[162] §210 of the judgment.

[163] § 220 of the judgment.

[164] § 221 of the judgment.

[165] § 2009 of the judgment.

concept of people[166]. Similarly, in its jurisprudence on Darfur, the African Commission drew heavily on the quasi-jurisprudence of the United Nations Committee on Economic, Social and Cultural Rights regarding the right to health.[167].

More systematically, the report of the group of experts, after quoting the provisions of Article 60 of the ACHPR, expresses its understanding thereof. In dealing with communications submitted by persons identifying themselves as indigenous or in examining States' periodic reports, the African Commission should have recourse to, and "draw inspiration" from divers international human rights instruments. Although only a few States have ratified ILO Convention 107 of 1957 and none has ratified ILO Convention 169 of 1989, these two conventions are part of international law. An important point to consider is that ILO Convention 169 of 1989 recognises the principle of self-determination as an important criterion. It could be said that although many African states do not recognise the existence of indigenous peoples on their territory, or that some believe that the concept of indigenous peoples is inapplicable to Africa, Article 1.2 of Convention 169 of 1989 grants rights and protection to peoples who identify themselves as indigenous to Africa"[168].

What has been observed in the study of the system formed by sections 60 and 61 of the ACHPR therefore has particular application here. The interpretation that has been made of these provisions borders on heterodoxy because it goes beyond mere " inspiration" and tends to serve as a basis for powers that the States party to the ACHPR never intended to confer on human rights protection bodies. By way of openness to external sources, obligations that States have never formally subscribed to are, so to

---

[166] §§ 104 et s of the judgment.

[167] §209 of the judgment.

[168] Report cited above, p.86.

speak, imposed on them. The extracts from the just quoted report give an extensive, and others would say abusive, interpretation of the Parties' commitments. In short, the African system would be doubly adventurous: not only does it confer immediate protection on peoples, but States' obligations in this area could be drawn from legal instruments that would not necessarily or formally be enforceable against them, but which would simply reflect "trends" in international law. The binding nature of the African approach is striking.

Not only is it so in absolute terms, but it also remains so from a relative, i.e., comparative, point of view. The originality of African protection of the rights of peoples becomes apparent when we compare it with the protection afforded in Europe and America.

In the European system, the preservation of the rights of specific human groups is doubly indirect. On the one hand, the prerogatives enshrined do not form part of an autonomous body of rules that could be linked, for example, to a minority right. Secondly, they are preserved obliquely, through the rights of individuals, and not, as in Africa, in an open, assertive, and direct manner. In the case law of Council of Europe bodies, it is through provisions such as Article 9 (freedom of conscience and thought), Article 11 (freedom of association) or Article 3 of Protocol No. 1 to the European Convention on Human Rights (right to free elections) that the rights of peoples are affirmed. In other words, they are not, in principle, the addressees of these statements since the beneficiaries of the rights enshrined are people. The relevant legal instrument here could have been the Framework Convention for the Protection of National Minorities, adopted on 10 November 1994. But this document is not binding. According to legal scholars, it remains "a multilateral instrument with a programmatic and purposive function"[169]. The only commitments it stipulates, which are weakly worded, are for States to comply with a few general principles in their national legislation, with a view to protecting minorities. Moreover, the framework convention, faithful to the idea of protection that is only indirect and not direct, intends to cover only persons belonging to national minorities, i.e., individual subjects first and foremost, determined secondarily by their minority status. In other words, there is no such thing as a minority as a subject of law. One need only read the convention to realise this immediately. The holder of the rights set out is "every person belonging to a national minority", not the minority itself. This expression runs through almost all the provisions of this convention[170].

In the European human rights protection system, not only are human entities protected through the rights and freedoms of individuals, but the case law has a special feature: it refers almost systematically to the concept of "democratic society" or "democratic pluralism". The European Court of Human Rights in *Gorzelik and Ors Vs. Poland* on 17 February 2004, held that "respect for minorities is a condition without which there can be no democratic society"[171]. A few years earlier, the same Court had also observed that "pluralism, tolerance and broadmindedness are the hallmarks of a (democratic society)" and that "democracy requires a balance which ensures the fair and proper treatment of minorities and avoids any abuse of a dominant position"[172]. Other rulings could be cited.

---

[169] Rouland N ; Pierre Caps S., Poumarède J., *Droit des minorités et des peuples autochtones,* Paris, PUF, 1996, p. 236.

[170] Articles 1,3,4,5,7 to 13 of the Framework convention –.

[171] §88 of the Judgment.

[172] § 63 of the judgment of 13 August 1981, « Young, James and Webster Vs United Kingdom ». More generally, Tulkens F. and Piedimonte S., « La protection des minorités nationales dans la jurisprudence de la Cour européenne des droits de l'homme », Advisory

It is important to understand here that the justification of protection by the concept of "democratic society" reflects the absence of conventional resources, an absence that the European Court must face up to. The concept of a democratic society acts as a lifeline; it is what remains when the texts are silent. The notion, as a justification, is a mishmash , a convenient and unifying concept in the sense that so many things can be lumped together under its banner. In the absence of a precise and specific justification for the rights of people, the European system resorts to a general, elliptical justification, even a philosophical justification. The protection of minorities here – peoples elsewhere - is therefore a matter of a certain classicism. While the aim of protecting minorities is desirable, the means are very well tried and tested. So, there is nothing innovative about it. One must therefore admit that the preservation of such rights is somewhat unpredictable. By leaving it up to States to define the concept of minority, by managing to limit the binding effect of the framework convention to a modest area, by resorting to rather impressionistic concepts such as "balance" or "abuse of dominant position", European practice provides a breeding ground for "national discretion", another weapon conceded to States to limit the scope of recognised rights.

It is important to understand that this European, "Western" prevention, the reluctance to accept in principle a "right of peoples" is rooted in a fairly long history. The peace treaties drawn up in the aftermath of the First World War, while intended to protect minorities, were in no way intended to give legal recognition to the human person per se. The question did arise when these treaties were negotiated, but the option was clearly taken to gloss over it, in other words, to refuse to enshrine the legal personality of "peoples" or "minorities". Are we to conclude, then, that it is in Africa that awareness of the need to safeguard diversity has been

---

Committee on the Framework Convention on the protection of national minorities, 7th meeting, Strasbourg, 12-13 March, 2008.

more acute, and the concept of national unity less tyrannical? In truth, things are not so simple, and it has happened - as we shall see later - that in the field of African nation-states, an excessively unitary conception of society has been championed. But the fact is that, in terms of regional human rights protection systems throughout the world, the African continent is an exception. Not so much because the protection it provides is necessarily more "advanced" than others, but because it is the only mechanism that embedded national pluralism in its principle by conferring rights on communities of human beings in their own right and not on "persons belonging to ethnic minorities", to use the expression of the European Framework Convention. Moreover, leaving the realm of mere principles to consider the concrete content of the rights of peoples, it must be acknowledged that the ACHPR and its interpretation in case law go quite far. African distinctiveness is therefore more than just a façade. The interpretative activity of the African Commission and Court on Human and Peoples' Rights shows that the consequences of the choice of principle expressed in the Charter have been faced squarely.

Analysing the post-war treaties for the protection of minorities, S. Friedman wrote in 1927 that these treaties have in view only the minority nationals, the arithmetical sum of these, but not the moral unity constituted by the community [173]. When therefore, the authors write, the PCIJ talks about social groups (referring to these minorities) in the *Minority Schools in Albania* case, this should not be misunderstood. By no means does it intend to establish a community as a subject[174]. Reluctance to recognise minorities as subjects of international law therefore goes back a long way in Europe. It is this deep-rooted reluctance that explains the scanty

---

[173] Friedman S., *Le problème des minorités ethniques et sa solution par l'autonomie et la personnification,* Thèse, Toulouse, 1927, pp 133-134, cited by Rouland N et al, op cit, p.191.

[174] N Rouland et al, op cit, p. 191.

record of the European human rights protection system in this area. Moreover, even with a framework convention of modest effect, the European States seemed, in the relatively recent past, to be reluctant to enshrine peoples' rights[175].

If we now turn to the American continent and its protection mechanism, the African distinctiveness persists. In this part of the world, however, there is a solid tradition of case law defending indigenous peoples, and one might have imagined a convergence on this point with the ACHPR mechanism and its interpretation. However, there are two major differences between the two approaches.

The first relates to the very issue of indigenousness. In Inter-American practice, this concept refers to specific realities, which are not certain to exist on the African continent. More specifically, the African human rights protection mechanism has admitted some applications from entities that are not necessarily indigenous. And the protection bodies have not dwelt unduly on this "indigenousness". The rights of peoples referred to in the ACHPR have therefore benefited human communities that are not characterised by their prior presence on the national territory - which is what indigenousness ultimately boils down to. The black Africans of Mauritania or the Katangese of Zaire are not necessarily first inhabitants. While the African human rights protection mechanism deemed it necessary to set up a working group on indigenous populations or communities, as we have already seen, and while the report submitted did indeed describe situations of indigenousness and mention the dangers threatening the rights of the communities identified[176], it must be clearly understood that action before the supervisory bodies is in no way subject to the existence of this status conferred by history. Any people, even non-

---

175 N. Rouland et al, op cit, p 229.

176 Report cited above, pp 18 et s.

indigenous ones, may claim the rights set out in articles 19 et seq. of the ACHPR. Moreover, when asked to give an opinion on the United Nations Declaration on the Rights of Indigenous Peoples, the African Commission itself took the view that in Africa, the term indigenous does not mean "first inhabitants" in reference to aboriginality as opposed to non-African communities or communities from elsewhere. As far as it is concerned, the Commission considers that: any African can legitimately consider himself indigenous to the continent»[177]. In other words, the concept of aboriginality is inapplicable in litigation, which means that the protection of peoples is to some extent unconditional.

Indigenousness is, in contrast, a « marker » of American jurisprudence on "peoples'" rights[178]. The originality of the Americas, according to J. Dhommeaux, is, on the one hand, their ethnic plurality– nearly 400 ethnic groups for 30 million inhabitants – and, on the other hand, the persecution of certain groups[179]. These groups have been marginalised and subjected to physical and cultural genocide, dispossession of land and social contempt. In such conditions, the defence of the rights of peoples is imbued with the idea that the categories in question are essentially characterised by their vulnerability. The concept is taken up literally in certain judgments of the Inter-American Court: the " Sawhoyamaxa " of 29 June 2006, or " Yakye Axa" of 17 June 2005[180]. This overarching presence of indigenousness does not exist in the African human rights protection mechanism. In this respect, the African

---

[177] Legal opinion of the African Commission on Human and Peoples' Rights on the United Nations Declaration on the rights of indigenous peoples, adopted during the 41st ordinary session held in May 2007 in Accra, 2007, p.4.

[178] Dhommeaux J., « Les communautés autochtones et tribales dans la jurisprudence de la Cour interaméricaine des droits de l'homme », in Hennebel L. and Tigroudja H.(dir), *Le particularisme interaméricain des droits de l'homme,* Paris, Pedone, 2009, pp.183 et s.

[179] Dhommeaux J., op cit, p. 184.

[180] Dhommeaux J., op cit, pp 2002-203.

mechanism could give the impression of being less "closed" than the inter-American mechanism.

But above all, one of the limitations of the Inter-American system is that, like that of the Council of Europe, it understands the rights of communities only in an indirect, biased way, in the literal sense of the term: it is obliged to use a bias to give effect to these rights, the bias of individual rights. What the two systems - European and American - have in common, then, is that they have not thought of human entities as autonomous bodies, and that they only grant them rights belatedly and approximately, in other words analogically. The way in which the rights of peoples are preserved is not "primary", it is "derived", derived from individual rights, the only ones contemplated *ab initio*. The clearest proof of this relegation of *peoples*. The clearest proof of this relegation of *peoples* is that the Permanent Council of the Organisation of American States itself recommended, during the 39th session of the Organisation's General Assembly, the adoption of an American Declaration on the Rights of Indigenous Peoples. Furthermore, as pointed out by legal scholars, when the organs of the inter-American system are confronted with a case involving the rights of peoples, they are met with a quasi-legal vacuum[181].

It is the analysis of the decisions handed down by these bodies that provides proof of the indirect nature of the protection of peoples. The very legal basis of these decisions, i.e., the provisions of the American Convention on Human Rights of 1969, concern individuals and not peoples or populations. Articles 3 (right to legal personality), 4 (right to privacy), 5 (right to physical integrity), 22 (freedom of movement), 23 (right to participate in the conduct of public affairs), which may have benefited peoples , all begin with the enunciation "*Everyone has the right......* ". The Convention therefore enshrines individual rights, not, " collective" rights.

---

181 Dhommeaux J. op cit, p. 193.

Moreover, the decisions handed down quite regularly refer to individual rights, even though they concern indigenous peoples or communities. For example, the " Plan de Sanchez" ruling in 2004 states, in relation to the execution of more than two hundred people: " Given that *the victims* in this case are *members of* the Mayan people, this court considers that an important component of the individual reparation is the reparation that the Court will now grant to the members of the community as a whole"[182]. Ordering reparation that satisfies the entire Maya community, taking that community as a unit when awarding the reparation deemed most appropriate - this is what the Court says - does not make that human group a direct right-holder. The words just italicised clearly show that the Court is following a traditional approach, identifying individuals who are directly concerned by the proceedings precisely because they are the only ones to have suffered damage. The social context in which this suffering takes place, and the feelings of the community of which these primary victims are members, may be considered when determining the methods of appeasement that the trial is supposed to provide, but they are not technical elements of the trial and do not come into play in the judicial reasoning *stricto sensu*. In other words, peoples do not enjoy, in such a context, an immediacy of litigation, an intrinsic capacity to assert rights.

Other cases attest to this. In the *Sawhoyamaxa* ruling of 2007, collective suffering is mentioned, but it comes second, after the real and not just symbolic suffering of the "victims". The Inter-American Court considers that "the actions of the State contrary to international law have affected not only t*he victims as individuals,* but the very existence of the community "[183]. In the 2001 *Mayagna* case, the Court referred to "the right of *every person* to

---

[182] Ibid. § 86 de l'arrêt.

[183] Dhommeaux J ; op cit, p 195, § 201 of the judgment

simple and rapid remedy"[184]. In this context, certain statements in the case law should not be misunderstood. One of these can be found in the "Bamaca Velasquez" decision of 2000. Pertaining to the right to have one's case heard with the appropriate guarantees, the Court refers to a "right to the truth" as having a collective nature, which includes the right of society to " have access to essential information"[185]. However, this extract should not be misleading, for at least three reasons. The first is that, in the same paragraph, the Court states that " the State violated the right to the truth of the next of kin of *the victims* and of society as a whole ".; then in paragraph 201: " the right of the *victim* or his next- of-kin to obtain clarification of the facts… ". Secondly, and without playing too much on words, the concept used by the Court is indeed that of society, and not of people or community. The issue goes beyond aesthetics. A society is not a subject of law, nor can it be. On the other hand, a people can be a legal person, if we look at the context in which we live, which concerns precisely the rights of peoples. Finally, when the Inter-American Court, in the same case, enshrined rights for a people, it emphasised that this was the result of a dynamic interpretation of the human rights treaties. All of which shows that the legal protection of peoples remains indirect, and never direct.

Recourse to individual rights to ensure the rights of peoples in the inter-American system is not the only means used by the protection bodies. The rights of communities are defended in two other ways, which could be described as internal and external, respectively. The first is Article 29 of the Convention. In essence, it prohibits a restrictive interpretation of rights based on the Convention. Based on this qualitative pivot, on the virtuous dynamic induced by this article, the Court has been able to develop

---

[184] Dhommeaux J ; op cit., p 210, §104 of the judgment.

[185] Ibid., § 197 of the judgment.

case law recognising the rights of peoples. The afore-mentioned *Mayagna* judgment of 2001 and *Yakye Axa* judgment of 2005 refer to this protection clause[186]. External bias is the use of external sources. The resources of cross-fertilization, offer the inter-American judge the opportunity to preserve the rights of peoples. The solutions it finds are inspired by other legal or judicial systems. The function of this appeal to the outside world must be understood, like the European notion of democratic society discussed above, as a lifeline for a body wishing to guarantee a preservation that it is struggling to find in its formal reference standards. In the "Saramaka" judgment of 2007, the Court referred to a series of texts relating to the rights of peoples: resolutions adopted by the Inter-American Commission on Human Rights, General Recommendation No. 23 on indigenous peoples of 1997, the judgment of the European Court of Human Rights of 27 May 2004, *Connors v United Kingdom*, which considers the protection of the way of life of minorities as a means of ensuring equality before the law .

All in all, the rights of peoples in America have been safeguarded by interpreting the Convention in the light of specific indigenous and tribal characteristics[187]. Through several techniques, the most widespread and simplest of which is equating peoples with individuals and subsequently extending the rights stipulated to human communities, legal protection has been provided to entities that were not envisaged at the time the treaties were drafted. The derivative, indirect nature of the protection thus afforded does not in any way prejudge the quality of that protection. The inter-American mechanism is unique in that it has taken the methods of preserving the rights in question to a very honourable and original level. If we were to judge this

---

[186] §§ 147 and 124 of the judgments.

[187] Rinaldi K., « le droit des populations autochtones et tribales à la propriété dans le système interaméricain de protection des droits de l'homme », in Hennebel L and Tigroudja H, publication cited earlier, p. 220.

achievement, it would certainly be flattering rather than critical. But that is not what is highlighted here. It is the contrast that emerges from the confrontation with an African system that has, in its very philosophical foundations, i.e., at its origin, taken into account the rights of peoples, and not just of private individuals. The difference with its European and American counterparts is obvious on this point.

The choice made by the African states is not only striking because it is original. It is interesting because it has a kind of therapeutic quality, a dimension that we would describe as strategic in the sense that the adjective refers to something planned, coordinated, to resolve a difficulty. Hence, in the African approach, there is an immediately operational aspect, a topical dimension, and a strategic and preventive aspect, with both prophylactic and anticipatory virtues. It is this second aspect that we must now examine.

II. Strategic aspects of the break

The merits of the African position can be summed up in two points. On the one hand, the clear assertion of a right of peoples fills the gap in specific legal protection for minorities, particularly ethnic minorities. This is a crucial issue on a continent where ethnic explanations tend to become a kind of hackneyed ritual, a convenient way of reading social phenomena (A). Moreover, recognition of the rights of peoples is neither unlimited nor unconditional. It is kept within a reasonable perimeter, reconcilable with the requirements of the unity of the sovereign State. The consecration of a legal heritage takes place in relation to the imperatives of national unity and the indivisibility of the State, so that the danger of secession is contained, controlled, and circumvented (B). Under these conditions, it can be argued that the African position tends to strike a balance, to reflect a dialogue between diversity and unity.

A. Addressing ethnic and minority issues

African states born after 1960 have regularly been criticised for trying to gloss over the ethnic question, as if the modern state they intended to establish could not accommodate the human diversity that their societies were home to. In these circumstances, ethnicity was seen as a hindrance to development.

The truth is that these states did not share the same degree of ethnic concealment. The fact is that the former French colonies, once they had gained independence, reproduced the well-known hexagonal prevention of social diversity. A whole mythology of Unitarianism, inherited from French history, culminating in the Revolution of 1789, with the birth of the African states as a corollary. The myth of national unity and the dogma of the indivisibility of the Republic are being reappropriated in a way that is tantamount to denying the very history and sociology of these new State entities. From such a perspective, any affirmation of diversity is seen as the result of a centrifugal logic, and therefore dangerous for the survival of the State. As a result, the state itself is conceived in terms of authority, and its relationship with the population is seen as vertical. It is an essentially authoritarian, tutelary relationship. Under these conditions, there is no place for the rights of minorities. The nation is a unitary magma, a sociological block whose component parts are quickly perceived as undermining the social pact itself. As a result, particularist demands are at best stigmatised, at worst suppressed. A value judgment is applied to them: such impulses are considered retrogrades , backward-looking, at a time when the march is toward development and a modernity predicated on the blurring of ethnic singularities and the eradication of otherness is in full swing. From this point of view, the post-modern African state is being built in a certain atmosphere of intolerance, intolerance of bigotry that alters the unity of the nation.

Gourmo Lô describes very well the process by which the post-colonial African state, caught in the clutches of the colonial legacy, begins to reproduce the myths of the former dominator. This conception, he writes, is native to Europe and has a progenitor: France. It has a formal framework of expression: the " Nation State" and is supported by a general principle: the indivisibility of the nation, the meaning of which is expressed through two key concepts : national unity and territorial integrity, conceived in such a way as to exclude any possible legal coexistence between identity-based group components (ethnic groups, communities, nationalities)... Founded on the legal ideology of a single, culturally homogenous and territorially " indivisible", "nation" the post-colonial African state, like the French state of which it is the archetype, cultivates an assimilationist vision of inter-community relations, denying differences and even openly hostile to any real cultural diversity... [188].

Of course, colonial heritage is not everything. There are also purely local motivations behind this relentless quest for unity, this strenuous denial of difference. In the final analysis, the unitarian myth also applies to political power itself, to the government of these societies. Clearly, what is denied in the social sphere is also denied in the political sphere. Here too, any opposition must be defeated, any dissent must be presented as contrary to the principle of unity which alone guarantees development. The urgent needs of the moment do not allow for 'factious' tendencies, and anyone who is not part of the unitary train is putting themselves on the fringes of the march of society. It is not just governments that are using unity as a blackmail tactic. There was a time when analysts complacently entertained the idea that because these nations were

---

[188] Gourmo A. Lô, « Identité et statut des minorités en Afrique », in de Raulin A., Ould Abdallahi S.M., Lô G (dir.), *Droit, culture et minorité*, Proceedings of the GREDFIC conference, Paris, L'Harmattan, 2009, pp. 360 and 365.

fragile, an unfailingly open democratic process risked sowing the seeds of disintegration.

Of course, mistrust of ethnic considerations and social diversity has not disappeared. It still prevails in some national Constitutions and can take several forms[189]. One of these is the willingly systematic association between the principle of the indivisibility of the Republic and the ban on ethnic-based propaganda. Such links can be found in the constitutions, past or present, of Mauritania[190], Guinea[191], Benin[192], Burkina Faso[193] or Djibouti[194]. Another way of circumventing ethnicity is the obligation imposed on political parties, again in the Constitutions, not to identify with a particular section of the population[195], or to have a "national" representation, i.e., not limited to a part of the territory identified with an ethnic group [196].

All these data undoubtedly reflect a desire on the part of the newly independent African states to ignore the ethnic factor, to pretend that it does not exist, in the name of the imperative of national unity. In our view, however, this observation needs to be put into perspective in two ways at the present time. The need for this relativisation arises from considerations both internal and external to these States.

---

[189] Manangou V.R., « L'ethnie dans les Constitutions de troisième génération des Etats de l'Afrique francophone », http://publication.lecames.org.

[190] Article 1

[191] Article 1 of the 2010 Constitution.

[192] Article 3

[193] Article 168.

[194] Article 3.

[195] Article 4 of the Constitution of Senegal, article 13 of the Constitution of Burkina Faso, article 7 of the Togolese Constitution.

[196] Article 3 para 2 of the Constitution of Guinea, article 61 of the Constitution of the DRC, article 13 of the Constitution of the CAR.

From an internal point of view, it should be noted that the Constitutions have evolved. Even if we have not necessarily seen an upsurge in minority rights, we must admit that in many cases ethnicity is no longer a taboo, since the Constitutions not only name it, but also proclaim their desire to promote it. In other words, diversity is accepted, "internalised", and even valued. Many states declare their "pride" in their diversity and their attachment to sociological plurality. Better still, political constructs and institutional arrangements are designed with ethnicity in mind. States such as Rwanda and Burundi clearly admit to avowed forms of power-sharing based on the diversity of the nation. Others, such as Ethiopia, which have not necessarily had a troubled political history arising from ethnic tensions, have also arranged their constitutional public authorities - particularly in the context of a bicameralism based on identity - based on group disparities.

From an external point of view, the African human rights protection system, through the quasi-jurisprudence already mentioned, has made a major contribution to plugging the gap in minority law as such in Africa. Formally, such a body of rules may certainly be lacking, but materially, practically, the protection bodies have provided protection for minorities. As we have already seen, the African Commission and the African Court of Human and Peoples' Rights, through a very comprehensive understanding of the concept of people, have recognised that group entities are entitled to the rights stipulated in Articles 19 et seq. of the African Charter. The decisions handed down in this respect have objectively contributed to the defence of minorities on the African continent. This is one of the results of the interpretative inventiveness of African bodies.

The ethnic question is no longer ignored. The most eloquent testimony to this is the decisions made by the bodies themselves. Ethnic groups are mentioned, either expressly or implicitly. Several decisions can be cited in this regard, including the ruling handed down by the African Court concerning the Ogiek people of Kenya. The judges stated that:

> The enjoyment of the rights recognised ...to the constituent peoples of the population of a given State may be extended to sub-national *ethnic* groups and communities forming part of that population. [197].

Similarly, in its Communication of 27 May 2009 on Darfur directed against Sudan, the African Commission notes that the elements for identifying a people, include "language, religion, culture, the territory they occupy within a state, common history, *ethno-anthropological factors*... In States with a mixed racial composition, race becomes a determinant of groups of peoples, as does *ethnic identity*, which may also be a factor. [198]

In addition to the ad hoc solutions provided by these rulings, it is important to emphasise their strategic dimension: not only are the decisions handed down notable for the direct and immediate protection they afford to peoples, but they also settle, indirectly or by anticipation, the question of minorities. In our view, therefore, it is important to put into perspective the criticism that has been levelled at the African rights protection system on the grounds that it does not include a component relating to the rights of minorities. The truth is that case law has, to a large extent, made up for this shortcoming. This is not the only problem it has preventively addressed. If you read it carefully, you will realise that while it is very liberal in allocating rights to group entities, it remains careful never to open the Pandora's box of international sovereignty, careful to channel the prerogatives in question so that they never lead to a right to secession of peoples.

---

[197] §199 of the judgment.

[198] §199 of the judgment.

B. Containing the risk of secession

The rights generously conferred on peoples are contained within a perimeter that does not threaten the existence of the State in which they are located. The prerogatives conferred must remain compatible with the survival of the sovereign State. To put it another way, there is no right of secession for peoples within States.

This position is based primarily on the case law of the supervisory bodies. In the 2017 judgment of the African Court of Human and Peoples' Rights concerning the Ogiek people, it is stated that:

> "It is difficult to understand why the states that drafted the Charter would want, for example, to automatically recognise the right to self-determination and independence guaranteed by Article 20 of the Charter for the ethnic groups and communities that make up their population. In this case, this would amount to a genuine right to secession. "[199].

The same decision specifies that the rights granted to peoples by the ACHPR are only conceivable if " provided that these ethnic groups and communities do not undermine the sovereignty and territorial integrity of the State"[200]. Previously, in a 2013 case concerning Cabinda, a landlocked territory of Angola, the Commission also considered that "in post-colonial Africa, the right to self-determination can be enjoyed within the existing territories and with full respect for the sovereignty and territorial integrity of States Parties to the Charter"[201].

This position of principle has also been reiterated in a non-contentious context. Asked to give a legal opinion following the

---

[199] §220 of the judgment.

[200] §199 of the judgment.

[201] §199 of the judgment

adoption by the United Nations of a Declaration on the Rights of Indigenous Peoples, the African Commission on Human and Peoples' Rights stated that "the notion of self-determination has evolved with the growing demands of indigenous peoples whose right to self-determination is exercised in accordance with norms and modalities compatible with the territorial integrity of the nation-States to which they belong"[202].

This position of principle has also been reiterated in a non-adversarial context. Asked to give a legal opinion following the adoption by the United Nations of a Declaration on the Rights of Indigenous Peoples, the African Commission on Human and Peoples' Rights stated that "the notion of self-determination has evolved with the growing demands of indigenous peoples whose right to self-determination is exercised in accordance with norms and modalities compatible with the territorial integrity of the nation-States to which they belong"[203]. The statement by the African Group at the United Nations concurs, reflecting a kind of African *opinio juris* on the subject. In the Aide - mémoire produced by it in Novembre 2006, the Group considers that implicitly recognising the rights of indigenous peoples to self-determination (...) can be misinterpreted and understood as granting a unilateral right to self-determination and possible secession to a specific part of the national population, thereby threatening the political unity and territorial integrity of any country.

It seems that the position of principle of the African States is widely shared. The Declaration on the Rights of Indigenous Peoples itself makes a significant clarification in Article 46, which states that:

---

[202] Communication 328/06 « Front for the liberation of the State of Cabinda v Republic of Angola », 5 November 2013, §126 of the judgment.

[203] Legal opinion of the Commission, p.6 (electronic version available).

> Nothing in this Declaration may be interpreted as implying for any State, people, group or person any right to engage in any activity or to perform any act contrary to the Charter of the United Nations or construed as authorizing or encouraging any action which would dismember or impair, totally or in part, the territorial integrity or political unity of sovereign and independent States.

This position may be considered to reflect the state of international law. It can be found both in well-known legal instruments[204] and in the case law of the ICJ, the principal judicial organ of the UN[205].

African states make it a point of honour to assert the subsistence of the sovereign state and its borders because they understand that among the rights recognised to peoples by the ACHPR, there is one that smells of sulphur, and that is the right to self-determination stipulated in article 20, paragraph 1. It is around this prerogative that States are understandably edgy. If such self-determination does not or cannot lead to a right to secession, as we have just seen, then one may well wonder - unless, of course, this notion has a particular meaning in the ACHPR - whether it was appropriate to mention it among the rights of peoples. In any event, it should be emphasised that its formulation produces unease.

As we have seen, this is reflected in the position of African states at the UN. But this unease also exists within African human rights protection bodies. The report of the working group on indigenous communities stresses that members of the African Commission on Human and Peoples' Rights have expressed difficulty in grasping the content of this right to self-determination, particularly in the

---

[204] See for example convention n°169 of the ILO, §3 line 1.

[205] ICJ, Opinion of 16 October 1975 on Western Sahara, ICJ Law Report, p. 33.

Cabinda case[206]. The applicant's claim to independence was rejected in that case, but the basis in principle for such a claim is to be found in Article 20 of the ACHPR. Similarly, this time before the African Court, the judges said they had difficulty understanding how the concept of self-determination in Article 20 could lead to a right to secede[207]. We can only share their discomfiture, because admittedly, a right to self-determination that must never lead to secession is problematic from a logical point of view. In this respect, it would be desirable for the protection bodies to take the " bull by the horns" by giving a precise content to the right in question, by saying what precisely it covers, rather than simply making statements of principle and indicating in a somewhat cryptic and repetitive way that the right to self-determination is only conceivable if it does not lead to a right to secession.

This is not the only point on which the qualitative assessment of the protection of peoples in Africa needs to be somewhat nuanced. On at least two other points, the African mechanism calls for some reservations.

Firstly, the immediate legal protection of peoples. It has been shown that this is the specific feature of the treatment of minorities in Africa, and that in this respect, the African human rights protection mechanism was ahead of others. This point is well established, but it should not obscure the fact that this protection of peoples is also sometimes direct, as in the case of other regional mechanisms. In other words, Articles 19 et seq. of the ACHPR are not the only legal basis for peoples 'rights; other provisions aimed at individuals can also be used to assert a peoples' right. This is the case, for example, with the right to participate in public affairs, provided for in Article 13 for the benefit of anyperson, but which

[206] Report cited above, p.82.

[207] §199 of the judgment of 26 May 2017 handed down by the court, on the Ogiek people in Kenya.

the Commission invoked in the Katanga case. Similarly, in the case concerning the Ogiek people of Kenya, the Court found a violation of articles that did not really relate to the rights of peoples as set out in Articles 19 et seq: these were the provisions of Articles 1, 2, 8, 14 and 17. By extrapolating individual rights into the field of the rights of peoples, the African bodies, like others, are promoting indirect rather than direct preservation. If it is therefore asserted here that the rights of peoples are protected in principle, through direct protection, it must be understood that this protection is not exclusive and that it can coexist with its opposite, indirect preservation, biased - in the true sense of the word.

On the other hand, it happens that African human rights institutions " mutilate" the statutory specificity of the rights of peoples by lumping them together, so to speak, with individual rights. This is the case when the African Commission on Human and Peoples 'Rights considers, in one of its resolutions, that, « the right to development in Article 22 may be invoked by " individuals". This is still "an indirect approach", but it works in reverse: it is no longer peoples who are protected through individual rights, but it is individuals who invade the field of peoples' rights. In both cases, it is the specific status of peoples that is diminished, weakened, and watered down. This shifting ground of legal bases for claims, this kind of mingling, i.e., interchangeability of invocable provisions, may end up dissolving the African originality, which has consisted precisely in "isolating" a right of peoples, in devising a body of rules for these subjects of international law that other systems have tended to treat as latecomers, derivatives or secondary subjects.

This African originality must therefore be reaffirmed. It may be chipped away at, as we have just seen, but it remains robust and undeniable in principle. The history of international law must do justice to this fact: that it was on African soil, in modern times, that systematic and substantial protection of peoples was established.

CHAPTER 5

ALTERNATIVE JUSTICE: SWAYING THE HOLD OF THE DICTATOR'S SWORD[208]

The idea that people have of the law depends on the meaning they give to the world

Norbert Rouland, *Aux confins du droit*

On the ugly side of its history, the twentieth century will undoubtedly be remembered for two events that were traumatic in their scale and cruelty: the century-old racial segregation that held sway in South Africa until the 1990s and the genocide that devastated Rwanda in 1994. Two global shockwaves like few others, two spectacular manifestations of the inhumanity of human history.

From the outset, these events, which were collective traumas, raised the question of how to rebuild the societies that they had destabilised, so much so that these upheavals had shaken the very foundations of the affected communities. Rising from their tragedies, the South African and Rwandan societies found themselves obliged to re-establish themselves, to rebuild, to restore a social bond that had been severely compromised. The objective,

[208] This article repeats some passages from my last book titled *L'émotion et la Raison. L'Afrique face à la justice internationale,* Dakar, L'Harmattan, 2020.

was first and foremost to repair injustices and rehabilitate the victims. These countries initially had to adopt a compensatory approach. This approach consisted of a work of justice, a form of justice that soon came to be known as reconstructive or restorative justice. To meet the unique challenge it set itself, this justice system had to devise ways and means appropriate to its purpose, which, as we can easily guess, was incommensurable with that of traditional justice, that of normal times and ordinary crime. The challenge was therefore one of inventiveness, the ability to develop social and legal engineering, a re-establishment of justice as much as a social restoration. This post-conflict justice is therefore, first and foremost, a different kind of justice, an alternative justice.

Nearly thirty years on from these reconstruction efforts, it would appear that the mechanisms devised have proven to be rather novel, and rather effective, although a nuanced assessment of their design and implementation is still possible, as there is an abundance of critical literature on the subject. But the fact is that the national reconstructions undertaken in the two African countries gave rise to developments which, here again, not only responded to the exigencies of the time, but also, because of their success - an undeniable success to a large extent - stretched the limits of the classical approach to justice and its compensatory paradigm.

A few points need to be made, however, to ensure that what is said here is properly understood. Indeed, it is not only on the overall assessment of reconstructive justice that opinions must be measured. Caution is also called for when it comes to the very existence of an African specificity in this area. After all, Africa does not have a monopoly on this socio-judicial approach to resolving collective trauma or mass atrocities. Initiatives such as the creation of the Truth and Reconciliation Commissions is the most widespread institutional embodiment, have spread throughout the world. And according to a study by Amnesty International published in 2007, at least thirty-three Truth and Reconciliation

Commissions were set up in twenty-eight countries between 1974 and 2007[209].

Most of the time, it arises out of not being satisfied with the traditional judicial system for punishing the offences or behaviour in question and adding to the repressive dimension of the work of restoration, a component involving the rehabilitation of the social link. In this sense, it can be argued that alternative justice is intended to be plural in nature, as social and national contexts inevitably remain diverse. Intended to respond to needs, to local necessities that are irreducible to any other, alternative justice is in fact a blend of specific forms of justice.

A final clarification is in order at this introductory stage. It concerns the broad conception of the notion of alternative justice that has been adopted here. Indeed, the formulae used from one country to another vary considerably, and the question of the relationship between ordinary justice and alternative justice is subject to various adjustments. The subject cannot, therefore, be generalised, and it is even advisable to have a flexible understanding of the concept of alternative justice, which is by no means stereotypical. The characteristic features of this type of justice that are retained here are, on the one hand, the essential place reserved for narration and listening to the victims, and, on the other hand, the emphasis placed on repentance and forgiveness as a means of resolving the tragedies experienced. It is around this minimum standard that the concept of alternative justice mentioned above is built, and these criteria are undoubtedly found in both the South African and Rwandan cases. For the rest, there may be differences between these two models, such as the relationship with criminal law, which is evanescent in the case of

---

[209] Amnesty international, *Truth, Justice and Reparation. Establishing an Effective Truth Commission* 11 June 2007, International Secretariat, London, p. 5.

South Africa, but real in the case of Rwanda's *gacaca* courts, which can hand down sentences of up to three years.

Beyond their differences and nuances, they have a common denominator, as mentioned above. They reject exclusively penal solutions and invariably repressive recommendations. If we were to keep them within a judicial framework, we would say that from ordinary or classic justice, they retain less force than balance, less the sword than the scales.

Since Africa does not, so to speak, have a monopoly of alternative forms of justice, its original features should not be sought or found in any claim to precedence or even exemplarity. What is interesting about the cases considered here - South Africa and Rwanda - is two-fold. Firstly, the scale of the traumas involved: racial segregation and century-old repression in one case, genocide that was all the more violent because it took place on a national scale, and therefore across the board. Not all the countries that have introduced restorative justice mechanisms have experienced atrocities on this scale. Here, it was the scale on which the crime was committed that made the responses perilous and the challenge onerous.

On the other hand, and from what might be described as a qualitative, theoretical, or intellectual point of view, the South African and Rwandan approaches were, to a large extent, the antithesis of the traditional judicial settlement. Major general principles of ordinary criminal procedure were superbly subverted, deliberately ignored in favour of extra-legal considerations. The solutions adopted have thus served to shatter the limits or conundrums of hard criminal law, revealing by their very existence, and by their major success, that it is possible to have an approach to justice that is not only different, but far more appropriate to post-traumatic social therapy.

Our interest thus lies in the properties of these alternative forms of justice, in the same way that we talk about the properties of a medicine, virtues that are all the more worthy of attention because they are dissident, because they depart from the paradigm of ordinary or classical justice (I). It must be said, however, that while these responses have served their purpose well at national level, their acceptance at international level has not been a matter of course. It is as if the international community, too attached to traditional dogmas or inclined to ignore the need for justice to be socially rooted, was reluctant to make room for other, alternative forms of justice that were not part of the dominant, Western-centric model, because they were keen to rediscover their cultural roots. Recent relations between these methods of conflict resolution and the institutions of international criminal justice, particularly on the African continent, illustrate this muted mistrust (II).

I. INTERNALLY: A REDISCOVERY OF THE AMBIGUITY OF JUSTICE

Alternative forms of justice are substantially based on the principle of relativity. This relativity is two-fold. Firstly, it exists in relation to ordinary justice, that of the States and their law courts, a national or international justice system that only deals with the law and is essentially technical in nature. Relativity is also present at the very heart of this other form of justice because it is necessarily plural in view of the social rehabilitation it seeks to achieve. This implies considering the diversity of contexts[210]. It does not, therefore, accept the univocality of the rule of law or the verticality of the organisation of the bodies that express that law.In short, it rejects any authoritarian logic. In this sense, alternative justice effectively reveals that there is something else, another way of dispensing justice. The experience of reconstructive justice in general, and that of South Africa and Rwanda in particular, is

[210] This being the case, and with no real consequence resulting from this bias, the singular and plural will be used interchangeably: we will speak here of: alternative justice or « alternative forms of » justice.

evocative and reminiscent: it reminds us that justice is a plural concept, that there are different conceptions of justice, simply because justice ultimately refers to a social or mental representation, to a *weltanshauung*. This is true when we look at justice both in terms of legitimacy (A) and in terms of effectiveness, i.e., from the point of view of achieving the goal it has set itself (B).

A. On the question of legitimacy

The legitimacy of alternative justice stems first and foremost from its collective roots. This characteristic is desirable in a context where, by definition, it is a question of collective outrage, both from the point of view of the perpetrators of the acts being judged and the victims of those acts. So, there is nothing to do, as in a traditional criminal trial, with an offender and a victim. In such a trial, society is of course involved through the public prosecutor, but this social presence remains purely symbolic or mediatised. In mass crime trials, on the other hand, the community is affected first and foremost, and it is the community that reveals itself daily during the proceedings. There is nothing like the rigorously bilateral confrontation between executioner and victim, but a procession of victims with varied histories and conditions, all working together to highlight collective dysfunction and trauma. The trial is therefore a faithful mirror of society, which shows itself in the very materiality of the trial, without the need for a prosecutor. This is because the evil being judged is not an individual deviance but a collective vice.

African societies have a rather communitarian way of life and are therefore predisposed to embrace the paradigm of reconstructive justice. Norbert Rouland has expressed this relationship between African societies and justice in striking terms. Talking about African cosmogony, asserts the following:

> Continuous differentiation and the coherence of creation go hand in hand: differences create solidarity, and social

division is conceived in terms of complementarity (...). Political power is also subject to these kinds of divisions, a separation of powers that predates those of Aristotle and Montesquieu: little by little, the master of the earth, the master of the rain, the master of the harvest, the master of the invisible, and the political leader have emerged. No one can exercise power without the support of others. This does not mean that conflicts are absent from these societies. But they are prevented, cushioned by this system of representations, which poses the problem of justice in a different way: justice is less a question of individuals (...) than of global balances, which are always fragile, and in which everything is done to maintain order. The division between Good and Evil takes place at this level, which cannot satisfy our Western minds, which are more characterised by individualism. This focus on order leads to another construct, which is equally disconcerting for the Western jurist: the lesser weight of norms, understood in the sense of general and abstract rules, which fill our codes. [211].

Rouland speaks of traditional African societies, but the essence of the concept he describes is certainly present in the development of alternative justice systems in South Africa and Rwanda. It could not have been any other way, since once the collective nature of the vice had been diagnosed, the appropriate response could only be found in a return to oneself, in a rediscovery of oneself that remains a traditional resource, a return to one's roots. The therapy therefore draws on the common heritage of the members of the social body. Now that the social pact has been subverted, we need to go back to its origins to re-establish it. He further writes: "The backdrop to the

---

[211] Rouland N., *Aux confins du droit,* Paris, Odile Jacob, 1991, p.65.

trial, the context within which the protagonists of history will confront each other, is what they share, a common foundation. To judge is to relate a fact to the origins of the social pact.[212]

But the point is not to return to history to be exiled from it. The return to the founding social pact is only one stage in the process of reconstitution and is destined to be overtaken. For the reconstruction of the social bond must be open to the future. Without this projection into the future, it remains a purely nostalgic act, a shrinking and stunting. Rediscovering the essence of the social bond must not be a one-way ticket; it must be followed by a time of openness, which is a gamble on the future. The South African law setting up the Truth and Reconciliation Commission speaks of a bridge, a bridge between a traumatic past and a future full of promise:

> Since the Constitution of the Republic of South Africa, 1993 (Act 200 of 1993), provides a historic *bridge* between the past of a deeply divided society characterized by strife, conflict, untold suffering and injustice, and a future founded on the recognition of human rights, democracy, and peaceful co-existence for all South Africans, irrespective of colour, race, class, belief or sex.

A. Garapan writes more or less the same thing:

> This link between justice and construction, between justice and politics, between the past and the future, prevents the trial from being destructive (…). Law of the (victims) imprisoned in their suffering, the trial frees them (...). The trial thus acts as a bridge between the past

[212] Garapon A., *Des crimes qu'on ne peut ni punir ni pardonner,* Paris, Odile Jacob, 2002, p 238.

> and the future because it judges a period that is past, but under a new law and a new regime. [213]

The justice we are talking about, which is supposed to heal society from the severe shock it has suffered, will therefore be characterised by two things: a collective approach and a grounding in tradition.

It is a community that is at stake, if only because the crimes in question spared no one. Involving everyone in the search for a solution is both logical and fair. Logical because everyone has been involved in this tragic story - in different ways and to different degrees - and fair because the victims, in particular, have the right to be involved in restoring their rights.

The « people » is thus called upon to play a significant role in this process. The Preamble to the Rwandan Organic Law of 26 January 2001 "on the establishment of the *gacaca* courts and the organisation of prosecutions for offences constituting the crime of genocide or crimes against humanity committed between 1st Octobre 1990 and 31st Decembre 1994". In a preamble, it states that since the offences were "committed publicly in full view of the public", their "repression" and reparation for injuries must be carried out in public. The justice dispensed by the *gacaca* courts is indeed carried out in the public eye. The law also states that the aim is not "merely to punish, but also to rehabilitate Rwandan society, which is in a state of decay... ...". The Manual for judges of these courts is also revealing. It states "the fundamental principle of the *gacaca* courts is that everything works with the people and by the people. No decision is taken without first holding a meeting with the people. It is the people who make up the *gacaca* courts. They also provide information about what happened and the responsibility of the

[213] Garapon A ; op cit., p.264.

accused. It is the people who appoint the Inyangamuyago (judges) who take the decisions. [214]

Finally, the courts in question are deeply rooted in Rwandan society. They existed long before colonisation and were naturally exhumed in the aftermath of the April 1994 massacres. It is true that this resurgence was facilitated by the collapse of the Rwandan State's official judicial system, but the speed with which they were replaced and the government's acquiescence to this spontaneous generation of courts speak volumes about society's support for this method of dispensing justice.[215]

The introduction of restorative justice in the two countries studied was relatively easy because it was based on a principle of trust that only increased its legitimacy. Even the profile of judges was rigorously delineated, and in a manner as to allow them to secure the buy-in of the people for justice delivery. The *Inyangamuyo* of Rwanda are counterparts of the *ubuntu* described by Desmond Tutu in South Africa[216], and similar ones can be found in other African contexts as well [217]. These enlightened individuals are judges solely by virtue of their personal qualities and the social recognition they enjoy. The appointment of these arbitrators goes beyond individual consecration; it is driven by deep-seated motivations because it reflects a break in legitimacy, the abandonment of the old justice system in favour of a new one, dressed up in other finery and certainly better accepted, at least

---

[214] P. 5 of the Manuel. Cited by Garapon A, op cit., pp. 293-294.

[215] IDEA, Huyse L. *Traditional Justice and Reconciliation after Violent Conflict, Learning from the African Experience,* 2009.

[216] Tutu D., *No future without forgiveness,* London, Rider, 1999, p.34.

[217] Other examples include Sierra Leone, where the law of 22 February 2000 setting up the Truth and Reconciliation Commission provides for the assistance of traditional and religious leaders (§7.2), and Burundi with the (§7.2) « Umushingantahe » or the « Bashingantahe » (IDEA, Huyse (dir), op cit, p.164.

from the perspective of the social therapy made necessary by the immeasurable criminality we have just witnessed.

The reversal of legitimacy is obvious when the Rwandan law of 2001 establishes incompatibility between the current or past exercise of functions linked to the authority of the State - such as that of career magistrate, expressly excluded - and that of judge of the *gacaca*[218]. The reversal of legitimacy is obvious when the Rwandan law of 2001 establishes incompatibility between the current or past exercise of functions linked to the authority of the State - such as that of career magistrate, expressly excluded - and that of judge of the *gacaca* courts. It is therefore a question of turning one's back on a certain kind of justice, and not of cobbling together expedients to make up for the shortcomings of a judicial system in disarray. Nothing could be more erroneous, or more simplistic, than to regard the replacement of official justice as merely supplementary and temporary. In Rwanda, the return to the traditional courts was a veritable reversal of legitimacy, a de-legitimisation and re-legitimisation, albeit provisional, because it was simply a matter of clearing up a traumatic past and getting on with life, so to speak.

Local justice makes for better "control", of the justice delivery system, and in contexts where the national pride of a people may have suffered from a more or less open form of marginalisation or international ostracism, alternative justice has been the springboard to regaining lost dignity. This stage of justice is the stage of reclaiming the national history and sovereignty. By endowing itself with restorative institutions, the State is affirming to the world that not only does it have the means to pull through, but that it is prescribing the appropriate medication for itself. There is no denying the sentimental and somewhat vindictive dimension of this approach. These adjectives are in no wise demeaning. On the

---

[218] Article 11 of the above-cited law of 2001.

contrary, the point is to show that it is from national pride that we draw the strength to successfully complete the reconstruction project.

In fact, in the two countries, there were solemn moments, almost dramatic peaks, when sovereignty was affirmed.

It is as if mass atrocities gave rise to a feeling of dereliction in the communities that experienced them - a feeling that was often accentuated by the distant or curious way in which others looked at them - and then to a nationalist outburst. In our two examples, sovereignty was invoked both nationally (in South Africa) and internationally (in Rwanda).

In South Africa, the amnesty contained in the Promotion of National Unity and Reconciliation Act was challenged in the Constitutional Court, with the applicant challenging the constitutionality of the Act on the grounds that it failed to recognise the right of victims to protection. The Court's response is a mixture of reason and authority. On the one hand, it stated that the Amnesty Law is authorised by the Constitution itself. On the other hand, the aims of the law are put forward: It allows the victims to express their pain and the words of the victims help to reveal the truth. By giving a voice to those who suffered from the crimes of apartheid, the law not only restores to them a right that was apparently ignored under the racist regime, but also serves a social objective, which is to know the truth. Then comes the argument about authority: it consists of saying that the very principle of such a means of redressing suffering was laid down by the sovereign people through their representatives. Only the law, the embodiment of the will of the people, the repository of sovereignty, could bring about such a redistribution of the cards. Sovereign power is unconditional, which is why it is able not only to break with existing arrangements, but also to choose the path it deems appropriate for reconciling society. Thus, sovereignty is a power, a supreme power.

In the case of Rwanda, the sovereignty crisis occurred when the ICTR was created at the Security Council. It was sovereignty in its external dimension, i.e., independence, that was highlighted. Rwanda contested what it seemed to regard as a symbolic expropriation of its history, which was the UN body's decision not to establish the Tribunal in the country itself, but in Tanzania. Even though Rwanda had itself asked for UN support to set up an ad-hoc tribunal, it felt it had to vote against Resolution 955.

The country's representative on the Security Council listed seven reasons why his country could not support the resolution. One of these reasons was the location of the tribunal. It could even be said that this issue was at the heart of Rwanda's protest, as it was mentioned twice in the country's arguments. According to the ambassador, it is hard to accept that the draft statute of the International Tribunal proposes that those condemned be imprisoned outside Rwanda and that those countries be given the authority to reach decisions about the detainees. This is for the International Tribunal or at least for the Rwandese people to decide (...). My government called for the establishment of an international tribunal to prosecute those guilty of genocide because the international community is deeply concerned in this respect, but also and above all we requested the establishment of this Tribunal to teach the Rwandese people a lesson, to fight against the impunity to which it had become accustomed since 1959 and to promote national reconciliation. It therefore seems clear that the seat of the International Tribunal should be set in Rwanda; it will have to deal with Rwandese suspects, responsible for crimes committed in Rwanda against the Rwandese. Only in this way can the desired effects be achieved. Furthermore, establishing the seat of the Tribunal on Rwandese soil would promote the harmonization of international and national jurisprudence. My delegation was surprised to see that the authors of the draft still hesitate to indicate where the future seat of the Tribunal will be.[219].

This speech sums up Rwandan prejudices perfectly. Under these conditions, the exercise of international criminal justice is perceived as an inappropriate interference, as an aggressive intrusion, as a form of violation of national history. Rwanda feels it has been dispossessed of its own history. The international community has come to "plunder" a heritage, committing a kind of breach of trust by convincing a State to enter the intimacy of its history, but robbing it at the last moment of the power to judge, which is so symbolic of sovereignty.

This is about how justice is perceived, its social acceptability, and therefore its legitimacy on all the points that have just been addressed. But the changes suggested by alternative justice are not limited to the question of legitimacy alone. They also affect the very effectiveness of justice, in that the therapy proposed is not that of ordinary trials.

B. In terms of efficiency

Farewell to the obsession with repression and the "all-penal" approach, long live healing through storytelling and forgiveness! Because alternative justice has neither the methods of ordinary justice, nor its ends. It is deliberately far removed from the paradigm of classic criminal justice, with its afflictive and infamous method of reparation. It is the retributive nature of the punitive approach that is denied. Punishing a criminal is not the goal, nor is inflicting punishment, as is customary. In place of an individualistic and utilitarian approach that assumes that the seriousness of the act prosecuted, and the punishment inflicted match up - a match that is obviously problematic when it comes to atrocities committed on a humanly incommensurable scale - a more communitarian-

---

[219] S/PV.3453, p.16.

inspired approach is promoted, emphasising the need to re-establish the truth of the facts and the need to repair social ties. The executioner-victim face-off, possibly mediatised by a public prosecutor pursuing a purely individual responsibility, disappears in favour of a collective exercise in exorcism, where the main issue is the liberation of speech, the verbalisation of the past being seen as the means of freeing oneself from the nightmares of the past. Neither personal stigmatisation nor repressive obsession, alternative justice is quite simply justice without trial, in the sense in which the latter is often understood.

The storytelling dimension is healing through verbalisation. Alternative justice is first and foremost testimonial justice. The explanatory memoranda to the South African and Rwandan laws are very clear. The aim of the South African law is "the granting of amnesty to persons who make *full disclosure* of all the relevant facts relating to acts associated with a political objective committed in the course of the conflicts of the past during the said period ; affording victims an opportunity *to recount* the violations they suffered ; the taking of measures aimed at the granting of reparations to, and the rehabilitation and the restoration of the human and civil dignity, victims of violations of human rights ; *reporting* to the Nation such violations and victims… ". Regarding the law setting up the « gacaca » courts in Rwanda, it considers « that the offences (…) were committed publicly before the eyes of the population » and « that it must therefore *relate the facts, reveal the truth* and participate in the prosecution and trial of the alleged perpetrators», "that the *duty to testify* is a moral obligation, and no one has the right to shirk it for any reason whatsoever". The Judges' Manual of the *gacaca* further specifies the objective of "bringing to light the truth of what occurred during the genocide and the massacres associated with it"».

When the confrontation between the perpetrators and the victims does not necessarily aim to establish liability for punishment, when free expression of views and feelings is the sole purpose of the trial, it is clear that the aim is not so much to condemn individual behaviour as to seek absolution. Whereas conventional justice operates on the pessimistic or negative principle of determining culpable liability, the course of alternative justice reveals the positive side of human reality, since it must conclude with forgiveness: the Beast versus the Angel, Evil versus Good, Hobbes versus Rousseau.

We need to listen to the protagonists in the history of both countries, leading political figures, talk about the essentially absolutist vocation of alternative justice. For Bishop Desmond Tutu, whose book's title alone says it all [220], "there is another form of justice, reconstructive justice, which was the basis of traditional African jurisprudence. In this context, the aim is not punishment in line with the concept of *ubuntu*, the primary concerns are to repair the damage, restore the balance, restore broken relationships, rehabilitate the victim and also the guilty party, who must be given the opportunity to reintegrate into the community that has been injured by his or her misdemeanour or crime". Nelson Mandela himself, the leading figure in the fight against apartheid, stated that "forgiveness liberates the soul, it removes fear. That is why forgiveness is such a powerful weapon"[221]. The 1995 law on the Truth and Reconciliation Commission adds:

> Since the Constitution states that there is a need for understanding but not for vengeance, a need for reparation but not for retaliation, a need for ubuntu but not for victimization.

In Rwanda, the advocate of forgiveness is also the country's chief magistrate, Pasteur Bizimungu, who was Head of State when the Truth and Reconciliation Commission was set up. He asserts that:

---

[220] Tutu D., *No future without forgiveness*, Paris, Albin Michel, 2000.

[221] Cited in IDEA, Huyse L. (dir) p. 4.

" the nation must be rebuilt on new foundations, and it is up to the people who saw these bad things happen to bear witness, nothing can be envisaged without them (...). Some may *repent* and repair the damage done, others may *forgive,* and it is they, together, who must rebuild Rwanda"[222].

It is the retributive nature of criminal justice that is really denied: there is no question of punishing a criminal, of inflicting punishment, as is customary. In place of an individualistic and utilitarian approach, which assumes that the seriousness of the act prosecuted, and the punishment imposed are commensurate - a match that is obviously problematic when it comes to atrocities committed on a human scale that is incommensurable - a more communitarian-inspired approach is encouraged, emphasising the need to re-establish the truth of the facts and the need to rebuild social ties. The face-to-face confrontation between the perpetrator and the victim, possibly mediated by a public prosecutor pursuing a purely individual responsibility, gives way to a collective exercise in exorcism, where the main issue is the liberation of speech, the verbalisation of the past being seen as the means of freeing oneself from its nightmares. Neither personal stigmatisation nor repressive obsession, the alternative justice of truth commissions is quite simply justice without trial.

There is something else: the effectiveness of restorative justice can also be assessed in terms of comparative advantages. In other words, on several scores, its superior quality, its qualitative superiority over the institutions of ordinary justice, should be noted. The first point on which alternative justice is relevant is its ability to cope better than the ordinary justice system with the workload that mass crime entails. he formal justice system is

---

[222] Cited by Dumas H., « Juger le génocide sur les collines. Les procès gacaca au Rwanda », in Andrieu K and Lauvau G. (dir.), *Quelle justice pour les peuples en transition?* PUPS, 2014, p.269. Italics mine.

designed to deal with ordinary criminals, of the sort we come across daily. Their absorption capacity is therefore limited because the crime in question is marginal, exceptional. As soon as it becomes monstrous, i.e., reaches certain proportions, it can no longer be dealt with under the usual procedures. Overall, however, alternative justice bodies have succeeded in this challenge of stock management. In Rwanda, the cases of the one hundred and thirty thousand people imprisoned after the genocide, implicated in the massacre of nearly eight hundred thousand people, were dealt with in a timely manner, something that the official justice system would never have been able to do.[223]. In South Africa, more than twenty-two thousand people were heard by the Truth and Reconciliation Commission. [224]

Traditional justice is also unable to apply its rules of evidence to mass atrocities. This is difficult when the crime has spread its tentacles to the whole of society, when the status of victim and executioner is not fixed but confused in the muddled succession of events, and when systematic and deliberate policies and practices to dispel evidence are organised on a large scale. Under such conditions, it becomes impossible to maintain the evidential requirements of ordinary trials. The offences in question call for the invention of a new judicial paradigm, and this is precisely what alternative justice systems are trying to do. If we were to keep to the pattern of the ordinary trial, the trial of mass crimes would lead to dead ends or absurdities.

As despicable as they are in that they are the embodiment of evil, these acts have the value of encouraging inventiveness. And the unprecedented ways in which they were responded to, in South Africa as in Rwanda, show that justice is not a mechanical device, a

---

[223] IDEA, Huyse L., op cit., p. 56.

[224] *Truth and Reconciliation Commission of South Africa Report*, Capetown, Juta & Co, 1998, 5 vol., 2739 p.

technical arrangement, but refers to mental representations, to a vision of man and society. It is therefore never one and the same, never assigned to a single purpose, but remains full of relativity and ambiguity.

Undeniably original, the experiments in restorative justice in South Africa (the Truth and Reconciliation Commission) and Rwanda (*gacaca* courts) have, quite honourably, been able to meet the twin challenges of legitimacy and effectiveness. Their work is certainly not without criticism - we will come back to this - but the results of their action can be defended, particularly in view of the conditions under which they were set up.

It is therefore curious that at international level this record has not been fully appreciated. The international community has displayed a somewhat schizophrenic and paradoxical attitude towards alternative justice. On the one hand, it has paid it many tributes, and has even clearly conceded that it could be an appropriate remedy for the turmoil caused by mass crime. On the other hand, however, at the stage of collaboration with it or its concrete activation, it has shown prevarications which undoubtedly testify to the strength of habits and the difficulty of precisely internalising the ambiguity of justice.

II. EXTERNALLY: THE INTERNATIONAL COMMUNITY'S VACILLATIONS

The paradox lies in the fact that international institutions have in turn exalted and glorified alternative justice (A), then held it in contempt and distanced themselves from it (B).

A. Exaltation

National experiments in restorative justice have been well received throughout the world. It is hard to find, in the practice of States as well as in legal doctrine, any repudiation in principle of these novel approaches. Better still, the phenomenon has been showered with praise, both in a global international organisation such as the UN and in the more limited framework of regional organisations.

Within the United Nations, several declarations or proclamations can be cited that attest to this benevolence towards restorative justice methods.

One of the documents that systematise UN doctrine in this area is instructive. Title: "The rule of law in transitional justice in conflict and post-conflict societies"[225], it addresses the issue of the settlement of disputes arising from the crisis in clear terms that are worth reporting. Regarding truth commissions, the report states that "truth commissions have the potential to be of great benefit in helping post-conflict societies establish the facts about past human rights violations, foster accountability, preserve evidence, identify perpetrators and recommend reparations and institutional reforms. They can also provide a public platform for victims to address the nation directly with their personal stories and can facilitate public debate about how to come to terms with the past. "[226].

UN General Assembly Resolution 68/165 of 18 December 2013, Welcomes the establishment in several States of specific judicial mechanisms and non-judicial mechanisms, such as truth and reconciliation commissions (...) and Encourages the States concerned to disseminate, implement and monitor the implementation of the recommendations of non-judicial (...)[227]. In Resolution 2282 adopted on 27 April 2016, the Security Council for its part stresses that the adoption of an approach encompassing all aspects of transitional justice, aimed particularly at fostering appeasement and reconciliation, the establishment of security

[225] Doc S/2004/616, 23 August 2004

[226] Op cit., p. 22.

[227] §§2 and 3.

institutions (...) is essential to prevent States "from engaging or re-engaging in a conflict"[228]. UN Secretary-General Koffi Annan, on his part, stated the following: "due regard should be given to traditional indigenous and informal mechanisms for the administration of justice or the resolution of disputes, so that they can retain their often-essential role, in accordance with both international standards and local tradition"[229].

The European Union has had to consider alternative justice. Its Parliament has devoted several sessions to this issue and has adopted declarations encouraging this form of peace making, which is used in some countries.[230].

The statement adopted at the IV Conference of Francophone Ministers of Justice, organised by the Organisation Internationale de la Francophonie (OIF) on 14 February 2008, underscores the importance of para-judicial mechanisms in the context of peace making or peacebuilding in post-conflict situations.

Curiously, however, these expressions of good will do not seem to have been matched by concrete work with alternative justice institutions. It is as if alternative justice was only taken seriously on the diplomatic and official scene as long as it remained for internal use. Indeed, international institutions seem to have been in a state of doubt when it came to putting the matter into practice and incorporating national para-judicial bodies into the formal machinery of international justice.

---

228 §12 of the resolution.

229 Cited by IDEA, Huyse L., op cit., p. 3.

230 Flautre H., « La justice transitionnelle dans le prisme de l'Union européenne », Revue *Mouvements,* 2008/1, pp. 26 to 30.

B. Doubt

When it comes down to it, international institutions have found it difficult to domesticate alternative justice. It is as if a form of realist conservatism has taken over once the time for petitions of principle and empty entreaties has passed. Although they generally recommend recourse to this new form of justice in the name of respect for specific social characteristics, the major international organisations - first and foremost the UN and its bodies - are reluctant to take action, i.e., to regard restorative justice as a worthy partner that can be incorporated into the formal mechanisms of international justice.

It is immediately clear that it is in its relationship with criminal courts in general, and the ICC, that these latent reservations will find expression. As the system of permanent criminal jurisdiction can generally only be set in motion on condition that the national judicial system refrains from acting - a principle of complementarity that lies at the heart of the way the ICC operates - the question quickly arose as to whether experiments in alternative justice, with their dissenting features, could be considered as part of the exercise of justice in the classic sense in which the Rome Statute on the ICC envisages it. It was therefore the question of the procedural articulation of the two forms of justice that was raised, i.e. that of harmony or coherence in their respective deployments: Is the exercise of such justice comparable to the triggering of State justice, justice in the sense of the Rome Statute establishing the ICC, in which case its implementation could, in the name of the principle of complementarity, neutralise or freeze any intervention by the international jurisdiction in cases being dealt with at national level (principle of complementarity, i.e. subsidiarity of the ICC)? One could put it in more philosophical and systematic terms: can international criminal justice, so dominated by repressive considerations, admit the existence of a form of justice devoid of any punitive purpose, can it tolerate otherness, can it conceive of other forms of justice?

The debate is not purely philosophical. It has a definite practical dimension, given that this different form of justice exists in almost all the countries whose cases have been dealt with by the ICC, and that it has even claimed, at given times, to take over cases that the international court was investigating or wanted to investigate[231]. investigate. It should be added at this point that the prospect of a systematic replacement of criminal justice by truth commissions was, at least for a time, attractive to African leaders. The idea of setting up this model as a panacea was toyed with by the experts responsible for drawing up a report on the situation in Darfur, a group headed by former South African President Thabo Mbeki. The conclusions and recommendations of this Panel go beyond the case of Darfur and clearly have a regional ambition. It is clearly specified that, beyond Darfur, the aim was to *make generic recommendations on integrated justice and reconciliation responses for Africa as a whole* [232].

The statement adopted at the IV Conference of Francophone Ministers of Justice, organised by the Organisation Internationale de la Francophonie (OIF) on 14 February 2008, underscores the

---

[231] This is the case in the DRC (Act of 30 July 2004 on the organisation, powers and operation of the Truth and Reconciliation Commission), Côte d'Ivoire (Order of 13 July 2011 on the establishment, powers, organisation and operation of the Dialogue, Truth and Reconciliation Commission), Kenya (Bill of 9 May 2008 on the Truth, Justice and Reconciliation Commission) and Mali (Order of 15 January 2014 on the establishment of the Truth, Justice and Reconciliation Commission and Decree of the same date). The establishment of such commissions has been advocated in UN reports, for example in Sudan (Report of the International Commission of Inquiry on Darfur, addressed to the Secretary-General, S/2005/60, 1 February 2005, §617) or in the Central African Republic (International Commission of Inquiry on the Central Africa, Republic Final Report, S/2014/928, 6 December 2014, p.26).

[232] Centre For the Study of violence and reconciliation, *Africa Transitional Justice Police Framework: Expert's Consultation Report, Annex: African Union Draft Transitional Justice Policy Framework (ATFJ),* Pretoria, 12-13 March 2012, pp.4-5.

importance of para-judicial mechanisms in the context of peace making or peacebuilding in post-conflict situations.

Curiously, however, these expressions of good will do not seem to have been matched by concrete work with alternative justice institutions. It is as if alternative justice was only taken seriously on the diplomatic and official scene as long as it remained for internal use. Indeed, international institutions seem to have been in a state of doubt when it came to putting the matter into practice and incorporating national para-judicial bodies into the formal machinery of international justice.

The scepticism, indeed, the prevention, of international criminal justice first took the form of a distancing from such mechanisms, through what might be called a theorisation of the functional specialisation of the two forms of justice. This involved the ICC proclaiming to the African States that criminal justice and transitional justice should not be confused because they pursue different goals, because they have different purposes. This assertion may have appeared stringy or contorted, but it was nonetheless how the Court found a way of disregarding national settlement procedures in order to give precedence to an extremely legalistic and penal approach. This has given rise to a feeling of jurisdictional imperialism, as well as a feeling that justice is being suppressed at home. But it is not enough to note the deepening rift; we must highlight the inconsistencies in the claims of international justice.

The argument for the functional specialisation of justice systems seems to stem first and foremost from the Rome Statute itself, the terms of which suggest a kind of afflictive obsession. The Preamble to the text recalls the need to combat impunity in very forceful terms. The crimes covered by the international convention must not go unpunished and their effective prosecution must be ensured by measures taken within the national framework...... ; "it is the duty of every State to exercise its criminal jurisdiction over those responsible for international crimes". The repressive option is then echoed by the bodies of the ICC themselves. On 21 September 2012, the Prosecutor stated that the Court remained « It is not a truth and reconciliation commission, still less a body for resolving collective conflicts. [233] In a document systematising his policy in the specific area of assessing the interest of justice[234], the Prosecutor reiterates his understanding of his mission, which must remain very specific and very independent. Without naming alternative justice, he insists on the narrowness of his own mission and seems to leave it to the Security Council to assess any factor relating to the maintenance of international peace and security that could interfere with the course of justice[235].

In other words, and in relation to the debate before us, the ICC Prosecutor considers that he has no need to include alternative justice in his analysis. Not that he denies its possible relevance or impact in a given context, but he believes that, as it is extra-judicial, it should be addressed by a non-judicial body, which could be, at the international level, a political body such as the Security Council. To sum up, and in the debate on its relationship with alternative justice, the ICC champions a dual theory of separation of functions: separation of the functions of international justice (judicial prosecution of those guilty of crimes) and alternative justice (restoration of social relations and cohesion); then, from a perspective that is strictly internal to the Rome Statute itself, separation of the functions between the Prosecutor (judicial

---

233 ICC, Office of the Prosecutor, 2& September 2012, note 34.

234 Article 53 of the Rome Statute, making the « interests of justice » of the criteria for a request by the Prosecutor to open an investigation.

235 *Policy Paper on the Interests of Justice, September 2007,* p.8: « In situations where the ICC is involved, comprehensive solutions addressing humanitarian, security, political, development and justice elements will be necessary. The Office will seek to work constructively with and respect the mandates of those engaged in other areas but will pursue its own judicial mandate independently. The Statute recognizes a role for the UN Security Council to defer ICC action where it considers it necessary for the maintenance of international peace and security. Article 16 provides that….."''

investigations of alleged perpetrators) and the Security Council (assessment of political or extra-judicial considerations relating to the maintenance of international peace and security). There is a rationality that governs these distinctions, a profound meaning that runs through this distributive logic: the cult of the preservation of the judiciary, the refusal of political or sociological contamination, the stubborn desire never to mix law and politics or socio-anthropology.

Faced with an unprecedented level of criminality, the International Criminal Court has proven resistant to original remedies, attached to punitive approaches that no one would dream of rejecting in their entirety, but whose limitations in this case must be acknowledged. Above all, it has tended to forget the ultimate purpose of its office, which is the recovery of societies that have suffered mass atrocities, and to forget the principle of economy that should inspire it, economy of judicial means when other means to the same end may be deployed or are in the process of being deployed.

How then can one resist the temptation to remind the ICC of another line of conduct displayed by the judicial body of the United Nations - to which the Court is linked and with which it shares its universalist calling -? Admittedly, the facts of the case are not quite the same, the first difference being that the defendants are individuals or States. It is also true that the position of this judicial body is not systematically the same[236], but in a kind of wisdom imbued with finalism as well as the limits of the judicial method of dealing with problems, its predecessor, the PCIJ, has for a long time, and willingly, assumed the subsidiarity of its mission by

---

[236] In some cases, the Court in The Hague has refused to be « swayed » by an out-of-court settlement and has instead asserted that the pursuit of such a settlement does not in itself constitute an « obstacle to the exercise of its judicial function » (case of « Aegean Sea Continental Shelf », LR. 1978, p.12). See also « Diplomatic and Consular Staff of the United States in Teheran » (LR.1980, pp.22-23) and « Military and Para-Military Activities … » (LR. 1984, p.440).

allowing extra-judicial actions to take place in order to resolve the disputes that could be brought before it. In the Mavrommatis Concessions in Palestine case, the court held that « only cases that cannot be settled by negotiation should be brought before it »[237]. Then, in the Chorzów Factory Case, it took the view that "it seems highly desirable that a State should not take a step as serious as bringing another State before the Court without first endeavouring to establish clearly that a difference of view exists which cannot otherwise be resolved"[238]. Lastly, in a decision on the Free Zones of Upper Savoie and the District of Gex, it cast it's philosophy most memorably in the following terms: "the judicial settlement of international disputes for which the Court is established is no more than a substitute for the direct and amicable settlement of such disputes between the parties; it is therefore for the Court to facilitate such direct and amicable settlement to the fullest extent compatible with its Statute"[239].

It is not, it must be reiterated, a question of expecting a court that rules on individual behaviour to be as sensitive to political considerations as a court that judges only States. But apart from the fact that international criminal justice is also about States - that is to say, about national judicial systems as vectors of international trust - and not just about physical individuals, it should be added that the choice made by the ICC was by no means inevitable: it would have been perfectly possible to imagine it opening up more to non-judicial mechanisms in general, even if it meant monitoring their progress and regularly assessing their effectiveness. This was not the choice made.

However, objectivity dictates that the adoption of this strictly criminal approach should not be confined to the organs of the ICC.

---

237 Judg of 30 April 1924, series A, n°2, p.15

238 Judg of 16 December 1927, « Interpretation of judgments 7 and 8 (« Chorzov Factory ») », series A, n°13, pp.10-11.

239 Order of 19 April 1929, series A, p.13.

These bodies have undoubtedly been able to draw some arguments from the theses put forward on various occasions by certain human rights organisations. Insisting on the legitimate need to prosecute the perpetrators of serious crimes, these organisations have occasionally glossed over alternative justice and insisted on the criminal justice approach. A joint report by two organisations points out that "while the respective functions of truth commissions and courts are complementary, their tasks differ in nature, and they should not be conflated. Truth commissions are not intended to replace the courts, whether civil, administrative, or criminal. Most especially, truth commissions cannot replace a judicial process aimed at establishing individual criminal responsibility"[240]. It is even stated, with some temerity "calls for reconciliation to the detriment of justice (...) must not be taken into account"[241].

Clearly, the criminal law thesis needs to be seriously put into perspective. Let us be clear, however: it is not at all a case of questioning the fight against impunity and the subsequent need to punish those guilty of egregious violations of the law; it is simply a question of distancing oneself from a retributivist and hegemonic logic, which acts as if other approaches, relativistic and careful not to hurt local peculiarities, were not conceivable, as if the individualist conception of the criminal trial could not be surpassed by a more social, less intersubjective apprehension of things.

The very structure of the offences in question is the first element that should call for humility. Mass crimes, crimes against humanity and genocide are not ordinary crimes and cannot be adequately dealt with by ordinary means. Quantitatively and qualitatively, therefore, the traditional justice system is incapable of grasping and dealing with the criminal phenomenon that is the subject of

---

240 Amnesty-FIDH, *Looking for Justice: Recommendations for the Establishment of the Hybrid Court for South Sudan,* p.10.

241 Ibid. p 36.

international criminal justice. From this standpoint, the reparations envisaged are a kind of last-ditch effort, and even their symbolic value - not to mention their restorative value, which is unattainable by definition here - poses a problem. It seems that the victims of the atrocities themselves were very sceptical about the relevance of the reparations decided by the Hague tribunals, but could they not be relevant[242] ?

These data confound the traditional judicial trial model. They are an invitation to explore other keys to analysis, to approach the criminal phenomenon in question in a different way. Clearly, there can be no question of undertaking even the first steps of such a daunting task. But it is enough to denounce the pretence of subjecting such monstrous, disconcerting realities to the procedures of ordinary justice, of which the ICC recommends itself and of which it is, in a way, the institutional embodiment. In most cases, the type of crimes that the ICC is called upon to judge have subverted societies and traumatised communities, sometimes to the point of calling their very existence into question. Traditional judicial responses can of course be applied in such contexts, but it would undoubtedly be abusive and dangerous to make this method of treatment a recipe.

The example of South Africa, whose Truth Commission is so often cited as a model, proves that in this area, no truth is absolute, and no solution can be imposed cavalierly. This national experiment in alternative justice has shaken the dogmas of traditional judicial procedure and swept away the prejudice of retribution by going so far as not to threaten its « defendants » with punishment, but to reward them with a benefit, that of amnesty; what was at stake in the trial was therefore not punishment, but a reward. This unprecedented approach, which is certainly destined

---

[242] Hazan P, *La justice face à la guerre. De Nüremberg à la Haye*, Paris, Stock, 2000, p.247.

to remain exceptional, is proof of the sovereignty of societies in determining the means they deem appropriate to overcome their traumas, to conquer their demons.

It is obviously not the task of international judicial institutions to restore social bonds, as the organs of alternative justice do, but they cannot write off the work of these organs, they cannot ignore - i.e., despise - this work. Not out of diplomatic convenience or conventional deference, but because the classical judicial approach they embody is not an end in itself, but aims, like all criminal law itself, to put an end to strife and pacify societies. A judiciary that remembers its ultimate purpose is necessarily attentive to the work of pacification undertaken by other bodies, necessarily imbued with the idea that it does not have a monopoly over social regulation, either by itself (other regulatory bodies exist) or by its mode of action (non-legal regulations exist).

Has alternative justice in general, and that implemented in South Africa and Rwanda in particular, achieved its objective? The answer to such a question can only be nuanced. There is a fairly abundant critical literature on these two cases, some of whose conclusions are irrefutable - others less so. The value of such justice can therefore not be overestimated. It certainly remains imperfect.

There is a second element of relativisation, which relates more specifically to the subject of this book. It is that on the chapter in question, the African continent can claim neither total originality nor any kind of antecedence. It has been demonstrated from the outset that alternative justice is a global phenomenon, a mechanism that has been particularly in demand in recent decades, with all regions of the world being affected.

These two reservations having been expressed; it is nonetheless necessary to stress the interest of experimenting with such justice in our two African States. Though the alternative phenomenon is a worldwide phenomenon, its implementation here conceals specific features that certainly justify a doctrinal interest in it. The depth of the trauma is a first characteristic that is not necessarily shared: centuries of foreign domination and racial banishment on the one hand, with the unprecedented violence that goes with it, massacres on the scale of an entire country, all the more dramatic because they involve the two ethnic components that make up the bulk of the national population. The intensity of this kind of conflict does not exist everywhere, and it makes the challenge of national reconciliation even more daunting to meet.

The relative boldness of the solutions advocated constitutes the other interest in studying the South African and Rwandan cases. In Rwanda, traditional and alternative justice were not two parallels that never touched each other; more precisely, if the latter followed the pattern of the former by adopting a criminal approach and sanctions, the South African Reconciliation Commission dared to take a radical step, going so far as to overturn, in an absolutely revolutionary move, the pattern of the criminal trial as we know it: Instead of stigmatisation, a liberating confession; instead of condemnation, absolution; an inversion which, from the point of view of its creators, has the capacity to heal both the perpetrator and the victim. It has been written that this precedent constitutes "the only case in which reconstructive justice presents itself in its most complete state, that is to say, for its own sake and no longer as a substitute for justice"[243].

For all these reasons, it is important to highlight Africa's place in the international debate on justice. This is an international debate because, as we have said, justice is a global phenomenon, and our two cases would undoubtedly teach us a great deal. South Africa and Rwanda not only prove to us that justice is not unequivocal, they go further, dare we say it: they exhume, by their mere existence, an all too often forgotten truth, which is that justice rests on foundations, on a philosophical base and a social assent, and

[243] Garapon A ; op cit., p.283.

that, made for a time of peace, it must submit to the test of its substantial validity in times of unrest, when too high a level of deviance exposes its shortcomings.

A return to the foundations reveals the cultural relativity of justice, as we have written: "If we consider that what is universal is the reconstructive function and not the law or the trial, not only do we guard against the risk of cultural colonialism, but we discover that the influence is perhaps in the other direction: from foreign experiences - particularly African - to the West (...). The universal is no longer to be found only in the lawsuit (...) or in the law (...), but in a function: to make possible a new coexistence, to revive institutions (...)"[244].

---

[244] Garapon A., op cit., pp. 272 et 297.

CHAPTER 6

TWO WEST AFRICAN BRIGHT SPOTS: CONSTITUTIONAL TREATY AND GLOBAL CITIZENSHIP

For the soul of the city is nothing but its constitution....

Isocrates, *Areopagiticus*, 14.

The Constitution and European citizenship are two concepts that have fuelled abundant doctrinal controversy on the European continent. No doubt the unique way in which Europe was constructed and the resolutely exceptional nature of its legal order in relation to the classic principles of international law have contributed to encapsulating these debates, to making them a strictly continental affair, in short, to failing to look elsewhere and to consider or deal with the questions raised in a comparative context.

There are, however, similar experiences taking place in other climes, which could undoubtedly have shed some light on the controversies surrounding Europe. West Africa is a special case in that it has, without fanfare, experimented with two institutions that have hitherto been thought of almost exclusively in their European guise. The framework within which these innovative principles have been developed is that of a West African sub-regional organisation, the Economic Community of West African States (ECOWAS). This organisation was established by the Treaty of

Lagos on 28 May 1975, and now has fifteen member states. Within this Community, two major legal instruments have been adopted: the: Protocol on Democracy and Good Governance, adopted on 21 December 2001, currently being revised, and the Protocol on ECOWAS Citizenship, adopted in 1982.

One is very ambitious, in that it deals with eminently constitutional issues, and undoubtedly deserves to be properly described as a Constitutional Treaty. Perhaps more than the European document also known as the Constitutional Treaty or Constitution for short, which was the subject of debate between 2004 and 2005, this ECOWAS Treaty has a constitutional dimension. It would therefore be advisable to put into perspective the idea, which surfaced at the time, of a European distinctiveness on the subject: the claim or aspiration of a formally international legal instrument to assume a constitutional scope.

On the question of citizenship too, West Africa has had to devise pioneering rules. Long before the Maastricht Treaty formally enshrined European citizenship, ECOWAS established an international, specifically West African, citizenship, first in its founding treaty and then in a treaty adopted in 1982. The concept of citizenship appeared in the 1975 Treaty of Lagos. Article 27 of the Treaty, the only provision in Chapter IV entitled *Freedom of Movement and Residence*, which reads:

> **1**. Citizens of Member States shall be regarded as *Community citizens* and accordingly Member States undertake to abolish all obstacles to their freedom of movement and residence within the Community.
>
> **2**. Member States, by agreement with each other exempt Community citizens from tourist visas and residence permits and allow them to work and carry out commercial and industrial activities within their territories».

However, it was not until seven years later that the Member States codified Community citizenship in Protocol A/P.3/5/82 of 29 May 1982. As we shall see, the approach chosen was to some extent rather half-hearted, and this may well warrant criticism. But apart from the fact that the institutional development of this international organisation has generated a stream of elements tending to enrich this citizenship, what is important to emphasise is simply the pioneering, avant-garde nature of the African organisation's approach. It is indeed, unless I am mistaken, the first in the world to lay the foundations of international citizenship.

All these unknown or obscured facts deserve to be recalled. They relate to constitutionality (I) and citizenship (II).

I. ON CONSTITUTIONALITY

The ECOWAS Protocol on Democracy and Good Governance, adopted in 2001, is a genuine constitutional treaty, by which is meant a legal instrument that is formally international but materially constitutional in the sense that it relates to constitutional matters, i.e., matters concerning the organisation and functioning of power in the State. Understood in this way, a constitutional treaty is therefore a subtractive act, an international commitment that implies sacrifices of sovereignty on the part of States, sacrifices that are of course high since they concern symbols of sovereignty, and are of a constitutional nature.

It is a fact that in the debate on the European Constitution there were theses tending to give the concept of constitution a different meaning. However, there can be no doubt that in the minds of the drafters of this text, the temptation or intention to bring the European entity closer to a state entity was also an undeniable fact, if only from the point of view of terminological symbols: as you will recall, there was talk of a president of Europe, of European laws, etc. These terminological devices should not be treated lightly. By mimicking the figure of the state, the supporters of the European Constitution were conveying a substantial underlying message, that of a state achievement for the European Union, whether real or imminent, a crowning achievement completed or in progress. This tension towards statehood could not fail to raise the question of the concessions of sovereignty that the Member States had made to the EU. If only from the point of view of the symbols it carries, the draft European Constitution could not escape the debate on the volume and intensity of the transfers of competences from the States to the Union. It is only from this perspective of the transfer of competences that the question of constitutionality is raised here. In this respect, there is a striking contrast between the constitutional anchoring of the ECOWAS Protocol and the prevarication of the European Constitution.

A. The Actual Constitutional Underpinnings of the ECOWAS Protocol

In its current version, the ECOWAS Protocol touches on several areas that are unquestionably constitutional in nature. Specific obligations are set out in the document, and Member States are consequently required to amend their constitutional provisions in line with the Protocol.

First, the Protocol sets out what itself calls the principles of constitutional convergence. These include separation of powers, independence of the judiciary, transparency of elections and rejection of any unconstitutional means of acceding to power. Rules are then laid down on electoral matters, including a principle of fairness, particularly relevant on the African continent, which prohibits any revision of the electoral law six months before an election, if such a revision has not been agreed by the political players. Other demands include the reliability of the electoral register - the subject of so much recrimination from the political opposition - and the establishment of genuinely independent arbitration bodies. In addition to these purely political issues, the Protocol also mentions the fight against poverty and social policies in favour of women and children.

It should also be noted that the Protocol, which is a veritable international treaty, establishes a system of sanctions against defaulting States. In ascending order of severity, these sanctions range from refusal to support the candidature of a State in breach of the Protocol for an international position, through refusal by the organisation to hold meetings in that State, to suspension of that State from Community bodies.

Such provisions certainly constitute an overt interference in the domestic political affairs of States. The 2001 Protocol does have a constitutional dimension, as we have seen. In the light of its draft reform, under discussion at the time of writing, the text is even more revolutionary, with five or six major innovations being introduced.

The amendments concern the crucial and highly sensitive issue of presidential term limits. In an unprecedented move, and certainly the only one of its kind in the world, ECOWAS has established the rule that terms of office must be limited to a maximum of two. This is obviously a courageous step, given that the issue has been at the root of real political crises in many African states in general, and in West Africa, in particular. In recent years, countries such as Guinea, Togo, Côte d'Ivoire, and Senegal have experienced periods of tension and violence stemming directly from the issue of presidential term limits. And if the draft revised Protocol is still slow in being adopted, it is precisely because some of the Member States are opposed to this rule. Anticipating the tricks used by heads of state or governments to stay in power - allegations of external dangers, extension of the electoral calendar, manipulation of the Constitution - the Protocol states that presidential terms may not be extended, for any reason or in any form whatsoever. In so doing, the African sub-regional organisation is legislating on a matter that is certainly constitutional and is opening up a major gap in the principle of the constitutional autonomy of States, which is well known in international law.

It is also important to understand the symbolic significance of calling into question the national definition of the presidential term of office. One of the reasons often put forward for rejecting term limits is precisely the sovereignty of the people, who alone are entitled to decide on the duration of governments and therefore on whether, or not, it is necessary to limit the term of office of the President of the Republic in particular. Popular sovereignty is the bulwark of the advocates of non-limitation, whose argument is virtually founded on the notion of authority. By tackling such a fundamental political option, in a continental context characterised by such challenges, the ECOWAS Protocol delves into the heart of the sovereignty of States and takes responsibility for such a peculiar move.

There is also a new obligation for States as part of their commitment to uphold human rights. They are now required to report annually to the ECOWAS Commission on the measures they have adopted in this area. The organisation itself will have a new body, a special rapporteur for human rights, whose task will be to provide the head of the secretariat - the President of the Commission - with regular reports on human rights violations in the Member States, which the Mediation and Security Council will consider for follow-up action.

On the question of elections, another major factor in political tension and violence, the key rule introduced in 2001 prohibiting any amendment to the electoral law within six months of elections has been strengthened: from now on "consensus" is no longer a justification for change, so the prohibition becomes absolute, and only force majeure can legitimise such an amendment. This is a major restriction, as States are deprived of the right to legislate in certain circumstances. On the electoral chapter, this reform is undoubtedly the most spectacular, and it somewhat overshadows the other innovations of the draft, such as the obligation to create an 'inter-party advisory committee, comprising members of the election management body and representatives of the political parties, tasked to meet to review preparations towards elections and the general political environment of the country. ECOWAS is also devising the means to take more structural action on electoral processes: no longer a one-off observer missions, but institution of short term missions and long term missions, the latter designed to focus on conflict prevention, notably in relation to election participation or the establishment of electoral registers.

A more refined approach is taken regarding sanctions. Now occupying a whole chapter - Chapter 5 - this point of the draft Protocol defines what is meant by an unconstitutional change of government, which is a precondition for triggering coercive measures against the new authorities. It should be noted that the text takes a rather broad view, identifying six forms that such a change may take. The approach to sanctions is also more systematic: not only are the measures set out correlated with the Supplementary Act on Sanctions of 2012, adopted by the organisation's Authority of Heads of State and Government, but they are classified into political sanctions – of which there are twelve – and economic sanctions - seven in number -.

Finally, the draft Protocol expands its governance, dimension as it is, in fact, a Protocol on Democracy and Good Governance. In this respect, the ECOWAS Commission will have to set up a technical assistance programme for member states. Governance itself is broken down into eleven pillars, ranging from responsibility and accountability to the fight against impunity, poverty, and corruption, as well as the transparent management of public affairs and the equitable sharing of national wealth. All persons holding public office must declare their assets at the beginning and end of their term of office. Finally, Member States have a duty to introduce legislation to protect whistle-blowers.

If the draft revision is adopted, it will undoubtedly be a unique instrument in the world because of its specifically constitutional nature. It deliberately attacks the heart of State sovereignty, organising sectors that previously seemed to be impregnable bastions, impregnable sanctuaries of constitutional autonomy. The legal instrument is already remarkable in its current state and will be even more so if it is ever amended.

Moreover, its constitutional basis is not only material, as we have endeavoured to demonstrate so far. This constitutional grounding is also formal in the sense that the Protocol has, *de jure,* been enshrined as a constitutional norm in some ECOWAS Member States. In addition to this formal enshrinement, it should be added that national constitutional jurisprudence itself has not been slow to invoke this text to censure the erring actions of state public authorities. For those who doubted the constitutional nature of the Protocol, here then is proof in the affirmative.

At least two ECOWAS Member States have included a reference to the Protocol in their Constitution. The Preamble to the Guinean Constitution of 7 May 2010 states that the people of Guinea "proclaim their adherence to the ideas and principles laid down in (...) the Constitutive Act of the African Union, the African Charter on Human and Peoples' Rights and its protocols on the rights of women, as well as the revised ECOWAS Treaty and its protocols on democracy and good governance ". Similarly, the Preamble to the Constitution of Burkina Faso - revised in 2015 - proclaims that this State affirms its "commitment to the values and democratic principles, especially as set out in the African Charter on Democracy, Elections and Governance of 30 January 2007 and in ECOWAS Protocol A/SP1/12/01 of 21 December 2001 on Democracy and Good Governance". To this must be added the possibility of an implicit reference to the Protocol. Indeed, Togo has provided in its Constitution that "the rights and responsibilities provided in (...) international instruments relating to human rights ratified by Togo, are a part and parcel of the Constitution"[245]. The 2001 ECOWAS Protocol is certainly a human rights instrument, as the African Court on Human and Peoples 'Rights acknowledged in a judgment handed down on 18 November 2016 (Action pour la promotion des droits de l'homme vs. Côte d'Ivoire). Relying, on its own admission, on opinions issued by the African Union Commission itself and by the African Institute of International Law, the Court comes to the conclusion that in order to determine whether a convention is a human rights instrument, "Such an object is expressed either by an express enunciation of subjective rights for the benefit of individuals or groups of individuals, or by the prescription in respect of States of obligations implying the consequent enjoyment of the same rights"[246].

True to this logic, the Constitutional Court of Togo, in a judgment of 9 July 2009, expressly referred to this international treaty as the standard of reference.[247]. There is no trace of any provision of the 2001 Protocol being taken up in the judgment, but it is explicitly referred to in the reference standards at the outset of the decision, which would tend to establish that it is a standard of principle. As we have seen, the Togolese Constitution itself, in Article 50, opens up the possibility of incorporating the Protocol into its reference rules.

Even more interesting is the case of Mali, where there is nothing in the constitutional text that clearly allows the Protocol to be taken into consideration, but where the constitutional court did not hesitate to refer to the ECOWAS text following a referral invoking one of its provisions. The ruling of 8 August 2018 on the

---

245 Article 50 of the Togolese Constitution.

246 §57 of the judgment.

247 Ruling N°C003/09 of 9 July 2009.

proclamation of the final results of the presidential election responds to the request made on this specific subject, which is undoubtedly proof that for the Malian judge, the constitutional scope of the treaty is beyond doubt. [248].

It should be added that in this debate there is a fleeting reference to the constitutional dimension of the Protocol in a judgment handed down by the judicial body of ECOWAS itself. It was in its judgment of 13 July 2015 that the Community judge achieved this landmark, thus proving that in a dispute largely concerning national constitutional data, recourse to the Protocol could be relevant. According to the Court:

> If, therefore, the principle of constitutional and political independence of States incontestably implies that States are at liberty to determine the regime and political institutions of their choice, and to adopt the the laws they deem fit, that liberty shall be exercised in conformity with the commitments the States have undertaken in that regard. Now, there is no doubt that such commitments do exist, the impressive list of texts invoked the Applicants attesting to that fact. Within the specific context of (...)[249].

The constitutional underpinning of the treaty concluded within the framework of ECOWAS is therefore obvious. Substantive anchoring, insofar as its object or part of its object is undoubtedly of a constitutional nature, formal anchoring in the sense that it has

---

[248] Ruling 2018-03/CC-EP of 8 August 2018. Such a position, undoubtedly pragmatic and perfectly logical, is undoubtedly preferable to that of the Constitutional Council of Senegal, which consists of posing the problem in somewhat dogmatic and formalist terms and rejecting any reference to this Protocol on the grounds that it « is not one of the Council's reference standards...which are the provisions of the Constitution, the preamble and the international instruments referred to in that preamble» (Ruling N°3-C-2021 of 22 July 2021, §149).

[249] Judgment of the ECOWAS Court of justice, 13 July 2015, *« Congrès pour la Démocratie et le Progrès and others Vs Burkina Faso »*, § 31.

been established as a formal constitutional norm or as a norm of reference for the constitutional court. This obvious fact contrasts with the reality of Europe. Is the "European Constitution", as constitutional as this, subject to the clarifications made earlier? This is what needs to be considered.

B. The Ambiguities of the "European Constitution

Let us take a closer look. It may be thought that the term constitutional may not mean that the text deals with a constitutional matter, but only that it is endowed with a certain fundamentality in the European legal system, its constitutionality would then emanate from its fundamental nature, from the fact that it is part of the foundations from the European order. However, in addition to the fact that this understanding is not necessarily shared by all academic writers, the very idea of a European Constitution is not neutral and necessarily refers to what might be called here the tectonic plates of competences, the tendency to subtract from state competences in favour of the EU. The idea that by choosing the name European Constitution the drafters wanted to give the impression that Europe was tending towards a state form is all the more legitimate given that, as we have seen, the text itself is full of references that are in principle to be found in states, and not in an international organisation.

The very climate in which the European constitutional debate took place is another factor that needs to be considered. Rightly or wrongly, this public debate has often been reduced to a confrontation between pro-Europeans and anti-Europeans, between proponents and opponents of European integration, the question being framed in terms of the erosion of national sovereignties, the strengthening of Europe and the corresponding weakening of the States. Under these conditions, it is logical to probe what might be called the statehood of Europe, to assess the constitutionality of the European Constitutional Treaty.

To do this, we need to look at the content of this text, which was adopted by the EU's twenty-five Member States, but which was unable to enter into force in November 2006 due to opposition from certain States, when unanimity was required. It turns out that many of the provisions of this Constitution were merely symbolic and of only relative practical significance. This is true of certain names that have been introduced, such as Minister for Foreign Affairs or European laws, or of the innovation introduced by the establishment of a stable presidency of the European Council, which brings together the Heads of State and Government. Other reforms relate to the internal reorganisations, Some of the changes to the 'Constitution' were merely symbolic and of only relative practical significance. This is true of certain names that have been introduced, such as 'Minister for Foreign Affairs' or 'European laws', or of the innovation introduced by the establishment of a stable presidency of the European Council, which brings together the Heads of State and Government. Other reforms relate to 'internal reorganisation', such as the new conditions for appointing the President of the Commission or the greater involvement of national parliaments in the European legislative process.

Above all, the European constitutional process is far from breaking with the intergovernmental logic, and the irreducible diplomatic element (C.A. Colliard) hovers permanently over it. The Member States have a say in EU decisions. Thus, they are free to avoid certain strictures of European economic policy by refusing to join the Eurogroup, and new avenues are open for enhanced cooperation but insofar as the States concerned agree amongst themselves, the possibility of setting up new "common policies" on defence does not affect the position of Member States in relation to NATO and, more generally, the wave of "parlementarisation" observed through a number of rules is offset by the decision-making power of the Council of Ministers, as an inter-governmental body. In the final analysis, it would appear that the revolutionary contributions of the European Constitution, which must be assessed in terms of the relinquishment of powers from the States, are few and far between. Apart from the principle of co-decision and some relaxation of the unanimous decision-making procedure, the text does not make any substantial changes such that the choice of the constitutional route should be understood as a serious weakening of national sovereignty.

It should be pointed out that the dust kicked up by the "European Constitution" is perhaps a storm in a teacup. If one drew up an inventory of the essential reforms introduced by this text, one would be entitled to doubt its "constitutional" nature, doubt its revolutionary significance, if by such epithet one should read something that should bring the EU closer to a State or to the attributes of a state. All in all, it appears that some of the reforms introduced by the text are more symbolic than tangible. Others have a limited personal scope because they are not targeted at all the Member States, thereby reviving the hitherto much-abhorred spectre of a *Europe à la carte*, a persistent and undoubtedly forced tribute to the sovereignty of the Member States.

The logic of intergovernmentalism shines through at many points in this European Constitution. Moreover, it seems that form has been traded for substance, that in exchange for bold terminology and designations, a reminder of the irreducible nature of diplomacy has been conceded: through the requirement, for example, of unanimity on certain issues, through the reiteration of the principle of subsidiarity as a dogma, or through the inclusion of the right to denounce the treaty and leave the EU. If we were to draw up an inventory of the markers of the Constitution, which could revolve around the following three areas: the institution of co-decision (between the Council of Ministers and Parliament) as the ordinary decision-making method, the right of citizens to refer a European Bill and changes to the use of a majority or unanimity as a method of decision making.

What is more, the rest of the story suggests that the constitutional scope of the text adopted in 2004 should be put into perspective. In the end, the constitution never came into force, due to opposition from several States - or peoples, if you like. But the fact that, despite this failure, several provisions of the aborted Constitution were included in the Treaty of Lisbon - negotiations on which began a few months after the failure and which came into force at the end of 2009 - shows that the Constitution was perhaps not so revolutionary, since these changes precisely to respond to the exigences of the times were made without major difficulty. The nominal and symbolic rough edges of the document have been trimmed away – especially the references to a state reality - and the Treaty of Lisbon is, to a certain extent, a lighter version of the Constitution.

The political - one might say ideological - context has also changed in the meantime. The debates have become less passionate, but in terms of substance, reforms such as the creation of a full-time President of the European Council, several changes to the decision-making process, the co-decision system and the full incorporation of the EU Charter of Fundamental Rights have been achieved. And no one has said a word about a Constitution! So much so that one would wonder whether it is not the climate of the constitutional debate in 2004-2005 that was artificially charged; whether a certain obsession with words, a touch of militancy or somewhat dogmatic prejudices have not made the controversy needlessly worse.

In any case, the critical re-appraisal of the European Constitution and its biological revival in the form of the Treaty of Lisbon have almost in no way affected the constitutional autonomy of Member States. However, the European Constitution may have given rise to unease or mistrust because it may have been perceived as competing with national Constitutions, seen as the forerunner or even the embodiment of a European federal state. In the end, dare we say, there were no substantial upheavals.

It is worth examining the arguments of the proponents of the Constitution to see how far the European text is from the West African document, precisely in terms of constitutional content.

The first argument for the existence of an EU Constitution is based primarily on the specific, autonomous nature of the European legal order. The judges of the Court of Justice of the EC/EU are among those who have most often emphasised this autonomy of EEC/EU law. A judgment handed down on 22 April 1986 literally refers to the basic constitutional charter formed by the European treaties. The expression constitutional charter is repeated in an opinion of 14 Decembre 1991, European Economic Area, and the Parliament itself adopted an organ called the Committee on Constitutional Affairs.

Some publicists have taken the same line. In a report on the constitutionalisation of the treaties, led by Professor Olivier Duhamel, we read: "by signing the Treaty of Rome, the Member States deliberately gave birth to a community of law *sui generis,* with its own organs, independent from them, capable of spawning legal standards to guide them, and which may be directly applied to their citizens"[250]

Such a point of view therefore emphasises elements of supra-nationality as justifying the existence of a European Constitution: Such a point of view therefore emphasises elements of supra-nationality as justifying the existence of a European 'constitution': decision-making mechanisms, direct effect of decisions adopted, supremacy of the organisation's law over the national legal order, etc.

---

[250] Doc A5-0289/2000 of 12 October 2000.

The question is, however, whether such autonomy is sufficient to suggest the existence of a Constitution. Wouldn't the elements presented as decisive simply be those of advanced supranationalism? Do we have to escape from the theory of international organisations to account for this European reality? Is recourse to the category of Constitution useful?

The truth is that in the nature of the EU there are elements of supra-nationality - certainly - but also elements of intergovernmentalism. The European institutional reality cannot be reduced to the supranational dimension alone. From this point of view, the EU remains an international organisation, and there is no need to resort to new categories to characterise it. Of course, no one would question the profound originality of this system in the galaxy of international organisations. All its characteristics outlined above attest to this. But the irreducible diplomatic is far from outdated. In addition to the fact that the Union contains classic elements of the law of international organisations, such as the definition of the legal personality or competences of the latter, the recent history of the EU bears witnesses to a return to a form of inter-statism, which tempers the thesis of European exceptionalism: reiteration of the principle of subsidiarity, *de facto* enshrinement of the national constitutional identity, the right to withdraw from the organisation, etc.

The second argument for the existence of a European Constitution is based on a more material approach to the question.

It posits that the European acquis contains elements of a constitution, such as the enunciation of rights and values and the definition of the ways in which power is exercised. But this approach does not entirely break with the theory of the uniqueness of the European legal order, since by referring to the institutional system and the definition of competences, it highlights the singularity of the European order.

It would seem that here too, there is room for doubt if we are to infer from these realities the existence of a "constitution". What is in question is the link established between the indisputable singularity of the EU as an international organisation and the existence of a constitution. We can pile up the elements of originality, insist on the distinctive features of the European system, but this originality does not necessarily imply the existence of a constitution. Or rather: we must first agree on what makes a constitution special. Is it the result of an accumulation of specific features? Does it require conditions to be met, relating to the features of the organisation?

In any event, our approach to the concept is based on two elements. Firstly, elements of a material nature, as has already been emphasised: it is through its content that a constitution is understood; it exists because it refers to very structuring objects, such as the status of power within the institution, and the foundations on which it is built. Then there are elements relating to the definition of powers. This involves taking into account the phenomenon of the subtraction of competences from the State: have there been transfers of constitutional competences, i.e., on matters covered by the Constitution, from the State to the international organisation? This second criterion for defining a constitutional order therefore refers to the idea of translation, of migration of constitutional State competences. In our view, the debate cannot escape the dialectic of the tension between the competences of the state and those of the organisation. If it is understood without reference to the Member State, if it is considered *intra muros*, i.e., within the European system, in a closed and self-sufficient manner, then there is a risk of arbitrariness in attributing the term constitutional. In other words, without the reference to the State, the debate can lead to misunderstanding. The shadow of the State hangs over the constitutional debate, not only because it is in principle States that have "constitutions", but also because it is hard to see how the « constitution » of an international organisation - especially if it is understood as a qualitative crowning achievement, as was the case for Europe - could escape the question of the tectonic of competences, which in this case must consist of a subtraction of the State's powers.

Without the reference to the State, supporters of the established existence of a constitution will necessarily enshrine it, based on criteria that they will have unilaterally defined. Others, who reject the constitutional perspective, will find just as much " grist for the mill" since they will have defined a referential goal that is in any case inaccessible to Europe.

In truth, the variety of European doctrinal positions can also be explained by the substantial ambiguity of the very notion of Constitution. Two opposing viewpoints have been put forward on this point. Some, for whom the "European Constitution" already exists, have taken the view that the adoption of a formal document claiming constitutional status could only constitute "added value" insofar as it would specify the distribution of powers between the States and the Union, but also between the organs of the organisation itself. A Constitution, if it were to come into being, would therefore only have a procedural and not a substantive scope; it would only define territories.

Others, on the other hand, believe that the European Constitution is a novelty that must be accepted as such. It would have, so to speak, nothing to hide, marking Europe's entry into the federal era, the Constitution would herald the transformation of the EU into a state, quite simply. A politically bold position, which certainly has the merit of clarity, but whose realisation remains strewn with political pitfalls. With their sights firmly set on the State and taking the logical view that a debate on the Constitution necessarily implies looking at the only legal entity that, in principle, has one, the proponents of this thesis have argued that a European Constitution could not exist without a "European State", which would then take a federal form: where there is a constitution, there is a State.

This point of view thus pushes back the constitutional horizon, perhaps sending it back to the Greek calends. In a context where Europe is seeking to reassure its nation states, this thesis is almost tantamount to maintaining that Europe will never have a constitution, or that it will not happen soon. The persistence of the inter-governmental arrangement described above will block any constitutional prospects for some time to come. Since it is not a sovereign state and is dependent on its members to carry out the decisions taken by its bodies, the EU would be reduced to the status of a "mere" international organisation, much to the dismay of the advocates of its exceptionalism. It could not then claim to rely on a constitutional instrument.

The European constitutional debate was thus fraught with difficulties. Starting from different premises and understanding the central concept of a constitution in different ways, the contending parties were not likely to reach an agreement.

The debate on the European Constitution, in addition to revealing sharp edges and clear-cut positions, has also undoubtedly suffered from its fundamental, intrinsic ambiguity. This primary ambiguity is terminological and literal. The very expression constitutional treaty, also used to designate this text, reveals, at first sight, the hybridity that characterises it: an international act referring, at least, in the common understanding, to a national reality, to an attribute of the State. While the term constitutional is likely to suggest an analogy between the content of the State's Constitution and the treaty thus concluded, the procedures for adopting these two acts reveal fundamental differences insofar as the treaty resurrects the EU's simple status as an international organisation, which must moreover be adopted unanimously by the Member States. In constitutional treaty, we should therefore pay more attention to the noun than to the adjective: it is the conventional dimension that prevails over the constitutional dimension. Otherwise stated, while the constitutional nature of the legal instrument reveals an essential step forward in the construction of Europe, a major achievement of the Union, the procedure for adopting this instrument restores, as it were, the truth of things, bringing them back to their proper proportions by highlighting the Union's status as a non-State.

In a nutshell, it can be argued that there are at least two obstacles to the constitutional enshrinement of the European institutions. The first is the conceptual misunderstandings that have surrounded the debate. The concept of the Constitution, which was at the heart of the controversy, was not understood in the same way. As a result, there was very little chance of seeing any convergence or points of consensus. The positions were monological, the points of view stretched out like two parallels destined never to meet, and the discussion closed as it had been opened. Weighed down by considerations that must be described as political, given that they referred to the positions of one side or the other on the desirability of European integration itself, the debate was condemned to fruitlessness.

On the other hand, and more to the point here, the examination of the translation of constitutional competences has not produced convincing results. By this we mean that, from the point of view of our problem, the European Constitution has not really eroded state competences. The question of whether or not competences have shifted cannot be dismissed if we are willing to admit that there is such a thing as a constitutional matter, and that any legal instrument claiming to be a constitutional matter cannot completely ignore it.

The ECOWAS Protocol, on the other hand, has a truly constitutional dimension. It would not have been extravagant to call it a constitutional treaty or protocol. The use of the epithet would even be entirely logical in view of the constitutional repercussions of the text, i.e., the disruptions it is likely to introduce into the constitutional and political order of the Member States. The Protocol gnaws at the competences of States; it enters into the heart of sovereignty by regulating, if only partially, eminently political issues such as how power is acquired or maintained, retained and devolved.

It is regrettable that an international treaty with such a strong constitutional content did not attract any attention in a debate such as the one that prevailed in Europe in 2004-2005. A comparative approach could perhaps serve to illuminate the academic jousting, decentralise the discussion and shed light on what is being done elsewhere. The fact remains that the 2001 ECOWAS Protocol is an original instrument in the international order, and it will be even more so when the draft revision, faithful to the initial bold approach, is adopted.

There is another area in which the West African integration organisation has been a little-known pioneer: that of citizenship, which it also enshrined at least ten years before Europe.

II. ON CITIZENSHIP

In Europe, it was with the Maastricht Treaty that European citizenship was officially enshrined. Article 8 of the Treaty states that "every person holding the nationality of a Member State is a citizen of the Union". It is true that this Treaty on European Union did not, strictly speaking discover, the idea of citizenship. Although the concept was not mentioned as such, the prospect of conferring special rights on all nationals of the Member States was raised, in particular through the plan to set up a working group on this issue, referred to in the Paris Declaration made by the Heads coincidence in the history of the construction of Europe: the future European Council enters at the same time as the citizen, and it is the Treaty of Maastricht that will integrate them both.

In West Africa, however, ECOWAS conceived of and codified community citizenship as early as 1982, demonstrating a resolutely futuristic vision (A), albeit an incomplete one (B).

A. Precedence of the ECOWAS Protocol

In Europe, the very notion of *European citizenship* was first mentioned at the Fontainebleau European Council in 1984. Eight years later, it was enshrined in the Maastricht Treaty. In West Africa, ECOWAS citizenship was first mentioned in the international organisation's founding treaty, adopted in 1975, article 27 of which, on freedom of movement, refers to the status of "Community citizens". More specifically, citizenship is the subject of Protocol A/P.3/5/82 of 29 May 1982. This text defines the conditions under which citizenship is acquired and lost, as well as the conditions for reintegration. Its general philosophy is based on two main ideas: that of exclusivity and that of the effectiveness of the bond of nationality, a condition for acquiring Community citizenship.

The idea of exclusivity implies the exclusion of any competing citizenship and appears in the definition of citizenship through the idea of option. Under the terms of the Protocol, Community citizens are:

> **1.** Any person who is a national by descent of a Member State and who is not a national of any non-Member State of the Community,
>
> **2.** Any person who is a national by birth of any of the Member States either of whose parents is a national by sub-paragraph (1) above provided that such a person on attaining the age of 21 decides to take up the nationality of the Member State.

If the person concerned holds dual nationality before the entry into force of the Protocol, he or she must renounce the nationality of whichever of his or her parents is not a national of a Member State.

As for the idea of effectiveness, it means that Community citizenship must not be artificial or self-serving but must reflect reality. The effectiveness of the link of nationality, identified in particular by the 'Nottebohm' judgment handed down by the International Court of Justice[251], is reflected in the ECOWAS Protocol by the condition of fifteen years of continuous residence, required of a person naturalised in a Member State and having renounced another nationality, of a child adopted by a naturalised Community citizen and who has opted for the nationality of his adoptive parent, or of a person with dual nationality, adopted by a naturalised Community citizen, and who, having reached the age of twenty-one before the entry into force of the Protocol, has renounced any nationality of a non-Member State. For these three categories of persons, fifteen years of effective and continuous residence in an ECOWAS Member State is required for access to Community citizenship.

We do not wish to go into the details of this regulation here. Suffice it to say, once the West African precedence has been emphasised, that it is regrettable that ECOWAS has not gone further in defining the content of the citizenship it promotes. Indeed, the 1982 Protocol shows that citizenship is limited to freedom of movement, i.e., a prerogative already implied by the economic integration project. This legal instrument does not add any political value, even though the concept in question is essentially political, implying a relationship with the polity and participation in public affairs. The Protocol establishing citizenship is silent on this point. Forged a long time ahead of other parts of the

---

[251] According to the ICJ, in this 1955 case between Liechtenstein and Guatemala, "the grant of nationality is entitled to recognition by other States only if it represents a *genuine connection* between the individual and the State granting its nationality" (LR . 1955 p 23).

world, as an international citizenship, the West African initiative suffers from the fact that it remains in its embryonic form, and certainly still has the potential to be enriched.

B. The 1982 ECOWAS Protocol: Room for Improvement

This situation is all the more regrettable given that the elements for such a deepening do exist. In 1982, when this code was adopted, ECOWAS was not yet ten years old, and it was still understandable that its approach was timid, that it could not go very far in the approach to citizenship. Times have changed, however, and qualitative leaps have been made, but they have not been linked to citizenship, so that the latter has hardly evolved formally since the Protocol which established it.

First, it is possible to find in an instrument such as the aforementioned 2001 Protocol elements that are certainly linked to citizenship. One thinks of the possibility of relying on the inter-party advisory committees set out in the draft reform to bring about a convergence of certain democratic practices within the Community, thus capitalising on Community citizenship. Similarly, the existence of the ECOWAS national identity card, today now an established reality, could have led to the introduction of a community voter's card, at least with a view to the election of members of the ECOWAS Parliament by direct universal suffrage. The very fact that the 2001 Protocol deals with social issues could still have justified a move towards the creation of a minimum standard of treatment in the Community area, and even if this standard had to be formulated in programmatic terms, it would constitute a kind of social side of citizenship.

Similarly, some developments in the parliamentary body, through Supplementary Act No. A/SA.1/12/16 on enhancing the powers of the ECOWAS Parliament, could have been related to the issue of citizenship. One example is the introduction of the right of petition. Indeed, the prerogative to receive and process petitions is regulated by the Rules of Procedure of the ECOWAS Parliament. These stipulate that any citizen of the Community, individually or in a group, or any legal entity represented on Community territory, may submit a petition to Parliament on a subject within the scope of ECOWAS activities. Petitions, which are subject to certain conditions of admissibility, are referred by the President to the relevant committee of Parliament, which decides what action to take on them after possibly holding hearings and requesting all relevant documents from the Committee. The committee may, where appropriate, submit motions for resolutions to Parliament on petitions it has considered. In all cases, petitioners are kept informed of the action taken on their request.[252].

The institutional elements for strengthening West African citizenship therefore objectively exist. It is a pity that the pioneering work begun in 1982 has, so to speak, been left to lie fallow. That said, it remains undeniable that West Africa was one of the first areas in which international citizenship was conceived and codified. As we have seen, one has to go back even further than the 1982 Protocol on the Citizenship Code, since the notion of Community citizens already appears in the very founding treaty of the international organisation, which dates from 28 May 1975.

From a resolutely revolutionary and *de lege ferenda* perspective, it is not inconceivable to detach the question of international citizenship from the national State. Indeed, in the current state of the law, this international citizenship is conditioned and mediated by the State. It is through the nationality granted by this State that citizenship is acquired, and the possession of a nationality is a condition for the acquisition of citizenship. This persistent state screen exists for both European and ECOWAS citizenship. This is so because, as has been highlighted by the scholars, the concepts of nationality and citizenship are confused, whereas it is possible to

---

[252] Articles 81 to 83 of the Rules of Procedure of the Parliament.

separate them, at least from the perspective of our topic.[253]. Citizenship based on considerations other than nationality - such as the right to free of movement or the right of residence - could then be constructed.

---

[253] See amo,gst many other writings, Jacque J.P., *Droit institutionnel de l'Union européenne*, Paris, dalloz, 2ème ed. p 107 ; Morin J.Y., « La citoyenneté européenne comparée avec la citoyenneté dans unions de type fédéral », in Philip C. et Soldatos P (dir.), *La citoyenneté européenne,* 2000, p 97 ; Fallon M., « Les droits fondamentaux liés à la citoyenneté dans l'UE sous les regards croisés du TCE et de la Charte », in Carlier J.Y. et de Schutter O. (dir), *La Charte des droits fondamentaux de l'Union européenne, son apport à la protection des droits de l'homme en Europe »*, Bruxelles, Bruylant, 2002, p. 164.

CHAPTER 7

THE IMPERATIVE OF IMPARTIALITY OR THE FLAWED CONCEPT OF ELECTORAL LAW

The law is not just something arbitrary that can indifferently be one institution or another, but the result of the intimate link between a state and its history.

Friedrich Carl Von Savigny

Perceived as a continent plagued by political instability and electoral disputes, Africa has become a by-word for a land where democratic competition hardly unfolds peacefully. The power of this image and the deep rootedness of such prejudice have accounted for the failure of many analysts to realise that amidst all the fire and fury of the struggle for power, the continent has still been able to develop original mechanisms for managing electoral processes of its own, capable of guaranteeing what is expected from such a process: transparency, impartiality, neutrality.

Yes, transparency, impartiality. This statement may be disconcerting if all we remember about the political life of African states is the bitterness of opposition and the harshness of contests, some of which have certainly taken a dramatic turn, sometimes to the point of threatening the stability of the state.

The ingenuity recently observed in the management of the electoral process is remarkable not only because it is capable, with the exception of a few cases to which we shall return, of dispelling the suspicion that has long weighed on the sincerity of the elections organised by a State that has admittedly been partisan for a long time; it is also remarkable because it comes, so to speak, from the bowels of society, it is authentically endogenous. The age-old process of mimicry is receding into the background. Faced for a long time with a structural deficit of electoral credibility, many African countries set up electoral management bodies at the turn of the 1990s, which ushered in the era of political pluralism, in order to ensure the credibility of their elections. The new electoral law, which is being implemented under the aegis of the NECs and INECs[254], is not only the product of real social needs - and not pretended or artificial, as may have been the case in other fields or at other times - but is also of such an elaborate and ambitious nature that it is certainly not an exaggeration to present it as « exemplary». It is neither an immaculate conception nor a patchwork; it is carnal and essential, responding to a need and opening the way to a certain uniqueness.

The time has undoubtedly come to do justice to this local ingenuity and even to shift the paradigm: when it comes to the impartiality expected of electoral management bodies, the African continent could not only claim a form of singularity but could even claim to be setting an example. The thesis of the immobility and ineffectiveness of the electoral legal framework in Africa is not only contradicted by the facts in many respects, but it often carries with it, openly or covertly, the idea that in other regions, those of stale democracies or democracies considered to be stale, the electoral question is no longer raised from the point of view of the neutrality of the bodies responsible for it. On each of these two points, some

---

[254] ANEC: Autonomous National Electoral Commission; INEC: Independent National Electoral Commission. These are the most common names. It is possible to find other names (ELECAM in Cameroon, ONEL in Senegal, etc.) but the bodies remain similar or analogous.

truths need to be re-established. Not only does electoral regulation as practised in the "old countries" have its limits from the point of view of the impartiality expected of its bodies (I), but an exploration of the African path of this impartiality could prove capable of reducing these limits (II).

I. THE SHORTCOMINGS OF TRADITIONAL METHODS OF REGULATING ELECTIONS

Apart from the model of the independent body, which has been adopted by a large number of African countries, two main systems of electoral management can be identified in a country: a system in which electoral management is the responsibility of the government in general and the Ministry of the Interior in particular, and a system which could be described as politico- judicial in that the existence of a judicial or quasi-judicial arbitration body does not in principle exclude the possibility of political or partisan considerations intervening in the design of electoral bodies and procedures.

However, the requirement of electoral neutrality is so strong that all these traditional management methods have shown their limitations. As we shall see, none of them has succeeded in structurally dispelling the suspicion of partiality. In such circumstances, it may be appropriate to look at the African experience of electoral management. This is not because they have actually found a solution to the problem – far from it –but simply because on the African continent bodies have been set up which, if they are not institutionally « politicised – can undoubtedly be said to respond better to the imperative of impartiality than their counterparts in the old democracies. The shortcomings observed in these countries are common to the two systems of electoral supervision mentioned above, the governmental model (A) and the political-judicial model (B).

A. The Governmental Model

The shortcomings of this method of election management can be illustrated by looking first at France. In France, the organisation and management of the electoral process is essentially the responsibility of the Ministry of the Interior. Such a stranglehold is likely to pose problems in at least two respects. Firstly, from what might be described as an objective point of view, the Minister of the Interior often displays a partisan affiliation, and the party to which he or she belongs takes part in the electoral competition, so in some respects he or she is judge and jury. From a more subjective point of view, recent French political history shows quite clearly that this strategic position has been occupied by individuals who not only had a very strong political profile, but who clearly intended to use this ministry to promote a personal political career or even a presidential candidacy, the most personal of all in France.

If we are to be objective, we must admit that this is no figment of the imagination. For nearly forty years now, French political life has been regularly riddled with debates casting doubt on the impartiality of the minister responsible for elections in the way he and his departments handle electoral matters. Judge for yourself.

In 1983, the then Minister of the Interior, Gaston Deferre, was re-elected in the municipal elections in the city of Marseille. However, there were a number of grey areas surrounding this election. Firstly, there were the political and legal issues, such as the false invoices implicating the mayor and his team, and the suspicious deaths of two people well known in Marseille circles between the two rounds, which were quickly linked to the local political climate. Above all, the election showed that the winner had a minority of votes. While this paradoxical subtlety of the election is known to occur from time to time, its legalisation in this case had been criticised for being, according to some, a one-off and premeditated enterprise. We would therefore be dealing not with the case-by-case effect of a general rule, but with a circumstantial set-up. This somewhat surprising result had been made possible by the law, passed three months earlier and defended by the Minister-Mayor, relating specifically to the new organisation of the cities of Paris, Lyon, and Marseille (PLM) law. As a result of the division of these cities into sectors each electing its own council and mayor, with the municipal council being the emanation of these councils, the opposition, which had a majority in votes, found itself in a minority in terms of the number of councillors, since it controlled only two sectors out of six. The fact that he was both the Minister of the Interior responsible for decentralisation and a candidate in the election had the worst effect of all, as the former was suspected of having favoured the latter by voting for this law[255].

The organisation of elections by the Ministry of the Interior in France once again came into question in 1986 when, following a change in the parliamentary majority, a new electoral map had to be drawn up. The Minister of the Interior in charge of such a division was immediately suspected or accused of bias. President François Mitterrand refused to sign the orders issued, as an enabling law had been passed. Parties represented in Parliament (Communist Party, National Front) had made it clear that the new division and the introduction of a surplus of majority voting were openly hostile to them, while another political grouping, allied to the government - the UDF - feared a weakening of its representation and went so far as to threaten the government with a vote of no confidence.

---

[255] https://fresques.ina.fr/sudorama/fiche-media/00000000267/la-reelection-de-gaston-deferre-a-la-mairie-de-marseille.html. According to Virginie Martin, « Beyond the administrative window-dressing, the reasons for this reform are also eminently political. Gaston Deferre is said to have devised this new voting system to ensure his - uncertain - re-election as mayor of Marseille in 1983. In Paris, the law enabled the ruling Mitterrand government to weaken the power of Jacques Chirac, mayor of the capital and new leader of the opposition. Two excellent reasons, therefore, for passing this law and giving it the trappings of proximity and decentralisation. », « The « loi PLM » : an opaque, complex and undemocratic voting », *Revue politique et parlementaire*, 2020.

The Minister of the Interior, the driving force behind the reform, was clearly perceived as seeking to benefit his own camp, and on the walls of Paris, sarcastic posters portrayed him as a butcher with cutting tools. Two other factors served to illustrate this noxious climate: Not only was the new law adopted by the back door - the notorious article 49-3 of the French Constitution was invoked - but it seems that in a context of cohabitation, the government was compelled to "negotiate" with the President of the Republic, one of the elements of the barter, also a piece of Machiavellian anthology and Florentine refinement, having been that personalities close to the Head of State benefited from a kind of preferential treatment in the division of their own constituencies. Others, more distant from the Prince, were "sacrificed"[256]. Finally, it should be added that the confusion of genres induced by the governmental model of election management is sometimes pushed to its extreme limits, and assumed, so to speak, with an ease that borders on impudence. In France, the Secretary of State for the Interior and Local Government, Alain Marleix, had, before his appointment, been Deputy Secretary General of a political party, the RPR, with responsibility for elections (between 1988 and 1990) and then National Secretary of the UMP, the new umbrella party, with exactly the same responsibilities. In short, on a mission that excluded any bias, he was invited to show off his partisan experience.[257].

The appointment of future President Nicolas Sarkozy to the Ministry of the Interior (first in 2002) was yet another real-life illustration of the vices of the ministerial model of electoral

[256] www.lesechos-fr2008,08, « En 1986, un découpage mouvementé ». Also Chignier-Riboulon, « Le découpage législatif de 1986, une logique partisane. L'exemple de Lyon », *Revue de géographie de Lyon,* 1997, pp.173-176. The author writes that « the UDF-RPR were able to retain their seats since 1986 as a result of the carving of electoral districts tending to make the strongholds of the Left weaker ».

[257] Ehrhard Th, « Le découpage électoral des circonscriptions législatives : le Parlement hors – jeu ? », *Pouvoirs,* 2013/3, n°146, pp. 117 à 132.

oversight. It is quite possible that the Ministry of the Interior could be an ideal launching pad for a presidential ambition, in a national context of security overkill, and no one would dream of reproaching an ambitious politician for understanding this and drawing the necessary conclusions. But what is worrying about the French model is that it is in no way protected from the political or electoral manipulation of the office. It is that, at a given moment, this model of electoral governance sidesteps the conflict of interests, turns a blind eye to the interplay of legitimacies, and paves the way for the office to be used for partisan or personal ends. The career of Nicolas Sarkozy is ample proof of this. He had been party leader (since November 2004) and Minister of the Interior (from May 2002 to March 2004 and again from May 2005 to March 2007). Responsible for organising elections in this latter capacity, he held three positions simultaneously from 31 January 2007: Minister of the Interior, Chairman of the governing party, and its candidate in the presidential election.

Three events that took place during this period highlight the limits of the government's election management system. Asked to specify whether the minister or the candidate had been to London the day before he was nominated, Nicolas Sarkozy replied: " it was the political leader, the candidate in the election". It is easy to see how these distinctions are somewhat artificial, and the journalist questioning him is forced to remind his interviewee that he is "the minister for elections", and that being a minister and a candidate at the same time amounts to "fixing the match". Another important episode in this sequence was the statement made by President Jacques Chirac, on 14 July 2004, to the effect that it was inconceivable for him to hold both offices at the same time. However, nothing happened when the two offices were combined. Finally, it was during the same period that a newspaper revealed that the minister-candidate had asked his departments to investigate the assets of his political opponents, and even to tap the phones of one of them[258].

More recently, the government's mandate to lead the electoral process has been challenged by the LFI (la France insoumise – France unbowed) party. In the June 2022 legislative elections, there was controversy over the official results posted by the Ministry of Interior. The LFI party, a member of the left-wing coalition, accused the Ministry of understating its results, with the press release of 13 June 2022 that it issued denouncing " the dishonest practices of the Ministry of the Interior" as well as "a new manipulation that aims to artificially make the presidential coalition appear to be in the lead, when it is not so according to the reality of the votes". Above all, we should remember the consequence drawn by the LFI: "if we win majority votes..., we will set up *a real independent election authority*, shorn of the minister's dishonest practices..."[259].

The suspicion of partiality in election management is therefore a kind of constant in French political life. This shortcoming has not escaped the notice of observers and academics. For J-C Colliard, for example, "it is curious that elections should be organised by a government that has an interest in their outcome, since its very existence depends on national elections and may depend - as democracy of opinion requires - on mid-term elections or referenda. The fact that a minister signs all the texts organising an election in which he will be a candidate only adds the anecdotal to the permanent"[260]. L. Touvet et Y-M Doublet agree. For them, the

---

[258] https://www.vie-publique.fr/discours/165235-nicolas-sarkozy-31012007-ump-election-presidentielle-politique-etrangere. See also, on all these points Ruiz Rodriguez J.A., *La communication politique de Nicolas Sarkozy du 6 mai 2002 au 6 mai 2012,* Political Science Doctoral Thesis, Paris II, 2014

[259] https://www.lemonde.elections-legislatives-2022-article/2022/OG/13legislatives-2002-la-france-insoumise-critique-les-manipulations-des-resultats-par-le-ministere-de-l'-interieur_6130145_6104324.html

[260] Colliard J-C., Préface à l'ouvrage de Touvet L and Doublet Y-M, *Droit des élections,* Economica, 2ème ed, 2014, p.IX.

establishment of an independent authority on matters of election is justifiable from two viewpoints. On the one hand, the very strong presence of the Ministry of the Interior in the electoral process does not foster the feeling of transparency of the ballot. On the other hand, such an authority could help to put an end to or reduce the dispersion of electoral competences, which are essentially the organisation of the ballot, the exercise of an advisory power on the electoral process and the control of the regularity of the operations. Our two authors, therefore, prefer States that have devised mechanisms independent of those of the State, citing the examples of Australia, Canada (with a Chief Electoral Officer appointed by the House of Commons, etc.) and the United States (with a Chief Electoral Officer appointed by the House of Representatives, etc.)[261].

France is not the only old democracy to test the limits of its electoral management system. Until 2000, the United Kingdom also opted for the governmental model, since elections in that country were supervised by a Home Office headed by a Minister of the Crown. But here, as early as the 90s, voices were raised in favour of a structure independent of the Government, responsible for electoral oversight. Indeed, it was in 1999 that a report drawn up by the Committee on Standards in Public Life"[262] , itself set up five years earlier following a scandal over the influence of lobbies on the Westminster Parliament, recommended the setting up of a "fully independent Committee with wide-ranging executive and investigative powers and the right to take cases to the Electoral Court for judgment"[263]. Such powers, finally enshrined in the Political Parties, *Elections and Referendums Act 2000,* are exactly those of many electoral commissions in Africa. In other words, at a

---

[261] Ibid., pp 568-569.

[262] Committee on Standards in Public Life, CSPL.

[263] V. Thomas P.G. et Lorne R. G., *Une évaluation comparative d'organismes électoraux centraux,* Rapport commandé par Elections Canada, mai 2014, pp. 55 et s.

time when a democracy as tried and tested as that of the United Kingdom is sketching out what it considers to be its "ideal", model of arbitration, which has already been a reality in several States on the African continent for nearly ten years.

In any case, the limits of the governmental or administrative standard of election management have been laid bare, and the French case illustrates this perfectly. It should be pointed out here that such a model is not rejected in all African states. It still applies today in many countries on the continent, but as you can imagine, the suspicion of partiality that hangs over the Ministry of the Interior is frequent in these countries. Political players there regularly call for the establishment of an independent body. But while the ministerial model was in use in almost all states before the era of pluralism began in the 90s, it is an independent body that has now been chosen in many states. The imperative of impartiality on the part of the management body can no longer be reconciled with a ministerial stranglehold on the electoral process. An election run by a partisan ministry cannot escape suspicion.[264].

The same applies to a ballot whose regularity is supervised by judges with proven, "internalised", and often openly acknowledged partisan affiliations. This is the model we have described as politico-judicial, and which can be found in many countries, including the United States of America. What these two modes of electoral management have in common is the constancy of the partisan element and their common inability to promote electoral neutrality.

---

264 In New Zealand, the « governmental » option was swiftly discarded by the working group charged with considering the reform of electoral adjudication, which considered that « while the ministerial model favoured a highly efficient and accountable administration, it risked creating the perception, at home and abroad, that New Zealand did not grant the same independence to electoral administration as other countries». Ibid. pp 48 and 49.

B. The political and judicial model

In the United States of America, the shortcomings of the choice that has been made are manifest, as shown by the two spectacular failures in the presidential elections of 2000 and 2020.

In the first contest, between George Bush and Al Gore, it was the saga that pitted the Florida Supreme Court against the Federal Court that left its mark.[265]. The federal court stepped in and ordered the state court to stop counting the votes because the deadline had passed. This order, requested by George Bush's lawyers, sealed the victory for George Bush. The Supreme Court's order was criticised not only for ignoring the democratic requirement that all votes cast be counted, but also for claiming a deadline for counting the votes that did not exist. On the other hand, the Florida Supreme Court's actions appeared to many scholars to be entirely consistent with the law. In any event, this political and judicial saga has conveyed the distressing image of a democracy in disarray, that of a state incapable of extricating itself from an electoral entanglement at a decisive moment. Two facts illustrate the scale of the fiasco. On the one hand, as in previous cases, the winner of the election was in a minority - an electoral triviality perhaps, but a definite aberration in terms of the postulate of democracy. On the other hand, the Supreme Court of the United States itself literally split in two, its decision having been adopted by five justices to four. And Justice Stevens, in his blunt dissenting opinion, gives an idea of the Court's unease: "Although we may never know with complete certainty the identity of the winner of this year's presidential election, the identity of the loser is pellucidly clear. It is the nation's confidence in the judge as an impartial guardian of the rule of law."[266]

---

[265] For all subsequent developments, see Rosenfeld M, « Bush c. Gore : trois mauvais coups portés à la Constitution, à la Cour et à la démocratie », *Les Cahiers du Conseil Constitutionnel,* Dossier « La sincérité du scrutin », janvier 2003, n°13.

[266] Ibid.

The most important thing to remember here is that this electoral failure was directly linked to the political opinions of the judges. In short, the Florida Supreme Court and the Federal Supreme Court were opposed to each other because the former was a Democrat and the latter a Republican. Such an accusation may be disconcerting to non-American observers, but it is not overly shocking in a country where the political leanings of judges are not a taboo. And the Bush / Gore case had precisely the merit of exposing the shortcomings of such a system of electoral regulation. We are no longer in the governmental model of electoral management, but the suspicion of bias remains, and it also affects the political / judicial model. As Professor Rosenfeld writes, "what is clear from the Bush v. Gore decision is that it is necessary to draw a line separating the purely political, the partisan (...) and on the other hand the domain reserved for the judge (...) who is ethically committed…). The best we can require of our judges is that they hand down rulings that quell the quarrels of the political world and soften its mores. The majority opinion in *Bush v Gore* did exactly the opposite"[267].

The 2020 presidential election was another grim moment for American electoral democracy, and a further revelation of the hold of partisan considerations over the electoral process. It was not the decision of an arbitration body that was at issue here, but the "permissiveness" of an electoral system, its porosity to partisan considerations. The actions of a large part of the losing camp - the Republicans - and of the outgoing President Donald Trump complete the picture of the exposure or vulnerability of the American electoral system to a form of delinquency that is truly astounding. First there was the pressure exerted on individuals by the President: on the Governor of Georgia to call a special session of the State Legislature to cancel Joe Biden's victory in that State, on

[267] Ibid.

the Speaker of the Pennsylvania House of Representatives, on the Georgian Secretary of State Raffensberger to "find enough votes to win this election"[268] etc. Then, even more astoundingly, there was the mobilisation of constitutional bodies to serve the ends of this factious enterprise: declarations by members of both Houses (Representatives and Senate) opposing the certification of the results of the Electoral College (to provoke a debate on the results in Congress itself). Declarations, again, by at least 140 Republican members of the House opposing the counting of votes in five states lost by Trump, and so on.[269].

We must, of course, look beyond these egregious and sometimes ubiquitous manifestations of electoral controversy in the United States. In this democracy, it is important to understand that it is the partisan factor that structurally and institutionally undermines the neutrality of the supervision of the electoral process. Arbitration decisions, including those of the country's highest electoral court, are almost systematically suspected of bias, as we saw in the 2000 election. At state level, the management of elections is often devolved to a secretary of state or lieutenant-governor who is himself affiliated to a political party.[270]

The political pressure on electoral arbitration is not only reflected in squabbling. It also manifests itself in the desire to keep elections away from prying eyes. Politics, and the elections that define them, are a kind of sanctuary that must be protected from inquisitorial regulation. A major effort was therefore made to circumvent the arbiters of elections, even to weaken them, and to curtail the powers of the oversight bodies. This almost instinctive reluctance to subject the election to regulation beyond the control

---

[268] Words spoken by President Trump himself.

[269] For a fuller account of these events, see: New York Times of 2 January 2021, « Washington Post » of 5 January 2021

[270] Hall Dr Thad E., *Guide d'information sur le système électoral des Etats Unis,* IFES, 2011, p.6.

of the political players has been demonstrated in at least two countries whose democratic quality no one would doubt in principle: Australia and the United States. In the first case, the MPs clearly intended to limit the powers of the Australian Electoral Commission to only technical and administrative matters, to the exclusion of electoral policy[271]. The aim was to reduce the Commission to a body that is merely executive, to keep it far from politics. In the United States, limiting the powers of the Federal Election Commission (FEC) was the outcome of a long legal battle. The principle of transparency was weakened as a result. In a ruling handed down in 1976[272], the Supreme Court of the United States carried out an actual dismembering of the powers of the American Electoral Commission, the result of which was to exclude from the jurisdiction of this body everything to do with the crucial issue of politics and money, and in particular the financing of political parties and election campaigns. The Court agreed with the petitioners that the members of the Commission performed executive rather than legislative functions, and that their appointment by the President of the United States therefore required the prior approval of the Senate, in accordance with a well-established rule. One of the consequences of this decision was that the Senate could no longer deal with issues relating to the financing of political activity. In this respect, the situation in the United States should be compared with that in a country such as Australia, where the National Electoral Commission is hampered by the persistent refusal of the political parties to allow it to acquire any competence in matters of electoral policy, its remit being limited to dealing with purely technical and administrative issues[273].

---

[271] Thomas P.G. et Lorne R.G., op cit, p. 41.

[272] Thomas P.G et Lorne R.G. ,op cit p 41.

[273] Thomas P.G and Lorne R.G. ,op cit p 41.

In addition to the threat of politicisation of its composition, the powers of the US Electoral Commission are being eroded. In fact, the body is characterised by a certain weakness, and electoral finance expert Thomas E Mann is right in asserting that Congress designed this oversight body to function like a watchdog trained by its master"[274]. Like several countries that have adopted the ministerial model of election monitoring - France in particular - the American model is plagued with structural deficiencies. The presidential election episodes of 2000 and 2020 should therefore not be interpreted as disruptive events or accidents of history, but as the "awakening" of volcanoes that are still active, revealing deep-seated institutional deficiencies.

While countries with a certain democratic tradition are reluctant or averse to setting up fully independent mechanisms, and while their political parties are slow to internalise the imperative of impartiality, African countries have succeeded in this challenge. In this respect, a cross-reading of the rulings handed down by the Supreme Court of the United States - on the *Buckley* case - and the Constitutional Court of Benin - about the National Electoral Commission - is instructive. The contrast is striking. On the one hand, there is a relentless effort to dismantle, and on the other, a deliberately positive approach. The following extracts attest to this.

According to the U.S. Supreme Court, in Summary, we sustain the individual contribution limits, the disclosure and reporting provisions, and the public financing scheme. We conclude, however, that the limitations on campaign expenditures, on independent expenditures by individuals and groups, and on expenditures by a candidate from his personal funds are constitutionally infirm. Finally, we hold that most of the powers conferred by the Act upon the Federal Election Commission can be exercised only by Officers of the United States, appointed in

[274] Cited by Thomas P.G. and Lorne R Gibson, op cit, p.66.

conformity with Art.II,2, cl.2, of the Constitution and therefore cannot be exercised by the Commission as presently constituted.

In a completely opposite perspective, the Constitutional Court of Benin magnifies the mission of the Electoral Commission: "Considering that the creation of the CENA, as an independent administrative authority, is linked to the search for a formula making it possible to isolate, within the administration of the State, a body having a real autonomy in relation to the Government, the ministerial departments and the Parliament, for the exercise of powers concerning the sensitive field of public liberties, in particular fair, regular, free and transparent elections (...). Considering that the creation of an Independent Electoral Commission is an important step in strengthening and guaranteeing public liberties and human rights; that it makes it possible, on the one hand, to establish a tradition of independence and impartiality with a view to ensuring free and transparent elections and, on the other hand, to win the confidence of voters and political parties and movements"[275].

This judicial opinion reflects the new state of mind in many African states. The proliferation of electoral commissions in Africa after the 90s, and even today, is not only a demonstration of remarkable local inventiveness but could well serve as an example for countries that are usually presented as models of democracy, but which are struggling to put in place mechanisms to ensure the neutrality of electoral arbitration. Of course, the establishment of NAECs and other INECs cannot be a panacea. Not only has the experience not been conclusive everywhere, it has even resulted in bitter failure in some cases. But these bodies are certainly not the magic potion that will cure Africa of its political ills, some of which are endemic. One should, therefore, not be under any illusion regarding their curative virtues, as we shall come back to later.

---

[275] Constitutionals Court of Benin, Judg. DDC 34-94 of 23 December 1994.

However, the challenge of electoral neutrality has, technically speaking, largely been met. Many African countries have taken the step that other countries hesitate or refuse to take, under conditions that sometimes indicate a certain boldness.

II. THE AFRICAN PATH TO IMPARTIALITY

The creation of electoral commissions on the African continent disqualifies the age-old reproach of mimicry. These bodies respond to a real and genuine political and social need. They thus emerge from the bowels of society (A). But these Commissions do not form a unified whole. There are many variants, but some of them, from a comparative perspective, are undoubtedly bold. (B)

A. A homegrown creation

It is important to understand that the new electoral arbitration bodies are the result of a genuine, real need. The historical conditions in which they were set up attest to this.

The Electoral Commissions were for the most part set up in the context of the choice of political pluralism in the 1990s. Breaking with one-party regimes - de facto or de jure - and withdrawing from the State Administration the power to organise and arbitrate elections, the new Constitutions that were adopted drew the consequences of the democratic approach chosen in the field of electoral competition, precisely by creating these independent Commissions, intended to deliver transparent elections. The National Electoral Commissions (NAECs/INECs) thus derive directly from the national conferences, these bodies for national dialogue which do not hesitate, in a revolutionary mode reminiscent of the *Etats généraux* of 1789 in France and the famed *Tennis Court Oath*, to exercise a constituent power attached to a self-proclaimed sovereignty. The new Constitutions of Sierra Leone, Ghana, Niger, and The Gambia were adopted against this backdrop of restive protest.

NAECs/INECs are created either to stem the tide of contestation over the integrity of elections, whether latent or patent, endemic or eruptive. The establishment of ONEL[276] in Senegal, in the mid-90s, was prompted by a concern to remove the suspicion of illegitimacy from the results of elections organised solely by the State"[277]. The creation of the ONEL was dictated by the serious disputes arising from the 1996 local elections. In Mali, the INEC was set up in 1997 at a time of tension between the government and the opposition, one of the bones of contention being the organisation of elections, which until then had been the responsibility of the Ministry of the Interior. In Guinea, the creation of the Electoral Commission was part of a package of measures adopted against a backdrop of paralysis throughout the country, marked by general strikes and deadly repression (January 2007). In Togo and the DRC, the body responsible for overseeing the electoral process was part of the political agreements intended to break the deadlock in the country: Comprehensive Political Agreement of 20 August 2006 and Comprehensive and Inclusive Agreement of 17 December 2001.

We are indeed witnessing a "manifestation of the African imagination in terms of legal engineering"[278], and the development of" an appropriate response to the distrust shown towards electoral administrations moulded in the culture of the one-party system[279]. But these arbitration institutions are not only remarkable from the point of view of their mode of generation - carnal generation, one might say -. They are also impressive in terms of the powers conferred on some of them -. Whereas in countries such as the

---

[276] National Election Observatory

[277] Zekaria O.A., « L'observatoire national des élections au Sénégal. Une neutralité sous surveillance », in Quantin P. (dir), *Voter en Afrique. Comparaisons et différenciations*, L'Harmattan, 2004, p. 149.

[278] Du Bois de Gaudusson J., « Les élections à l'épreuve de l'Afrique », in « La sincérité du scrutin », *Cahiers du Conseil Constitutionnel*, cited above.

[279] Mbodji El H., « Faut-il avoir peur de l'indépendance des institutions électorales en Afrique? », Revue *Afrilex.*

United States, the United Kingdom and Australia, political parties have opposed or continue to oppose any enhancement of the powers of these bodies, which are clearly seeking to keep them away from the political and financial stakes of electoral competitions, a few African states have taken the opposite position, that of a clear assumption of the arbitration mandate, by recognising the electoral commissions' decision-making powers in this respect.

B. Ambitious mechanisms

Clearly, not all electoral arbitration bodies have the same powers. The emphasis here is on the strongest amongst them. The decisive criterion in this respect is related or collateral competences to the electoral operation itself, its material organisation or even its ad hoc arbitration. From a logical but also empirical point of view, based on the experiences of electoral disputes on the African continent, it appears that it is before the elections that a lot of things happen. A body will therefore be considered as strong or active according to the control it exercises over the entire electoral process, over the determinants prior - above all - and after the election itself. One thinks of prerogatives such as those concerning the maintenance of the electoral register - that famous bone of contention in Africa , the demarcation of constituencies, which we have seen has been able to undermine the sincerity of elections in France and the United States in particular, the financing of electoral campaigns, and even of political life in general, the financial implications of elections and their often shady backgrounds creating the temptation, in manyold democracies, to circumvent the powers of the arbitration body.

On all these crucial points, African countries have resolutely opted for transparency. Ghana's electoral commission, for instance, not only ensures that the elections are held properly, but also registers and monitors the activities of political parties, checks that their financial accounts are in order, ensures that the electoral boundaries are consistent and fair, and collects and distributes the material and financial resources intended for the competitors. In Liberia, the Commission constantly monitors the relevance and proper application of electoral laws, it has the power to propose amendments to the texts, it registers and accredits the political parties, it is a party before the court's ruling on electoral matters, and it audits the financial expenditure incurred by these parties. The Gambian body has more or less the same powers, to which must be added that of drafting the code of ethics governing the electoral campaign and that of issuing permits for holding rallies during the campaign. The Burkina Faso Commission has a say in the financing of elections, in addition to its traditional remit, and the Nigerian Commission even exercises powers relating to civic education and access to the media, as in Côte d'Ivoire.

Of course, this picture should not be misleading. One could say that there is a yawning gap between the texts and reality, and when the facts are put to the test, attractive arrangements on paper may have been shattered and expectations disappointed. But apart from the fact that such disillusionment has not occurred everywhere, and that arbitration bodies are still today correctly fulfilling their noble democratic mission, it will be argued that the simple development of these techniques in the service of electoral neutrality is not an insignificant fact, when in other, more long-established democratic jurisdictions, such mechanisms are simply difficult to conceive of, or are even fiercely rejected, thus assuming a reluctance to draw all the logical consequences of democracy.

What is also remarkable is that the arbitration mechanisms developed by African states are being promoted to a form of international standardisation. Not only are the NAECs/INECs approaching an international standard of arbitral credibility, but they are tending, on the African continent itself, to be set up as instruments of democratic standardisation, as a yardstick for measuring electoral transparency. In this way, a kind of upward levelling is taking place, a beneficial process; the independent electoral commissions are having a virtuous knock-on effect on the political and electoral systems of the Member States.

The first sign of this qualitative improvement in electoral law is to be found in the constitutionalising of arbitration bodies. States such as Ghana, Sierra Leone, Guinea, Nigeria, and Niger have not hesitated to undertake this constitutional promotion. In this way, the Electoral Commission is raised to the level of a constitutional body and becomes a party to the State authority. It goes without saying that it is thus protected from the well-known vulnerability of being abolished or transformed by the parliamentary majorities emerging from the elections.

From a strictly international point of view, the independent electoral commissions in Africa are much closer than the mechanisms in place in many European, American or Asian countries to the demands made by an organisation such as the Inter-Parliamentary Union, the world organisation of national parliaments, whose Governing Council in a Declaration adopted in Paris on 26 March 1994, expressed the wish that in States, "disputes relating to the electoral process should be dealt with effectively and promptly (...) by an *independent and impartial authority* such as the courts or an electoral commission"[280]. And as part of the responsibilities of the State, the body prescribes "the establishment of a neutral, impartial or balanced mechanism for the administration of elections"[281]. A United Nations Declaration adopted in 2012 by nearly 160 election observation organisations

---

[280] Interparliamentary Council, Paris Declaration on criteria for free and fair elections, 154th Session, 26 March 1994.

[281] Idem.

recommends "impartial observation and monitoring of elections" as well as the "independent monitoring of the electoral process"[282].

On the African continent itself, in 2007 the African Union adopted a Charter on Democracy, Elections and Governance, which is an international treaty, and which sets out the obligation to "establish and strengthen independent and impartial national election management bodies".[283] The Economic Community of West African States (ECOWAS) and the Southern African Development Community (SADC) have established the imperative of impartiality as a regional standard binding on member states. The former has done so through its Protocol on Democracy and Good Governance, adopted in 2001 and currently under review. A veritable international treaty stipulating legal obligations that are actionable before national and international courts, the Protocol states that "the bodies responsible for elections must be independent and/or neutral and have the confidence of all political actors"[284], that "the preparation and conduct of elections and the announcement of results shall be done in a transparent manner"[285] and that "adequate arrangements shall be made to hear and dispose of all petitions relating to the conduct of elections and announcement of results" [286]. The African Court on Human and Peoples' Rights has itself shown the extent to which it is committed to the imperative of arbitral impartiality. When the matter was referred to it in connection with the Côte d'Ivoire Electoral Commission, the Court first confirmed that the ECOWAS Protocol referred to above was indeed a legal instrument relating to human

---

[282] The Declaration of Principles for International Election Observation and the Code of Conduct for International Election Observers, adopted on 3 April 2012 at the United Nations.

[283] Article 17.

[284] Article 3.

[285] Article 6.

[286] Article 7.

rights and therefore a potential reference standard for the Court. Above all, it considered that the Ivorian commission did not meet the requirement of impartiality. An electoral body, in the opinion of the court, is independent when it enjoys administrative and financial autonomy and offers sufficient guarantees as to the independence and impartiality of its members. The Court goes on to state "that institutional independence itself is not sufficient"; where representation is on a political and partisan basis, its composition must also be balanced. In the instant case, this condition is not met, since " .... there was an imbalance in the numerical representation of the ruling coalition"; moreover, the decision-making method used - simple majority - is likely to encourage unfairness. As a result, the court "holds that by adopting the impugned law, the Respondent State violated its commitment to establish an independent and impartial electoral body ", an obligation arising from Article 17 of the African Charter on Elections and Article 3 of the ECOWAS Protocol. The Court's view of the impartiality of electoral bodies is particularly noteworthy, as it takes into account the public's perception of such impartiality. According to the African Human Rights Court, "institutional independence alone is not enough to guarantee the holding of transparent, free and fair elections as advocated by the African Charter on Democracy and the ECOWAS Protocol on Democracy. The electoral body set up must, moreover, be composed in accordance with the law in such a way as to guarantee its independence and impartiality *and to be perceived as such*"[287].

There is, therefore, undoubtedly, a regional principle of arbitral impartiality in electoral matters. It is curious that this fact has eluded many electoral analysts, who are outspoken critics of the regional "governmental" or "partisan" model in Europe, America, or Asia, but have never thought of highlighting the African counter

---

[287] ACHPR, Judg of 18 November 2016, « Action pour la promotion des droits de l'homme Vs CI », §123.

example, which could then perhaps have been held up as a model for the rest of the world. The problem of electoral neutrality is an area in which African exemplarity, which is as remarkable as it is systematic, has been somewhat dismissed, through ignorance or prejudice. This is a sector in which no one will say that the institutions set up are mimetic or disembodied.

Reporting on a book on electoral law published by two French authors[288], Stéphane Bolle is rightly surprised by the absence of any reference to African experiences of electoral arbitration, even though the book is particularly critical of the French model. Bolle points out that " the book studiously ignores the responses - under debate - that the constitutions, laws and judges of French-speaking Africa have provided and are providing to the universal problem - dealt with in international law - of the independence of the authority organising elections. If the existence of a homogeneous francophone legal culture can be questioned, if the notion of francophone law is not easy to grasp, why should France first turn to the Anglo-Saxon world to review and correct its electoral law? Why should it draw on the post-authoritarian or post-totalitarian standards of Europe or Latin America and not on the standards of today's French-speaking Africa, which are clearly related to French law and aim to consolidate the rule of law and multi-party democracy? "[289]. However, Stéphane Bolle's assessment, which is difficult to refute, relates only to the French-speaking African world. The point of view espoused here is even broader, more disambiguated: it is both trans-regional and trans linguistic, open to the world and to all its languages and legal traditions. It therefore suggests taking into account experiences in English, and Portuguese-speaking African countries. More generally, the

[288] Doublet Y-M and Touvet L., *Droit des élections*, Economica, 2007 (1st edition).

[289] Bolle St., « Droit des élections. Et les CENA, CENI, CEI, ONEl et autres ELECAM ? », site www.la-constitution-en-afrique.

question of Africa's place in comparative law can be raised, as Alioune Badara Fall has shown[290].

This being the case, and to return to our theme, we understand that resolving the issue of the principle of electoral neutrality does not mean that the problem of elections in Africa has disappeared. Many problems relating to the fairness of elections remains acute and persistent, and it must be acknowledged that in many countries the illusions of the 1990s have fizzled out. Several provisos must therefore be issued at this stage.

First, it is certain that the establishment of independent electoral commissions on the African continent has not necessarily meant the end of controversy and tension, nor an unassailable guarantee of change of government. Governments in power have been able to set up such bodies while retaining power in other ways. Arbitration bodies are therefore not magic wands, recipes for the circulation of political elites or for improving political governance across Africa. These bodies have even failed spectacularly in their regulatory mission. Elections in Mali in 1997, Togo in 1998, Congo and Kenya in 2007 and Zimbabwe in 2008 were all marred by the failure of the monitoring system. In addition to these one-off setbacks, there are structural or latent institutional weaknesses, such as the non-permanence of commissions and the erratic allocation of human and financial resources. In countries such as Senegal under ONEL (mid-1990s), Benin and Niger, the late allocation of resources may have been perceived as a deliberate manoeuvre by the ruling governments to weaken the monitoring powers of the commissions and thereby secure electoral victories.

---

[290] Fall A. B., « Le droit africain, a-t-il sa place dans le droit comparé ? », in which the author provides an in-depth analysis of the conditions under which African states « receive » and « adapt » the law of former European colonial states; in *Le développement du droit comparé en France,* Journées d'études du 23 juin 2004, Institut de France (Paris), Groupement de droit comparé, GDR 1199, presses universitaires d'Aix - en- Provence, 2005, pp.162-184.

It should be added that the celebration of independence here does not sit well with the politicisation of the composition of certain arbitration bodies. Rather than having recourse to persons who are not affiliated to political parties, some States have made the strictly opposite choice, that of a composition based on political affiliation, the more or less balanced representation of the different parties and coalitions then constituting, it is argued, the guarantee of a certain impartiality. Clearly, however, such an approach is not entirely consistent with the imperative of neutrality as championed here, since the impartiality advocated should literally be understood as the absence of bias, the avoidance of any partisan consideration in the composition of electoral commissions. It is easy to admit that « partisan » commissions run the risk of reproducing political cleavages and that they are therefore exposed to the risk of paralysis. The recent history Côte d'Ivoire attests to this. Not only did the commission fall apart when the results of the 2010 presidential election had to be announced, but the African Court of Human and Peoples' Rights, in the afore-mentioned decision of 18 November 2016 on the IEC in that country, emphasised how the mechanism of systematic party representation could create situations of unfairness.

It is therefore appropriate, in conclusion, to put into perspective the effectiveness of electoral commissions in accomplishing the mission entrusted to them. We do not seek, by any means, to present them as a panacea but only as the manifestation of a homegrown genius on the one hand, and a remarkable institutional shaping of the principle of impartiality, on the other. It can therefore be accepted that there is a specific African feature to electoral arbitration, from which models tried and tested in other parts of the world would undoubtedly draw inspiration.

CHAPTER 8

AN UNIDENTIFIED LEGAL OBJECT: THE OHADA COMMON COURT OF JUSTICE AND ARBITRATION

The Kingdom shall be one and indivisible.
Article 1, Title II of the French Constitution of 4 September 1791

There shall be a single Court of Cassation for the whole Kingdom.
Chap.V, art.19 of the French Constitution of 4 September 1791

On 17 October 1993, in Port Louis (Seychelles), a group of African States, now ten, signed a treaty establishing an Organisation for the Harmonisation of Business Law (OHADA). The aim is to achieve legal integration through the development of « a single business law » for all Member States. The treaty, which is open to all African States, "even non-AU Members "[291], replaces " national business laws " a single set of rules, described as "community" rules. The aim is to give legal certainty to transactions by unifying the applicable rules, diversity being a factor of uncertainty. Ultimately, the aim is to encourage and develop investment in Africa.

OHADA is based on an institutional quartet: a Council of Ministers, which has legislative powers under ordinary law, in

[291] Article 53 of the treaty.

particular the power to adopt the organisation's " uniform acts"; the Permanent Secretariat, which reports to the Council of Ministers and acts as an integrated body; the Common Court of Justice and Arbitration (CCJA); and the Conference of Heads of State and Government, a fledgling body since it was created as part of the 2008 revision of the treaty. To achieve the desired legal integration, the OHADA bodies have two standard-setting instruments at their disposal: uniform acts and regulations. Uniform acts are used to adopt common rules covering the entire spectrum of commercial law. Criminal law is left to the discretion of Member States. Regulations are adopted "whenever necessary for the application of the Treaty". So far, they have covered proceedings before the Court of Justice, arbitration, the finances of the institutions of the organisation and the status of officials.

The CCJA plays a central role in the effort to unify the law. On an international level, it performs the functions of a court of cassation. It therefore hears appeals against decisions of the courts of appeal of the Member States. OHADA is thus an organisation whose originality is based on its unifying ambition, the desire to unify all business law (substantive revolution) as well as the centralisation and internationalisation of a procedure that is all too often forgotten to be the result of the strengthening of the State and therefore of sovereignty (procedural revolution). Unless I am mistaken, this last dimension is unique in the world. The internationalisation of an eminently national procedure, the "hijacking of an objective" of an essentially sovereigntist objective into a transnational and integrating instrument, is undoubtedly an original find, which is also a masterpiece of a balancing act, as we shall see.

I. A SUBSTANTIVE REVOLUTION

OHADA's legal work and its organic architecture are original in two respects. The desire to bring all business law under the umbrella of the Organisation is remarkable. States are thus stripped of significant aspects of their legislative power. But the astonishing thing is not only this wilful dispossession; it is also to be found in the way in which the common rules are drawn up, reflecting a high degree of supranationalism, the equivalent of which cannot be found, in the African field itself, in any other international organisation, particularly those which set themselves the objective of economic and monetary integration. In the original construction of OHADA and its jurisdiction, a distinction must therefore be made between quantitative aspects, relating to the volume of powers devolved to the international organisation (A), and qualitative aspects, relating to the high degree of institutionalisation of the decision-making procedure (B).

A. Quantitative Aspects

Article 2 of OHADA's founding treaty covers eight areas of legal integration. Coming under the heading of business law as the very name of the Organisation suggests, these areas are the legal status of traders, company law, securities law, debt collection and enforcement, company reorganisation and winding-up, arbitration law, accounting law and transport law. In principle, « Uniforms Acts" containing legal instruments with far-reaching unifying powers were to be adopted.

This is already an impressive list. However, there is every reason to believe that the process of unification will continue, and that the list in Article 2 is not restrictive. Article 2 clearly states that "any other matter which the Council of Ministers" decides to bring within the scope of business law may be the subject of unification. Furthermore, under article 11 of the Treaty, "the Council of Ministers shall, on a proposal from the Secretary General approve the annual programme for the harmonisation of business law". The Council of Ministers meeting in Bangui in 2001 decided based on this provision, to include in the harmonisation programme matters such as the law on cooperatives and mutual societies, banking law, competition law and contract law. This fact clearly attests to the expansive dynamics of OHADA law.

Apart from the elements of positive law, doctrinal readings tend to highlight the expansion of the boundaries of « business law ». It has thus been clearly questioned whether the scope of OHADA is not, *mutatis mutandis,* "unlimited"[292]. For others, the addition of an area such as securities law to the Organisation's remit was precisely a kind of legislative imperialism since it was not clearly a matter of business law[293]. The very resistance of the national courts of OHADA Member States to relinquishing their jurisdiction to the CCJA is further evidence of the reality of the feeling that the legislative dispossession of member states is not always justified.

OHADA's ambition is not only remarkable in terms of its scope, which is at least virtual. It is also remarkable in terms of the strong institutionalisation of the procedure for adopting Uniform Acts.

B. Qualitative aspects

The status of OHADA regulations is primarily a product of the decision-making process. What is at work here is an institutional quartet. What comes to mind is the European "institutional triumvirate " ...). But the Conference of Heads of State and Government, which was only grafted on the institutional structure in 2008 only, acts as a forum for resolving problems that the Council of Ministers has been unable to solve. Originally, therefore, it did not exist (like the ECC/EU). This highly political body is therefore overshadowed in the normative activity of ordinary law, and the

---

[292] Lohoues-Oble, J., « La création d'un nouvel environnement juridique de l'entreprise », colloque d'Abidjan du 2 avril 2001 sur *L'environnement juridique des entreprises dans la zone franc : quel bilan ?*, unpublished.

[293] See Presentation by Fometeu J. at the Conference on OHADA held at the University of Ngouandéré (Cameroun), 21 March 2007, cited in *OHADA. Traité et Actes uniformes commentés et annotés*, Juriscope 2008, p.35, under the dir. of Issa – Sayeg J., Pougoué P.G., Savadogo F.M.

scenario highlights the following players: the Council of Ministers, the Permanent Secretariat, the CCJA and the Member States. More specifically, Article 6 of the Treaty provides that draft Uniform Acts shall be "prepared by the permanent secretariat, in consultation " with the Member States, and then deliberated upon and adopted by the Council of Ministers after receiving the opinion of the CCJA. Three Treaty bodies are thus involved in the standard-setting process, along with the Member States.

Such a legislative process appears to have two advantages in our view. The first is the involvement of the Member States, which are requested to comment within 90 days of receiving the draft Uniform Acts. This collaboration with the States whose courts will be responsible for applying the adopted texts is likely not only to reduce the risk of "bad legislation" (since it is assumed that the comments requested from the Member States will cover all aspects of the issues and will possibly be critical or suggestive). It will also address national judicial sensitivities, which are always possible, as we have seen, when the reduction of national competences is perceived as being achieved " in a rush". Moreover, in this case, it is reasonable to assume that the existence of institutions such as the "OHADA national commissions" set up by Member States – another unique feature of the system -, comprising lawyers, will make it possible to gather relevant comments. This codified and formal process of involving States in the standard-setting process is regrettably non-existent within the African Union or the Regional Economic Communities.

The second advantage of the system is the involvement of the CCJA, which is responsible for applying the law. Involving the Court in the actual drafting of the law saves time and is a preventive way of resolving any difficulties or conflicts that may arise between legislator and judge. For a moment, it must be admitted, that judge becomes legislator; the OHADA mechanism temporarily blurs the lines between the legislative and judicial functions of the law. The dogmatism of the purists must be rejected here, and the blurring of reference points must be validated for pragmatism and speed. The work of both legislator and judge will be healthier as a result, and the alliance between theorist and practitioner will make the regulations appropriate, relevant, and welcome. What judge would not dream of such dualism to be able to shape his own rules of reference? For the Uniform Acts in question are precisely the bases on which the CCJA delivers his judgments. Therefore, it must be assumed that these Acts are designed to strike a balance between national constraints - reflected by the States themselves and their OHADA commissions, and the international requirements of integration - expressed by the CCJA.

Lastly, the systematic nature of the intervention of this supranational judicial body is remarkable because, in the international organisations where it exists, it is generally carried out only in an advisory capacity. The court is asked for an opinion and delivers its opinion. It is true that the systematic nature of the CCJA's intervention is also due to the specific and limited purpose of the organisation, which is to achieve legal integration. That said, no one would have been moved by the absence of the judiciary in the very process of drafting the Organisation's regulations. For this reason, OHADA is adopting the opposite approach, and the uniqueness of the mechanism put in place must be emphasised.

The "status" of OHADA regulations should also engage our attention, given the high degree of institutionalisation that characterises their legal force and their entry into force. The intergovernmental approach is obviously very much in motion, as Uniform Acts and regulations are adopted unanimously. OHADA's object and purpose lends credence to the enduring interstate argument. Legislative disparities cannot be smoothed out without the consent of the States. But the institutional approach remains present through the rule that the Uniform Acts in particular "are directly applicable in and binding on the

Contracting States notwithstanding any prior, or subsequent, contrary provision of domestic law"[294]. Its drastic, overriding effect is explained by the ambition of the objective: not "coordinate" or even "harmonise"[295], but "unify", i.e., abolish all national discordances. The CCJA itself has confirmed the power of the Uniform Acts to override national law. In its Opinion of 30 April 2001, it stated that "Article 40 contains a rule of supra-nationality, since it provides for the direct and mandatory application of the Uniform Acts in the Contracting States and, moreover, establishes their primacy over earlier and subsequent provisions of domestic law (...). Article 10 therefore appears to be the only provision capable of enshrining the supra-nationality of the Uniform Acts, as confirmed by the specific articles of each Uniform Act".

As regards the conditions for the entry into force of the Acts in question, it is stipulated that this takes place 90 days after their adoption, and that they are enforceable 30 clear days after their publication in the OHADA Official Journal, while it is still possible to publish them at the national level. The centralisation of the conditions for entry into force of the Acts also reflects the highly institutional nature of the Organisation's Law-making.

The same logic applies to the definition of the authority of judgments handed down by the CCJA. They « have the force of *res judicata* and enforceability. They are enforced in each State Party under the same conditions as decisions of domestic courts. In any case, no decision contrary to a judgment of the CCJA may be enforced in a State Party"[296]. Three things are clear from this

---

[294] Article of the treaty.

[295] If only in view of the purpose of the «Uniform Acts » (which is therefore to « unify » or « standardize »), it is reasonable to wonder whether OHADA does not go further than the mere « harmonisation » of business law, which does not in principle exclude the subsistence of national differences or « nuances ». OHADA may then be a misnomer. It should be added that regulations also have full binding force, even though Article 4 of the Treaty says nothing about this effect.

[296] Article 20 of the Treaty.

provision: the force of *res judicata*, the enforceability of the decision and the superiority of the CCJA over national courts. However, the essential originality of OHADA and its jurisdiction must be highlighted on another point: on the "outsourcing" of the appellate procedure and all the assumptions and implications of such a choice.

II. A PROCEDURAL REVOLUTION

Everything here is a break with the past. The system established by OHADA is revolutionary because it completely calls into question the hitherto prevailing approach to appellate jurisdiction. Whereas it used to be associated with the construction of the State or the assertion of its authority, appeal is now used to dispossess States in the interests of supranational integration. The technical conditions under which the CCJA performs its role are a departure from many of the dogmas of international litigation, both from the point of view of the regulations to which the judge refers and the sanction of the review it exercises. The CCJA version of judicial review thus disrupts the best-established dogmas, both from the point of view of the function of judicial review (A) and from that of the classic principles of international litigation (B).

A. From the appellate standpoint

The CCJA de-nationalises the appellate procedure. Initiated at the national level, the proceedings culminate in the international arena; they are heard successively by the national court and by the international court.

This continuum is original. Usually, the international judicial system only agrees to discuss a national trial or certain aspects of it on one condition: the condition of a watertight separation of the two procedures, which is based on the idea that although the factual raw material is the same, the legal issues and arguments are not similar, and the stakes are different. We will come back to this.

For the time being, let us just remember that the OHADA mechanism consists of a national procedure that continues at international level. This is a somewhat strange mix, but we need to unravel it by first recalling the close link between the appeals procedure and the sovereignty of the State itself.

There is no doubt about this link. It should be remembered here that the mythology of the State is a unitary one: unity of the territory, unity of the nation, unity of the application and interpretation of the law produced by the State. It is the Supreme Court of the State, the Court of Cassation, which is the judicial body par excellence and standard setter of the sovereign State. There is a relationship of concomitance, of correspondence, between the assertion of State authority and the establishment or strengthening of supreme courts charged with overseeing the uniform interpretation and application of the law. The essential unity of the State must be matched by the interpretative unity - or uniform interpretation - of the law. Obtaining the legislative power alone is not enough. Such power needs "regular maintenance" to ensure consistency and certainty in the interpretation and enforcement of the rules of law.

This unitary horizon, the obsession with uniformity, is not specific to the unitary state. They are necessary even in States with a more complex structure, even in federal States which, as we know, combine diversity and unity very well. As we shall see, the Supreme Court of the United States and the Court of Appeal of Germany - both federal States - were involved in the formation and consolidation of these two States.

In a unitary State such as France, from which so many OHADA member States have inherited their legal system and philosophy, this link between the consolidation of the State and the power of appeal is even more obvious. According to Jacques Boré, the role of the Court of Cassation was to "ensure that the courts and tribunals respected the unity of legislation that the Revolution had just established"[297]. In the minds of the revolutionaries, the Court of Cassation was the judicial ally of the centralising State, a sentinel dedicated to censoring centrifugal tendencies. The direct dependence of the Court of Cassation on the legislature itself is almost a caricature of the court's "instrumental" and "repressive" mandate. The well-known procedure of "judicial deference" clearly demonstrates the subordination of the judge to the legislature, but it is in its power to quash flawed judgments that the Tribunal's major raison d'être lies. At the parliamentary sitting of 9 November 1790, the MP Prieur declared that the Court of Cassation was " a watchdog established to uphold the law "[298].

The link between the court and the legislature reflects the idea that the court is the adjunct of the legislature. During the French Revolution, "the Constituents wanted the Court to be attached " to the legislature" because it seemed logical to them that the authority that interpreted the law should be close to the authority that made it "[299]. In fact, Article 1 of the law establishing the Court states that " there shall be *a* Court of Cassation established within the Legislature", after the Constitution of 4 September 1791 had stipulated that " there shall be *a single* Court of Cassation for the whole Kingdom...... ". It should be added that the Decree of 27 November 1790 specified that the court "shall be sedentary". This was intended to rule out the idea, mooted at the time, of entrusting the review of trials to "itinerant judges", as it would have, no doubt, been said today-. While such a plan was justified by the need to bring justice closer to litigants, it had the disadvantage of ignoring what must be called the political aim of the appeals procedure: the construction of uniform case law, the judicial expression of the sovereign State and legislator.

---

[297] Boré J., *La cassation en matière civile,* Paris, Sirey, 1988, p.4

[298] Boré J., op cit., p 5.

[299] Boré J., op cit, p 7.

It is therefore important to understand the decisive importance of these "logistical" elements. From the perspective of the role of the *juge de cassation*, they are undoubtedly important. Proximity to the legislature, which is first and foremost geographical proximity, means two things: not only is the court "watched" (« it has to be watched » in the literal sense of the word), but there is also an organic dependence between the watcher and the watched. The sedentary nature of the court is not insignificant either. A sedentary judge is not only better "supervised", and the risk of case law wandering and splintering is not only better avoided, but sedentariness is the " situational" side of unity : unity of the body of a judge that is physically accessible, destined to remain in the court dedicated to ensuring the unity of the interpretation and application of a body of laws produced by a State which, in turn, now affirms its unity in the Constitution: " one and indivisible Kingdom ", " one and indivisible Republic" are, in fact, formulae dating back to the Revolution.

The appeals procedure would, of course, evolve over the following years. The revolutionaries' conception of it was quickly overturned. Not only did the Court of First Instance gradually free itself from dependence on the other arms of government, particularly the legislature, but the appeal itself, as a procedure and as a technique, continued to be refined (especially by broadening the scope of review and introducing new ways of "preparing" cases). There is, however, one constant, one point that remains unchanged, and that is the remit of appeals, its "political value" as Jacques Boré puts it, i.e, " as an instrument for ensuring compliance with the law and jurisprudential unity"[300]. The quest has always been for the public authorities to keep a firm grip on a legislative process that does not stop with the enactment of the rule but extends to its understanding and interpretation. The French

[300] Boré J., op cit, p 127.

revolutionaries did not, therefore, have a substantially minoritarian conception of the judicial function, nor did they consider that judging was *in itself* an almost null power, to use Montesquieu's expression. They were even aware of the subversive potential of such a power - the still fresh experience of the parliaments of the *Ancien Régime* is a reminder of this - which is why they set out to circumvent it. The review of judgments is precisely a means of containing the virtual weakening of legislative power that results from plurality and freedom of interpretation. Plurality is always dangerous for the survival of a government precisely because it forces it to fight on several fronts. On the other hand, unity - unity of the players, of the issues at stake, of the authority that sets out the rule - is reassuring for any government concerned about its survival precisely because it removes the feeling of a multiple front adversity, a confusing and dangerous dispersion.

There is therefore a clear relationship between the appeals procedure and the authority of the State as legislator. What is true of France is also true of the United States of America, Germany, and Canada. In the United States, the Supreme Court has played an essential role in the idea of American and national citizenship. When it was necessary to assert the authority of the federal entity, a system of "itinerant courts" was devised " not only to consolidate the government in remote areas, generally, but also to improve the popularity of the law on jurisdiction in the States"[301]. The very birth of federal criminal law followed the United States vs Worall ruling of 1793. The case was the prologue to a centralising jurisprudence championed by Justice Peters. He states: "the existence of the Federal government would be precarious .... if.... an appeal must be made to the State tribunals, or the offenders must escape with absolute impunity ". This means that the supreme court of the

[301] Delaney E., « Promouvoir la fédération : la Cour suprême des États Unis au cours des années 1780 », in *Fédéralisme et fédérations dans les Amériques : utopies, pratiques, limites »*, 2008, § 7.

federation is the guarantor of the unity of the law and its application, and that such a guarantee would be undermined if it were entrusted to the plurality of states that make up the federation. The US Supreme Court, as a court of appeal, has therefore clearly played the federalist card when it comes to bolstering central authority. It has acted as a teacher in this respect, a veritable "republican schoolmaster ", to borrow from Ralph Lerner[302].

The same observations apply to the political and judicial history of Germany. The affirmation of national unity went hand in hand with the establishment of "Supreme courts" whose purpose was to help strengthen the new State. The proclamation of the German Empire after Napoleon III's defeat at Sedan in 1870 was almost immediately followed by the creation of a Federal Court with jurisdiction in civil and criminal matters, an institution that " went hand in hand with German political unification"[303]. This Imperial Court sat in Leipzig from 1879 to 1945.

Finally, the example of another federal State, Canada, is worth mentioning. Here, the Supreme Court has interpreted constitutional provisions - in particular, Article 91 - in such a way as to guarantee the jurisdiction of the federation in certain matters, to the detriment of the federated states.[304].

This correlation between the authority of the State and the power of cassation was, moreover, clearly highlighted by the African courts themselves, when they were called upon to consider the conformity of the OHADA treaty with the Constitution. In at least

---

302 Lerner R., « The supreme Court as Republican Schoolmaster », *The Supreme Court Review,* 1967, p.1.

303 Dike, Groupe de recherche sur les cultures juridiques en Europe, *Histoire des justices en Europe, 2. Devenir une Cour suprême,* 2017, p 28.

304 Bérard F., « Le fédéralisme canadien et la Cour suprême », popups.uliege.be. ; Leclair J., « The supreme Court of Canada's Understanding of Federation : Efficieny at Expense of Diversity », *Queen's Law Journal,* vol 28, 2003, p. 423.

four States, "the judges of the Constitution" have engaged in such an exercise. The devolution of cassation jurisdiction to the CCJA was immediately perceived as anomalous, and the competent national authorities, with a remarkable level of synchronicity never seen before on any other subject, referred the matter to the courts for clarification of the scope of the Port-Louis Treaty. It was clear that there was something strange and disconcerting about this story. To outsource the appellate procedure, to de-nationalise it, amounted to an undue sharing of the power to judge, so symbolic of sovereignty. To concede such a dispossession in the solemn and imperative domain of cassation, would this not be a scar on the power to judge, an infringement of a major sovereign prerogative?

Asked to rule on the matter, the Constitutional Court of Senegal held that the agreed transfer of jurisdiction does not imply « any change to the international standing of Senegal as a sovereign and independent State, or any modification of its institutional arrangements ». Furthermore, the national Constitution also includes provisions allowing for the transfer of jurisdiction to an international organization in the pursuit of African unity.[305] The Constitutional Court of Benin established the same link between the de-nationalisation of the power of reviw and the sovereignty of the State. According to the judge, " a partial ceding of sovereignty within the framework of a treaty cannot constitute a breach of the Constitution insofar as (...) the said treaty is justified, moreover, by the need for regional or sub-regional integration affirmed by the preamble and article 149 of the Constitution"[306]. Reference may also be made to the case law of the Supreme Court of Justice sitting as the transitional Constitutional Court in the Democratic Republic of Congo, handed down in 2010. The court ruled that the provisions referred to it constituted "clauses ceding jurisdiction and limiting

305 Décision n°3-C-93 du 16 décembre 1993 rendue par le Conseil constitutionnel du Sénégal.

306 Décision DDC 19-94 du 30 juin 1994 rendue par la Cour constitutionnelle du Bénin.

the sovereignty of the Member States to OHADA, which may be adopted pursuant to Article 217 of the Constitution, which states that "the Democratic Republic of the Congo may conclude treaties or association or trade agreements with other States: the Democratic Republic of the Congo may conclude treaties or association or community agreements involving a partial cession of sovereignty in pursuit of African unity"[307]. Finally, mention should be made of the Opinion issued by the Supreme Court of the Congo on 1 October 1998. The only dissenting opinion in this chorus of consensus was that the OHADA Treaty, by conferring appellant jurisdiction on the CCJA, violated the provisions of the Fundamental Act of 24 October 1997[308].

What is remarkable here is not the greater or lesser harmony in the answers ultimately given to the problem in the case law, but the convergence of the Problem Statement, the similarity in the way the problem is posed.

In fact, all the courts immediately put the question before them in terms of sovereignty and the State's power of self-determination. By transferring part of its judicial power, which is so symbolic of its very unity, the State is cutting off an element of its sovereignty. The States that considered that the internationalisation of the appellate procedure was not contrary to their Constitution relied on a provision authorising a "total or partial relinquishment of sovereignty". The other State took the view, arguably justifiably so, that the absence of a constitutional provision authorising such a "relinquishment" made the treaty contrary to the Constitution and a Constitutional review was, therefore, necessary if the authorities wished to commit themselves to the internationalisation of the cassation procedure. The Congolese court clearly decided that " the

---

307 Judg. Const.112/TSR of 5 February 2010, delivered by the Supreme Court of the DRC.

308 Opinion n°037/CS/98 of 1st October 1998 delivered by the Supreme Court of the Congo.

adjudicative function, whether exercised by the courts of first instance or appeal or by the Supreme Court, is a constitutional function at the same time as it is the expression of national sovereignty and independence" and " the power to enforce on national territory a judicial decision handed down by a foreign court or an arbitration award (...) also derives from national sovereignty and independence"[309].

The CCJA and the Treaty of Port Louis that established it are revolutionary and unprecedented. The treaty is not only innovative because it symbolically dispossesses states. It is also original in the institutional tinkering it does, in the procedural engineering it introduces through the hybridisation of a national procedure by an international procedure, the cross-fertilisation between the jurisdiction of fact, or facts, confined within the national framework, and the jurisdiction of law, transported to the international level. The OHADA treaty establishes a judicial procedure that is part national and part international; it is an unconventional and confusing construction, the uniqueness of which has not been sufficiently emphasised in our view. Hitherto, out of respect for State sovereignty, a watertight separation had been established between national and international proceedings; however, the OHADA system breaks with this logic of procedural discontinuity to adopt an approach based on continuity, precisely by instituting a genuine judicial continuum, the same proceedings having a national phase and an international phase. For while an appeal to the CCJA may well be analysed as a " domestic" - appeal - from the perspective of " exhaustion of domestic remedies" -, the international nature of the competent court is not in doubt, as we shall return to later. There is therefore something unusual and unsettling about this procedure in terms of the classic principles governing judicial procedure.

---

[309] Text of the Opinion in *revue Penant,* 2002, p 171.

B. From the point of view of the classical principles of international litigation

The CCJA exercises the power of judicial review in the event of censure of the decision submitted to it. Article 14 of the Treaty is precise in this respect:

> The CCJA shall be responsible for the interpretation and common application of this Treaty, the regulations adopted and the uniform acts in the Contracting States (...). In the event of an application for appeal on point of law, the Court shall rule on decisions handed down by the courts of appeal of the Contracting States in all matters relating to the application of the uniform acts and regulations provided for in this Treaty, except for decisions imposing criminal sanctions. In the event of cassation, it shall hear and determine the merits of the case.

This is in stark contrast to the way in which litigation is usually organised in the international arena. The systematic nature of such appeals shows that arbitral or judicial awards are challenged laterally rather than frontally. By this we mean that it is the environment of the decision that is challenged, the procedural conditions under which it was made, rather than its very merits. [310]. The focus is on collateral breaches committed while handling the case. This is borne out by the number of appeals for decisions to be declared null and void. The relevant disputes show that the cases that give rise to an action are often the following: breach of an essential procedural rule (failure to comply with the adversarial principle, partiality of the members of the court, etc.), judicial overreach (*ultra petita*) and failure to state adequate reasons.

[310] Santulli C., *Droit du contentieux international*, Paris, Montchrestien 2005, pp. 372 et s.

Of course, actions for reform may exist, but they are very limited in the international legal system. On the one hand, they are "internalised ", almost never "externalised " as in the case of the CCJA. In other words, it is within the same body, understood in the broad sense of the term, that the double level of jurisdiction is established. This is the case for appeals to the WTO Appellate Body, appeals to the Grand Chamber of the European Court of Human Rights, and appeals to the Appeal Chambers of criminal courts. In all these cases, the desired review is undertaken in the same forum, so to speak, and the appeal procedure is not " transported" elsewhere. This is what is meant by internalisation.

On the other hand, there are cases of "outsourcing" the appeal procedure, but these are residual. This is illustrated by the International Court of Justice (ICJ) in The Hague, the principal judicial organ of the United Nations. Decisions of a judicial nature handed down by the Council of the International Civil Aviation Organization (ICAO) may be appealed at the ICJ, under the terms of the Chicago Convention which created the ICAO[311]. Arbitral awards constitute the remaining cases in which the ICJ exercises appellate jurisdiction. Even then, it is not certain that the intervention of the UN judge can relate to the substantive aspects of the award. Here again, it could only be a question of a lateral review, relating to the circumstances surrounding the delivery of the verdict, and not to the merits of the verdict itself.

The CCJA's remit is a far cry from this judicial model, which is dominated by a form of reverence for the decision under appeal. The OHADA judicial body exercises " frontal" oversight over the judgments of the appeal courts, and the sanction for such oversight is just as decisive since it may lead to the quashing of the said judgments.

---

[311] Articles 84 to 86 of the Convention.

At this stage of the analysis, three distinctive features may be noted. Firstly, the CCJA is an international court of cassation, which hears appeals against national judicial decisions. It is also a court that refers to "Uniform Acts", which are in fact unilateral acts of international organisations, acts that are directly applicable and binding in their entirety. Thirdly, the CCJA is not only a court of cassation, it also has supervisory jurisdiction,: a judge of the law and a judge of the merits, a judge of cassation, he is a judge of a higher court, precisely through this power of appeal. It judges in the manner of a national court of appeal. The combination of so many qualities is striking from the point of view of the classical theory of the trial.

We still need to agree on the very " international " nature of the CCJA, since it is this label that has often been used here. But before attempting to answer this question, it is necessary to clear up an ambiguity. The African Court of Human and Peoples' Rights, called upon to consider the rule of exhaustion of "domestic remedies", has held that an appeal to the CCJA is indeed a "domestic remedy"[312]. The Court reached this conclusion based on a set of indicators. First, " the provisions of the OHADA Treaty do not require a specific procedure to be incorporated into the domestic law of the States ; Secondly, the CCJA is a court common to seventeen States. It is the court of cassation for decisions handed down by the appeal courts of the States Parties in matters of business law[313]. Lastly, it "replaces not only the national supreme courts in appeals to the Supreme Court in matters governed by the OHADA Uniform Acts but also the national courts on the merits through its power of review "[314]. Accordingly, in the African

[312] ACHPR, Judg of 30 September 2021, « Ghaby Kodeih Vs Republic of Benin ».

[313] § 57 of the judgment.

[314] § 58 57 of the judgment.

Court's view, as the CCJA has "become part of the judicial system of the State", an appeal before it " is a local remedy"[315].

This is not the place to revisit or discuss such a conclusion. Let us simply consider that it should not be extrapolated: to say that an action before the CCJA is a "local remedy" in no way prejudices the international nature or otherwise of that court. In other words, the appeal can perfectly well be regarded as "national", since the appeal on points of law is one of the means of appeal provided for by the country's judicial system, without the "internal" nature of this appeal having any influence on the very nature of the court before which it is brought. To be even more direct: the appeal in cassation can be a "domestic" action, but the CCJA to which it is referred remains an international court.

An inventory of the relevant criteria shows that the Court "ticks all the boxes" or almost all, and that its international nature should be readily admitted.[316].

It is possible to assert that the CCJA is an international court even though its litigants, private individuals, are subjects of national law. The presence of a major subject of public international law - a State or an international organisation - in the courtroom is therefore not a determining factor in whether or not a judge can be described as international.[317] Secondly, while it has been argued that the composition of the court is not relevant either,[318] this debate does not arise for the CCJA because its members are nationals of States Party to the treaty, appointed according to internationally defined

---

[315] § 60 57 of the judgment.

[316] Two specific studies are referred to here: Cavare L., « La notion de juridiction internationale », *Annuaire français de droit international,* 1956, p. 496 and Santulli C., « Les juridictions de droit international: essai d'identification », same Journal, 2001.

[317] C. Santulli refers in this respect to the case of international administrative tribunals or international criminal courts, which do not judge States but private individuals. See also Cavare L., op cit, p.506.

[318] Santulli, op cit, p. 48.

criteria - by an international convention - and on the basis of an geographical balance, parameters that are well known in international organisations[319].

In the same way, if we pay attention to the institutional expression of the jurisdiction, " the entity of which the court is the organ", in the words of C. Santulli[320], we must recognise that the CCJA is also an international court, since it is the judicial organ of an organisation comprising sovereign States. The doctrine of legal validity, i.e., the system which confers jurisdictional power also confirms the international nature of the Court. The issue here is to identify the source of the obligation to enforce a court decision. In this respect, the CCJA must once again be qualified as an international court, since it is an international treaty - the organisation's founding treaty in this case - that sets out the obligation to comply with judgments handed down. Indeed, under Article 20 of the Treaty of Port Louis:

> "Judgments of the CCJA are *res judicata* (...). In any one case, no decision contrary to a judgment of the CCJA may be enforced in the territory of a Contracting State".

For our purposes, therefore, it should be noted that even on points that authors may have considered to be inconclusive, but which have been brandished in the debate, the OHADA court can lay claim to the label, it "ticks all the boxes" for being an " international court".

There may be some elements that cast doubt on this, but in our view, they must be cast aside. As we have seen, the presence of private individuals rather than States in proceedings before the CCJA is irrelevant. The international status of the Court cannot be challenged on this basis. The domestication of the applicable law

---

319 Cavare L ; op cit, p 508.

320 C santulli, op cit, p 50.

as an obstacle to such recognition is just as moot. Insofar as the Uniform Acts replace national business law, the temptation to doubt the international nature of the rules may arise, leading to a questioning of the international status of the court. Lastly, classifying an appeal in cassation as a "local remedy " - as the African Court of Human and Peoples' Rights has done - could lead observers to question the status of the Court. From our point of view, such elements are not overwhelming arguments.

On the other hand, and to conclude on this point, it should be remembered that there are at least four facts that give rise to the opposite perception, which incline one to consider that the CCJA is indeed an international court, even if these criteria, as earlier observed, are not necessarily compelling. In terms of its composition and organisation, the Court is governed by internationally agreed rules. The rules it applies, which are its reference standards, are unilateral acts of an international organisation, even if they are domesticated. The institution from which the CCJA is derived is OHADA, an international organisation. Finally, the basis of validity of the decisions of this Court, and the authority attached to them is derived from an international treaty, which is also the founding treaty of the organisation. These are four facts based on which the thesis of the international nature of the court can be sustained.

On a final point, the CCJA defies the ordinary rules of international litigation. This relates to the extent of its power over the matters brought before it. More specifically, it has the power to quash, the equivalent of which is hard to find on the global jurisdictional landscape.

It is commonplace for an international judge to have to deal with certain aspects of a matter determined by a domestic court that has been concluded. But for the sake of sovereignty, as we saw earlier, the intervention of the international judge is draped in a veil of modesty. It is a traditional principle, particularly in cases of human rights violations, where the treaty judge intervenes after the national judge, that successive trials are not the same, that they do not have the same implications. At the international level, a State that owes commitments set out in a treaty relating to the rights of individuals is what is judged, and not to "touch" what remains the preserve of the sovereign State, which is precisely the main trial or the "first" trial. From this point of view, every international judge wishes to show restraint, to express their reverence for the exclusive domain of national jurisdiction. This concession is expressed through the assertion that the international judge is neither a judge of a higher court nor a court of Cassation. The dogma is so entrenched, the refrain so frequently repeated, that in these circles, an application that is "manifestly ill-conceived" is deemed to be one that ignores the judicial non-aggression pact...

This judicial diplomacy is at work in all the jurisdictions that fall within the scope of our discussion. The UN Human Rights Committee, in its Views under article 5, paragraph 4, of the Optional Protocol to the ICCP ", states that it " has taken note of the author's allegation that Mr Arutyunyan's trial was unfair. While regretting that the State party has made no comment in this regard, the Committee notes that this claim primarily relates to the assessment of facts and evidence by national tribunals. It recalls that it is in general for the courts of States parties, and not for the Committee, to evaluate the facts and evidence in any case, and to interpret domestic legislation, unless the evaluation was arbitrary or amounted to a denial of justice. [321].

In a similar vein, the European Court of Human Rights stated in *Kemmache vs France* that " in principle, it is not for the Court itself to assess the factual elements that led a national court to adopt one decision rather than another, subject to examination of compatibility with the provisions of the Convention. Otherwise,

[321] HRC, Communication n°917/2000, Arutyunyan A. Vs Ouzbekistan, 2 April 2004, § 5.7.

the Court would be setting itself up as a court of third or fourth instance and would be disregarding the limits of its jurisdiction"[322].

In *Fermin Ramirez v Guatemala,* the Inter-American Court of Human Rights on 20th June 2005, affirmed this position in its ruling. According to the Court, " it is important to reiterate in this Case, in which the actions within the framework of a criminal process are being questioned, that the bodies of the international American System of Human Rights do not act as an instance of appeal or review of the judgments delivered in domestic judicial procedures. Its role is to determine the compatibility of the actions carried out in said processes with the American Convention. This is what the Court will limit itself to in the present Ruling "[323].

The African rights protection mechanism is similarly restrained. The judgment handed down on 3 June 2016 by the African Court on Human and Peoples' Rights is a good example. In it, the Court "reiterates its position of principle that it is not a court of appeal against judicial decisions handed down by national courts (...); more generally, this Court would only act as a court of appeal if, *inter alia,* it applied the same law to the case as the Tanzanian national courts, i.e., Tanzanian law. However, this was not the case before it since, by definition, it applies exclusively, in the words of Article 7 of the Protocol, "the provisions of the Charter as well as any other relevant human rights instrument ratified by the State concerned"[324].

Such circumspection, shared by many international judges, is not appropriate before the CCJA. This court has genuine power to set aside judgments handed down by the courts of Member States, and such a power is certainly not common in the international legal

---

[322] HRC, Judg « Kemmache Vs France », delivered on 24 November 1994, § 44.

[323] IACHR, « Fermin Ramirez Vs Guatemala », Judgment of 20 June 2005, §62.

[324] ACHPR, *Mohamed Abubakari vs United Republic of Tanzania* , Judgement delivered on 3 June 2016, §§ 25 and 28.

order. It is therefore a rather curious judicial body: organically international - in many respects - but functionally national, if one dares say so, since it mainly exercises a function; cassation, that is part of the normal course of national judicial proceedings.

The institution and activities of the CCJA take on another, somewhat unexpected, dimension. They constitute an unprecedented facet of functional dualism. Traditionally, this concept, theorised by the French internationalist Georges Scelle, refers to the replacement of a deficient international legal order, which requires the assistance of national bodies so to do, which thus become, temporarily, agents for the enforcement of international law. Here is what Scelle writes: "in the inter-state order where there are no specific international governors and agents, the inter-state agents and governors who replace them are vested with a dual role. They are national agents and governors when they operate in the state legal order; they are international agents and governors when they act in the international legal order. This is what we will call the fundamental law of functional dualism"[325].

By being an international body and performing a domestic function - appeals - the CCJA also performs a kind of functional dualism, but in a novel version, different from the traditional archetype of this: it is not the State or its organ that makes up for the deficiencies of the international order by placing itself temporarily at the service of the latter, but it is the international organisation that performs a domestic function. The classic version of functional dualism highlights the limits of the international order, its incompleteness, and the subsequent need to fill its gaps. In this case, the idea of deficiency must be discarded. It is not the powerlessness of the substituted body that is at issue, but a political

---

[325] Scelle G., « Règles générales du droit de la paix », *Collected Courses of the Academy of International Law*, 1933, IV, p.358.

will to integrate that entails a sacrifice of sovereignty. In the traditional perception of functional dualism, the substitution of the relegated order is sporadic (in space) and episodic (in time). In the case of the CCJA, this substitution is systematic and planned. One might even venture the following assertion: the first version reveals a weakness in international law, the second its strength. While the notion of functional dualism itself may not imply any idea of deficiency or failure - and there is nothing to indicate that its meaning can be confined to this restrictive perspective - there is nothing to prevent us from considering that the CCJA practises functional dualism, understood in the admittedly less orthodox sense of an international body assuming a domestic function.

Ultimately, there is a series of "markers" of the CCJA that make it a special body in the field of international jurisdictions, a kind of unidentified judicial body, conferred with an international status, but forming part of a judicial continuum that originates in national systems, exercising a frontal - substantive check? - on the judgments referred to it, with a real power to set aside these judgments, practising cassation as much as a review, as judge of the law and judge of the fact all at once. This African jurisdiction undoubtedly has no equal in the world. It is an original piece of work, as much as a masterpiece of a balancing act, as has already been said, since, like any international institution, it is obliged to deal with the sovereignty of States. Having been in operation for more than a quarter of a century, it has undoubtedly proved that ambitious and effective local structures are not only possible, but that they can inspire other parts of the world.

CHAPTER 9

REFORMING DEMOCRACY: BUILDING NEW SPACES FOR DIALOGUE

" Our regimes may be democratic, but we are not democratically governed.

This is the great gap that feeds contemporary disenchantment and disarray "

Pierre Ronsavallon, *Le bon gouvernement*, Seuil, 2015

Democracy is in crisis, that much is known. Given the variety of ways in which the phenomenon is expressed, and the diversity of explanations put forward, it would even be appropriate to use the word in the plural and speak of *crises* of democracy (I).

Given the scale and universality of the phenomenon, we will look at two African experiences and examine their relevance as responses to the democratic crisis: national conferences and the *Espace d'interpellation démocratique* (Forum for democratic debate - FDD) (II). The first modality was used mainly in the 1990s, in the context of transitions to political pluralism. While it remains a provisional democratic experiment, limited in time, nothing prevents us from attempting to sustain it or renewing it from time to time, according to modalities to be defined. The other is a purely national initiative, in Mali to be precise, since, as far as we know, research has not revealed any other national experiments in the

FDD. It therefore has a spatial limit, but nothing prevents us from exploring how this local invention could be "duplicated" and extended to other countries.

Conceived and experimented with on the African continent, in contexts where democracy was certainly fragile, these two forms of popular expression had the merit of reintroducing the people and the citizen into the political arena. Yet democratic crises highlight the marginalisation of these two players. The National Conference and the FDD should not be seen as mere facts, but as part of their underlying philosophy. They represent a departure from conventional forms of democracy, the very forms whose relevance is being questioned today. Beside their exportability, which is always debatable and certainly conditional, it is their novelty and the finesse of the engineering behind them that should be remembered. As illustrations of local democratic inventiveness and tangible manifestations of endogenous creativity, they are not only African legal singularities, but they also shatter the essentialist prejudice that runs through the segregationist visions of democracy, for which some peoples or historical circumstances are more "prepared" for democracy than others.

I. THE CRISES OF DEMOCRACY

The disenchantment with democracy that is so often described in contemporary societies is multifaceted. While all theorists agree that there is a malaise in contemporary democracies, they tend to disagree about where the problem lies. However, despite the many manifestations of the crisis and the many explanations for it, there are two constants on which there should be ready agreement. On the one hand, the crisis takes the form of a challenge to constituted political power. This contestation itself is likely to take several forms, covert or overt, open, or concealed. In addition to the rejection of what already exists, there may be a more "constructive" dimension to the crisis, which consists of going beyond the protest phase to find substitutes for the impugned aspects of democratic practice, to find alternative forms of democracy. They claim to be qualitatively superior to conventional or current forms of democracy, and advocate returning power to its original holders: the people, the citizens. In so doing, they claim to be reviving the orthodoxy of democracy. They claim to be more "authentic", a kind of back to the roots.

The democratic malaise can be summed up in two ways: the challenge to established power (A) and the search for lost power, a quest suggested by reform projects in some of the world's leading democracies (B).

A. Challenging established power

This challenge is mostly "passive", but more exceptionally "active". In its first instance, the disavowal of political power is expressed in the form of mistrust. The established political powers no longer seem trustworthy, from the citizens' point of view. The mechanisms of checks and balances, by which power conceals its own checks and balances, no longer function. The separation of powers, which Montesquieu saw as the power that "restrains power", has shown its limits under the influence of a party government that the *Baron de la Brède* could not, in his defence, have suspected. Instead of a system of authorities dedicated to preventing any lurch by one of them, we are witnessing a collusion of powers, because between those who hold them, it is less a question of reciprocal surveillance than of connivance.

Power will only check power if we are counting on a form of selflessness on the part of political players. The institutional arrangements that have been put in place tend to emphasise the general interest, giving the political profession a somewhat priestly dimension. But when politics precisely becomes a matter of coalitions of interests - partisan and even personal - when it finds its own end and men and women, who have thus become "political entrepreneurs", live off it, not only can power no longer be stopped, but it becomes the property of a caste, and government is naturally transformed into an oligarchy. The age of modern politics is also an age of suspicion. We no longer have much confidence in those in power or in the mechanisms that are supposed to prevent their abuse: " democracy of distrust", as accurately diagnosed by P. Ronsavallon[326].

This is because modern democracy tends, among other reasons, to think of itself only in electoral terms. It culminates in the electoral moment, which thus becomes its be-all and end-all. Focusing on the electoral contest is likely to produce a rift, because once the contest is over, the elected representative eludes the voter and the representative body, in line with an obvious law of organisational sociology, displays "organicists" tendencies. Power is then no longer exercised, *de facto*, by its legitimate holders, the constituents, but by agents who tend to substitute their own will for that of the people. Modern public law, by prohibiting the imperative mandate, has facilitated this separation and almost legalised the hijacking and confiscation power by the proxy elite.

It is based on this observation that the need to invent a less intermittent democracy, which is less dependent on elections, has been advocated: "continuous democracy", according to Dominique Rousseau for example, the expression meaning what it means. In any case, intermittent democracy is stigmatised. This is one of the facets of the crisis: instead of being a daily practice, the exercise of democracy has become increasingly rare. Electoral democracy is a pathological democracy. If we want to restore the lustre and purpose of this political choice, we need to go beyond the horizon of electoral jousting.

Mistrust is also fuelled by the sense of alienation amongst citizens: government seems remote and aloof. The feeling of civic

---

[326] Cited by Halpern C., « La démocratie est-elle en crise? », *Mensuel n°192,* 2008.

dereliction will give rise to two things. On the one hand, it will give rise to the invention of democratic forms that embody the idea of proximity. Since political power is distant, local forms of democracy will be invented; a popular democracy. Alexis de Tocqueville, ever since*Democracy in America,* has sung the praise of grassroot democracy. The expression participatory democracy has been used to describe a return to the citizenry. It is not uncommon, in this age of big government, to find proposals for reform that suggest giving back power to neighbourhoods and other grassroots communities. From this point of view, democracy sheds its politics, depoliticises itself and, most of all, endeavours to meet real local needs. It becomes less dependent on political and ideological agendas and programmes, and once again becomes a citizen's affair. Local democratic practices restore the deliberative dimension of politics, with community affairs debated by all. The myth of the ancient agora has been revived. L. Rouban finds illustrations of this in the forms of expression recently seen in France, such as "Nuit debout" in 2016, or the Yellow Vests movement[327].

Traditional analytical approaches are also being called into question by the ways in which democracy now tends to be exercised. We are referring to new communication technologies, which are leading to networked practices and enabling citizens to express their views instantaneously on issues of interest to them. How should we interpret these new practices, this internet community [328]? Are they just another manifestation of the crisis? Or is it a way out of the crisis, insofar as it reflects a circumvention of the democratic forms that have been denounced, and an

[327] Rouban L., *La démocratie représentative, est-elle en crise?* Paris, La Documentation française, pp.8-9.

[328] Mathias P., *La cité internet,* Paris, Presses de Science po, 1997.

appropriation by citizens – at least, in terms of discourse - of society's problems?

However, we need to remain conscious of the limits of this democracy, which is both media-based and horizontal, and of these open and instantaneous deliberative exchanges. Instant democracy is not necessarily a deepening of democracy. Cyber-democracy tends to lack robustness and continuity. It seems to be condemned to remain locked up in transience and therefore in the outcropping of things. It lacks durability and depth. Another variant of participatory democracy, engaging in virtual debate may well not represent a genuine democratic breakthrough, and may ultimately prove to be no more than an instrumental mutation, the advent of a simple means of expression that does not necessarily give citizens any greater capacity to influence the political decisions that affect the community. The virtual space in which these open, horizontal exchanges take place is not necessarily democratic, as Paul Mathias has also noted. It is volatile, inconsistent, gaseous. It lacks both staying power and depth, the capacity to grasp plurality to produce an identifiable ideological unity posing as a proposition or an alternative. Without denying the innovative nature of cyber-democracy, we should resist the temptation to see it as an antidote to the crisis. We could even, perhaps, record it as a symptom of the crisis rather than a solution to it.

To complete this clinical picture, we should add something infinitely more worrying, which is the violent excesses that challenging established authority can lead to in today's *democracies*. One of the current afflictions of democracy is " populism". The phenomenon is remarkable, at the turn of the 2020s, in the Americas[329]. North America first, and the United States in particular. The presidency of Donald Trump (2016-2020)

[329] Nardon L., « Trump and the Crisis of American Democracy », *Politique étrangère,* Vol. 82, No. 1, Spring 2017.

undeniably was a distinctive moment in this crisis. The manifestations of this anti-democratic populism are manifold, and we do not seek to attempt a full or in-depth analysis of them here. Be it simply stressed that it has an intellectual side, based on positions that are deliberately hostile to scientific truths (on climate change, for example, or medical prescriptions, as the Covid pandemic from 2019 has shown, at the highest level of the Unted States) and allergic to the forms of compromise that had hitherto been the genius of American democracy and explained its smooth functioning. With the populist drift comes a challenge to the " system" and the elites, an assertion of the power of money and a revival of xenophobic, even racist, rhetoric. In short, all the errant ways exemplified by the Trump presidency.

Anti-democratic populism is not just an intellectual posture, it is also an action, a violent action that challenges institutions. The United States of 2020, which saw the victory of Joe Biden over Donald Trump, experienced the trauma of the attempted invasion of the Capitol by Trump supporters in a surreal post-election climate (January 2021). The storming of the seat of Congress was seen by some as a real coup attempt. Then it was Brazil, on the same continent, and two years later almost to the day (January 2023), illustrated by the outrageous behaviour of the supporters of far-right President Jair Bolsonaro.[330]. The National Congress, the Presidency, and the Federal Supreme Court of Brazil were stormed at the same time. These extreme and violent forms of protest are part of the indictment of democracy. Populism sees democracy as monopolised or "betrayed" by elites and believes that political power should be returned to the people.

Moreover, this continental American populism is not always strictly speaking a challenge to established authority. It is

[330] Clemenceau F., « La démocratie en Amérique du Sud, est-elle en crise ? », *Le Journal du Dimanche,* 19 October 2019.

sometimes used by governments in power, as shown by the path taken by countries such as Venezuela (with the regime of Nicolas Maduro) and Nicaragua (with the Sandinista regime, liberator turned oppressor) since the mid-2000s. These national experiments are obviously not of the protest type, but they are "pathologies" of democracy to the extent that some of their practices can be described as undemocratic.

The crisis of democracy is multifaceted and ever-changing. Based on the kaleidoscopic picture that has just been painted, a wise and reasonable mind might wonder whether the analyst is not tending to lump all manifestations of the democratic phenomenon together under the banner of crisis; in short, whether the diagnosis is not erring on the side of pessimism. The debate would undoubtedly be relevant, but we will not open it here. Suffice it to say that while the extent or depth of the crisis may be debatable, and while the assessment of the crisis may be nuanced, there is virtually no one who would deny that the classical forms of democracy that we have known or are knowing deserve to be re-thought, and that democracy needs a new lease of life. But the way out of this predicament is not so original in principle. It consists of finding the patented holders of power and putting them back in the saddle. In short, if democracy is in crisis, it is because it has tended to break away from its "fundamentals", to escape from its beginnings. What we need to do, then, is go back to basics and rediscover the original powerholders, the people, and the citizen. The proposals for reform put forward in several Western countries are in line with this truth, which, it must be said, makes some sense. The challenge to established power must therefore be followed by a search for lost power.

B. In Quest of the Lost Power: Re-discovering the "People" and the "Citizen"

We need only look at the options for reform being considered in countries with an established democratic tradition, but which are experiencing an acute crisis to realise that the solutions being devised are, quite simply, a return to the roots of the democratic principle. In other words a restoration of citizen participation and people power.

In Great Britain, the Labour Party has been working for almost two decades now on ways to reintroduce citizen participation in public affairs. It all started with a deep-seated mistrust of the British political class. When Labour decided to investigate the matter, nearly 71% of the public said they no longer had confidence in politics.[331] The Tony Blair government endeavoured to give citizens back their voice by fostering the setting up of "local groups", within the neighbourhoods, i.e., at the grassroots. There was talk of a New Deal for Communities and a National Strategy for Neighbourhood Renewal. The idea was to invent a form of democracy that would somehow survive elections, that would continue after the vote by giving ordinary citizens back their say and decision-making power, as Graham Smith and Corinne Wales write: "Although periodic elections act as a continuous discipline on elected officials to take constant notice of public opinion", the mandate that representatives enjoy extends over a period within which citizens have very little impact on decisions made in their name"[332].

To respond to the crisis of democracy, the British Labour Party therefore suggested setting up Citizens Juries, whose role, according to our two authors, was " to whip up interest in local

---

[331] Survey cited by Fons J.P., « Démocratie délibérative en Grande Bretagne : la rhétorique participative à l'épreuve », *Revue électronique d'études sur le monde anglophone,* 2009.

[332] Graham S and Wales C., « Citizen Juries and Deliberative Democracy », *Politica Studies,* 48, 2000, p.51, cited by Fons J.P., op cit., §23.

politics and overcome cynicism towards, and distrust of, local authorities"[333]. It seems that these theses have largely borrowed from the theories of the American political scientists John Dewey and Benjamin Barber, who advocate, as a way out of the democratic crisis, replacing our current political practices, characterised by the passivity of political subjects, with a new approach, deliberately promoting the participation and empowerment of a citizen freed from their uni-dimensionality as a voter[334].

In France, there is a consensus on the need to reintroduce citizens into the democratic process, in other words to move beyond institutional and electoral democracy. This is reflected first and foremost in theoretical thinking. The citizen is at the heart of continuous democracy advocated by Dominique Rousseau. Based on the principle that citizens are not in the body of representatives, this author considers that it is therefore necessary to recognise the constitutional autonomy of the body of citizens, who would then be able to make demands of the authorities who hold the power of decision, those who are supposed to represent this body. Going even further, he envisages the possibility of the citizens directly contributing to making laws. The revolutionary nature of such a proposal is obvious, as the author himself admits that it would be a question of breaking with the representative system [335].

The French political class has also felt the need to review democratic practices, or those that are still presented as such. First and foremost, in political projects. In 2012, when Ségolène Royal, the Socialist Party candidate, formulated her one hundred proposals for a Presidential pact. The aim was a "New Republic", in which " debates would be revived". More precisely, this would involve introducing participatory democracy into all public

---

[333] Graham S et Wales C, op cit, p.56. Cité par Fons J.P., op cit, §24.

[334] Fonds J.P, op cit., §27.

[335] V. Rousseau D., *Six thèses pour la démocratie continue*, Paris, Odile Jacob, p.57.

authorities (citizens' juries, participatory budgets, etc.). Any major social reform should be preceded by systematic consultation with citizens and should of course give rise to negotiations. The return of the citizen to democracy signals the end of a rule by decree and top-down power structures.

Ten years later, a political party in France, *La France insoumise,* included in its programme the establishment of " a Republic allowing popular intervention", with a key feature of " giving citizens the power to make the law or to dismiss those who make it". *L'Avenir en commun* (A Common Future), submitted for the 2022 elections, advocates the convening of a constituent assembly of the Fifth Republic, to show that the crisis of democracy is profound and to suggest that its resolution calls for drastic changes, a real cultural revolution in the perception of the relationship between governor and governed.[336].

The need to reconnect with citizens is clearly a shared recommendation, since it is to be found, *mutatis mutandis,* in the recommendations made by " experts"- and not by political players - in the *Bernasconi Report* presented to the French Prime Minister on 22 February 2022. The report, which looks at the democratic crisis and how to remedy it, contains fifty proposals, many of which focus on the return of the citizen to the political arena. The report recommends that, at the « local level », the possibility of a " shared initiative referendum " should be introduced, as well as a general principle of public involvement in all major decisions concerning local authorities with more than ten thousand inhabitants, and the exercise of a right of local petition . At national level, the plan would involve lowering the thresholds for shared-initiative referendums

---

336 Mélenchon J.L., « Changer de République pour faire place au peuple », https :avenirencommun.fr/livret-assemblee-constituante. V également Montebourg A and Bastien F., *La Constitution de la VIème République,* Paris, Odile Jacob, 2005. One reads in page 11 that « today, the 5th Republichas become a government by one person, without the people and against the people ».

to one-tenth of members of parliament and one million voters and to transforming the National Commission for Public Debate (CNDP) into a High Authority for Citizens' Participation tasked with ensuring quality participation, and including stakeholders other than those from Parliament, the Economic, Social and Environmental Council or associations of elected representatives. Lastly, citizens would have a direct say in the decision-making process through an arrangement that would allow some of them to take part in deliberative procedures as well as in the work of Parliament itself.

Almost everywhere, then, there seems to be a sort of civic deficit in democracy. Democratic practices have forgotten the citizens, as surprising as that may seem. The aim, then, is to reintegrate these citizens into public life and political deliberation. Is this therapy, which is not all that surprising in principle, likely to be extended to the populist pathology of democracy, another face of the crisis of democracy, and whose vibrancy can be seen on the American continent, in the United States itself and in some Latin American countries?

Any solutions that might be suggested in this area can only be relative, or contextual. Each country has its own reality, and while the diagnosis of the crisis is widely shared, we cannot prescribe recipes, or one-size-fits-all solutions. Bearing this need for caution in mind, however, it is possible to suggest that restoring the power of citizens could, in certain respects, constitute an antidote - among others, no doubt - to the populist pathology of democracy.

Indeed, the deliberative process, advocated by almost everyone, is by its very nature interactive and contradictory. It is the antithesis of the populist discourse that insists on the passivity of citizens, a passivity that is somehow imposed on them by institutions. And yet, by definition, exchange excludes passivity, the passive reception of a discourse. Without exchange, discourse is monological. Interlocution and the invitation to participate, by themselves, break such unilaterality. Populist criticism of democracy is neutralised by the factual demonstration of its inaccuracy: genuinely involved in the deliberative process, the citizen can no longer claim to be the poor relation of democracy.

Giving individuals back their rightful place is interesting even when they are the sometimes-complacent recipients of the populist "vulgate". It is important to remember that while citizens may assume a "passive" posture, they nevertheless articulate a precise criticism: that of the democratic shortcomings of institutions, which generates the search for a political and ideological "elsewhere", however toxic. The aim is precisely to break down this prejudice, to take the wind out of the sceptical citizen's sails by offering him or her the institutions " on a silver platter", so to speak. Are they criticised for being aloof? Then they decide to get closer to the aggrieved citizen. If you do not go to the democratic institutions, the democratic institutions will come to you! The reintroduction of citizen's participation in the political arena is therefore an act of good faith, as much as an optimistic gamble. It reveals the benevolent disposition of the institutions and the gamble they are placing on the intelligence and open-mindedness of the citizen. In this way, the return to the roots - for the return to the people or the citizen is simply a return to the foundation and principles of democracy – as advocated in many countries could perhaps prove useful in contexts where civic disaffection and democratic disillusionment are likely to fuel the abuse of power.

In the face of this debilitating picture, and the subsequent urgent need to reflect on the ways and means of rediscovering democracy, it may be worthwhile to look at something else, to take a step back in time and space: to unearth democratic practices that are unknown or out of fashion, to look at the experiences of other countries, other regions, other cultures. It is with this in mind that we present here two African experiences in which the aim has been to give a voice back to the governed, which is the goal of all the solutions we have just reviewed. On a continent that is still the scene of many attacks on democracy, it is worth recalling that two unprecedented arrangements have been put in place to restore the voice of the people and the individuals who make them up.

II. TWO AFRICAN RESPONSES

These two responses are of unequal scope and scale, but it does not matter. One of them was almost systematic in the 1990s; its purpose was to ensure a transition to political pluralism, and it was therefore tried out in a number of countries, the contagion effect being undeniable: these are the national conferences (A). The other, on the other hand, is neither general nor systematic since as far as we know it is practised in only one country, Mali. However, unlike the national conferences, it continues to exist: the *Espace d'interpellation démocratique* – the Democratic debate Forum (B).

A. The National Conferences

The national conference is the brainchild of several African countries that initiated a transitional phase that was to lead to political pluralism. The experiment took place roughly between 1990 and 1995. It was Benin that led the way, the process having apparently been preceded in the same country some twenty years earlier (1979), when the then President of the Republic, who organised the 1990 national conference, invited the country's leaders to discuss major issues of national importance for ten days or so. In fact, alongside the countries that have expressly resorted to the national conference approach, there are countries that have opted for initiatives that do not necessarily have the same format as these conferences, but which, like them, are deliberative forums designed to produce recommendations for the political direction of the country. The former include Benin, Gabon, The Republic of Congo, and the Democratic Republic of Congo (DRC), Niger and

Chad, while the latter include countries such as Ethiopia, South Africa, Kenya, Guinea Bissau, and Nigeria.

On the other hand, the very powers of the national conference differed from country to country. In some countries, it is a "sovereign conference", a title that it readily attributes to itself, which suggests that it has significant powers and is reminiscent of the famous "*Tennis Court Oath* that prefigured the French revolution of 1789. In other cases, the conference is not "sovereign" and therefore in principle has fewer powers than its counterparts.

Whether Sovereign or not, these meetings, which bring together the nation's driving forces between five hundred and one thousand two hundred depending on the country[337], are first and foremost places for breaking with the past. It has been seen as an essentially transgressive moment[338] ; the national conference is first and foremost a deviation, a work of democratic disqualification of the past. This is clear from the legal acts that created and established it.

Here are three examples. In the Republic of Congo, the preamble to the Rules of Procedure of the National Conference states that "to *rethink* Congo and to *rebuild it,* it is important to *restore* to the Congolese people the full attributes of sovereignty (...). The core mission of the national conference was to *redefine* the fundamental values of the nation (...)". In Togo, Act n°1 adopted by the national conference of 16 July 1991 indicates that the core mandate of the national conference is to *redefine* the fundamental values of the nation (…)", and in Benin, the Declaration on the Objectives and Competences of the National Conference, adopted on 25 February 1990, noted that the fundamental law had become obsolete and that all the political structures built up to that point were " illegitimate".

---

337 E Boulaga, *Les conférences nationales en Afrique noire: une affaire à suivre,* Paris, karthala, 1993, p. 142.

338 Besse M., « Afrique : la conférence nationale souveraine, un pouvoir constituant original », amitie-entre-les-peuples.org

In such circumstances, it is hardly surprising that the national conferences initiated constitutional reforms, proposing the replacement of the fundamental laws in force by others more in keeping with the prevailing climate, i.e., the canons of democracy.

What is illegitimate cannot be allowed to persist. Logically, then, it was state power that was dismantled and rebuilt in a way that was obviously perceived and presented as more democratic. The national conferences reconfigured power by weakening the once omnipotent Executive, which was so symbolic of the excesses of the past, and by promoting a Legislative branch that sometimes took on the appearance of a "transition body". The perspective is, therefore, decidedly revolutionary. Political power is "overthrown", and the balance of power is re-adjusted. Almost systematically, the upheaval was reflected in the establishment or restoration of a bicephalous executive, which is already a way of decentralising it. But it goes further, because the bicephalous system in question, unlike its past versions, is deliberately unequal in favour of the newcomer, the Prime Minister. In almost all cases, the weakening of the powers of the president of the Republic enured to the benefit of a " transitional Prime Minister" elected by the Conference.

In the case of Benin, a forerunner in this field, decree no. 90-043 governed the public authorities pending the adoption of the new Fundamental Law. The incumbent president was stripped of most of the powers he had held until then under the 1977 Constitution. Real power was held jointly by the newly formed government and the High Council of the Republic, the legislative body of the "transition". The powers of this High Council are in fact those of a real parliament. The powers of the president had been reduced to make room for the office of Prime Minister, whose legitimacy derives directly from the National Conference.

In the Congo, the Fundamental Act of the "Transition", adopted on 4 June 1990 by the Sovereign National Conference did not even give the Head of State the right to separate from his ministers. As he opened the meeting, the President had to bow to the will of the delegates to exclude members of his political party, the *Parti Congolais du Travail* (PCT), from all bodies, and from the "Presidium of the Conference"[339]. They were also powerless to prevent the conference from proclaiming itself "sovereign"[340]. It was in this context that the chosen prime minister became "chairperson of Cabinet, and Commander of the army" (articles 40 and 41 of the 4 June 1990 Act), "directs the action of the Government" (article 42) and "exercised regulatory power" (article 43).

In Madagascar, it is the National Convention of 31 October 1991[341] on the arrangements pertaining to public authority during the transition, which gives the President only symbolic powers. As the "symbol of national unity and territorial integrity", he is the commander in chief of the armed forces, ratifies international conventions and treaties, exercises the right to pardon and confers State honours. If he accredits and recalls ambassadors, it is again, "upon the proposal of the prime minister" (article two). Conversely, the prime minister, as head of government, appoints and revokes the members of the government team, chairs the Government Council, is the head of the administration, appoints senior civil and military officials (...) and is responsible for maintaining public order and security (...).

Although they were not as systematic, the strategies of dispossession of the heads of state in place, implemented by the national conferences, were no less real in other states. In particular, the national conference took two highly symbolic measures to reduce the power of the president: the abolition of the « presidential

---

339 *Afrique Contemporaine* n°158, 1991, p.60.

340 Ibid; p 86.

341 Text of the Convention in *Afrique contemporaine* n°163, 1992, pp.56 to 58.

guard » and the withdrawal of his position as head of the armed forces in favour of the prime minister[342].

The cases of Chad and the Central African Republic attest to the same concern to limit presidential prerogatives, but as the rationale of dispossession was not taken to its logical conclusion, the head of state was sometimes able to oppose the prime minister in office. The 1993 Chadian National Conference set up a High Council for Transition (CST in French), which adopted a "Transition Charter " providing for the election of a prime minister by the Conference. The latter, who is accountable only to the CST and not to the president of the Republic, is commander of the army and oversees the public service in the implementation of programmes drawn up by the CST.[343] This powerlessness of the President was even more apparent during the transition in the Central African Republic. Although the Head of State managed to exclude the very concept of a « national conference », as if to exorcise the spectre of a decline, the " Great Debate" that replaced it was nonetheless an opportunity to seriously undermine his pre-eminence. The agreement of 26 November 1992 between the national political players obliged the president to choose the prime minister from the opposition side during the transition period leading up to the multi-party elections.[344]. The latter did not hesitate to oppose the Head of State on the choice of ministers[345].

Over and above certain national peculiarities, the institutional pattern of the transition thus presents some fairly striking similarities, typical of periods of revolutionary frenzy. Transfer of power to newly established bodies, dismissal of the authorities in

---

342 Ibid. n°161, 1992, pp.289-290.

343 M. AICADI de SAINT- PAUL «La Conférence nationale souveraine du Tchad », *Afrique contemporaine*, n°167,1993, p.44.

344 M. KOYT, M. MBRINGA, P.M. DECOUDRAS "RCA: les vicissitudes du changement" *Afrique politique*, 1995, p.243.

345 *Afrique contemporaine,* n° spécial, 4° trimestre 1993.

place and abrogation of the law they made, which implies "dissolution" of existing institutions , especially the National Assembly, control of the new executive arm by the legislative body set up, both of which are obviously provisional, and according to a model close to the " imperative mandate".

The disqualification of the past in the name of democratic requirements is not limited to "principles". It is also embodied in the transformation of the conference into a real tribunal. It was not only political and ideological orientations that were being challenged, but also the practices that they encouraged. The national conference sets in motion a principle of accountability, and those who exercised various tasks under the discredited regimes are specifically invited to "account" for their past actions. Such "interrogations" sometimes led to sanctions or proposals for sanctions. In Niger, a crimes and abuse commission was established to search, investigate, and compile all acts, behaviour, and facts likely to trigger the political, criminal, or civil liability of those responsible in previous years. In Togo, a decision was taken to freeze the assets of the sole party, the *Rassemblement du Peuple Togolais,* while in Benin, the conference's law and constitutional affairs committee suggested that the conference proffer " at least symbolic sanctions against perpetrators of serious violations such as torture, and their accomplices ».

It is important to understand that all these events are not just revolutionary in nature, and do not merely involve the overthrow of a political power. Beyond the dispossession of political power, we need to grasp the democratic stakes involved. National conferences , and it is in this respect that they can provide useful context to a general reflection on the crisis of democracy, attempt to put back in the saddle those who are presented as the forgotten people of our current democracies: the people and the citizen. Their return to the stage initially takes the form of a ministry of discourse. At least the national conferences give them a voice again. They are becoming the forum to, at least, have their voices heard. This must not be trivialised, on the pretext that the conferences remain but a hiatus. The fact is that these conferences have achieved what the electoral machinery does not always succeed in doing: creating a sense of citizen involvement, to give people the feeling that they not only have the right to speak, which is materially true, but that they are heard.

From this point of view, national conferences as a means of democratic expression deserve attention. They are not only moments of citizen or popular reappropriation, but, more structurally, a way of going beyond electoral democracy, whose limitations are almost universally acknowledged today. Objectivity dictates that we recognise this virtue of African-style conferences. They have an enthusiastic quality, and are a departure from the much-discredited citizen apathy, with a euphoric quality that traditional elections do not guarantee, at least in the countries concerned. Observing the Congolese national conference, the American NGO NDI noted in its report that " never have we seen people in Africa speak up so freely, with so much verve and passion"[346].

Going further in his analysis of this cathartic dimension of the democratic exercise, F Eboussi Boulaga links this expression to a certain African tradition. The national conference », he posits, " is a revival of the African palaver, which is a form of speech therapy. To put an end to the rise to extremes, to the unleashing of passions, a meeting is called (...). The great paradigms of the African national conference are undoubtedly therapy and palaver. These are a ritual of restoration. They re-enact the original establishment in reverse, starting from the dissolution of things, from terminal chaos"[347]. The

---

[346] Cited by E. Boulaga, op cit., p. 33.

[347] E. Boulaga, op cit., pp. 151 and 154.

national conference thus reveals its endogenous dimension, a "specifically African mechanism", as M. Besse readily points out[348].

Let us remember only their democratic and analgesic virtues. Unquestionably, and while certainly aware of some of their limitations, it can be argued that African national conferences have been a means of renewing the exercise of democracy. They have gone beyond the logic of formalist and electoral democracy. They have given a voice back to the people, in particular circumstances. For this reason, they certainly deserve attention. All in all, they were a living illustration of an aspiration expressed in other parts of the world, of giving the people back their say, as we have seen.

Moreover, national conferences are not necessarily confined to their historical sequence. Indeed, it would be tempting to exaggerate their cyclical significance, to consider that they were outdated moments in African political history and that they therefore remain no more than historical curiosities. Such a view would be mistaken. In some countries, the time of the conference is frozen in history, and is therefore engraved in the marble of the national constitution. The conference is part of the revolutionary and democratic gesture, part of the long history of the quest for democracy; part of the national historical heritage. A Constitution like the 1992 Constitution of Mali refers to it in its preamble, and the 2018 Constitution of Chad proclaims that the sovereign national conference " restored the confidence of the Chadian people and ushered in a new era". In Benin, where " the Conference of the Vital Forces of the Nation has restored the people's confidence, enabled national reconciliation and heralded an era of democratic renewal", and the constitution of Niger, which acknowledges its virtue of having "consolidated the gains".

---

[348] Besse M. op cit.

Is it just a matter of principle, or just a symbolic proclamation? Nothing is less certain. To such a sceptical temptation, forgetting that a constitution is also a bearer of history and symbols, it is easy to retort that the positivity of a proclamation can be dormant and that, like an inactive volcano, it is always possible to activate it. This is neither a flight of fancy nor a fanciful gamble. Benin's constitutional court proved this in a seminal decision handed down on 8 July 2006, in which it conferred eminent legal value on the consensus reached at the national conference, thereby making ineffective a draft amendment to the Constitution aimed at extending the term of office of members of parliament. The evocative terms in which it was expressed are worth quoting, as follows : "Considering that this four (4) year term of office, which is a constitutionally established position, is the product of the *consensus reached by the Conference of the Nation's Vital Forces*, in February 1990 and enshrined in the preamble to the Constitution, which reaffirms the fundamental opposition of the Beninese people to... the seizure of power; that even if the Constitution has provided for the modalities of its own amendment, the determination of the Beninese people to create a State governed by law and pluralist democracy, the safeguarding of legal certainty and national cohesion requires that any review take into account the ideals that inspired the adoption of the Constitution of 11 December 1990, in particular the national consensus, a principle of constitutional value ; that, consequently, Articles 1 and 2 of Constitutional Law No 2006-13 adopted by the National Assembly on 23 June 2006, without respecting the principle of constitutional value thus recalled, are contrary to the Constitution"[349].

[349] Dec CC Benin, DCC 06-074 of 8 July 2006.

Quite understandably, reservations were expressed about the ruling. The very existence of a "consensus"was called into question[350], but that is not our focus. Here, the point is to agree on the fact that the judge or interpreter, tasked with interpreting a text or applying it, can refer to the "values" conveyed by that text, and that the national conferences have certainly been conveyors of value. It would not be an exaggeration, therefore, for the body that refers to them to draw reference standards from them.

B. The Forum for Democratic Debate

Mali is, if I am not mistaken, the only African country to have experimented with this unprecedented democratic practice; the *"Espace d'interpellation démocratique",* Forum for Democratic Dialogue. This is a practical, *in vivo* democratic exercise in which citizens take the floor and "call to account" those in power, who are obliged to respond.

The practice was set up by a decree of 31 May 1996, article 1 of which states that "an annual forum called the *Espace d'interpellation démocratique* is established in the Republic of Mali". Its " purpose is to inform national and international public opinion about the human rights situation in Mali, to contribute in an active and educational way to the creation of a national democratic culture and to give significant impetus to the policy of promoting and protecting citizens' rights and freedoms". Symbolically and systematically scheduled to take place on 10 December each year - the anniversary of the adoption of the Universal Declaration of Human Rights, which the United Nations itself has endeavoured to make coincide with the signing of other human rights treaties - the Forum for Democratic Dialogue is regulated by a decision of the

---

[350] See, especially, Sindjoun L., *Les grands arrêts de la jurisprudence constitutionnelle africaine,* Bruxelles, Bruylant, 2009, p.336.

Mediator of the Republic of Mali, setting out the institution's internal rules.[351].

The FDD has three bodies: a Permanent Secretariat, a Preparatory Commission, and an Honorary Jury. The Permanent Secretariat is responsible for preparing and running each session of the FDD. The main function of the Preparatory Committee is to examine the petitions and their admissibility. It is made up of representatives of the Prime Minister's Office, ministerial departments, civil society organisations and the Ombudsman's own staff. The Commission may also invite any "resource person", whose services or insights it considers useful. The Honorary Jury is made up of three foreign personalities, including at least two lawyers, four representatives of civil society organisations working in the human rights sector and two resource persons. The Ombudsman of the Republic is also free to invite national or foreign personalities to the FDD as "key witnesses".

The FDD is held according to a process that comprises the following five phases. Six months before the ceremony, the Ombudsman "informs the public, by appropriate means of communication, of the objectives and procedures for participating in the work". A ceremony to launch the FDD session is also held. Then, two months before the session is due to take place, the Ombudsman invites representatives of organisations, associations and traditional authorities to participate. Then, no later than one month before the session, the Ombudsman draws up a list of those invited to read their "contributions" on the day of the ceremony. As the FDD primarily concerns the public authorities, the Ombudsman keeps the chairpersons of the institutions of the Republic, the members of the government and the chairpersons or heads of independent administrative authorities informed. Finally,

---

[351] It is currently decision n°2021-015/MR of 2 July 2021.

the Permanent Secretariat receives and prepares the petitions and draws up the list of cases to be handled.

Several observations may be made at this stage.

What emerges from this organisation, first and foremost, is that the FDD is an all-encompassing democratic process that strives to embrace all legitimate interests. This is not an insignificant fact. By bringing together representative bodies of " traditional" legitimacy, for example, the FDD sees the democratic moment it constitutes as a " whole-of-society" business, and not only of the "State" and official structures. This is the sign of a democratic practice that is not only "citizen-based", but also " rooted". For anyone who doubted the possibility of a local or cultural version of democracy, the FDD is a fine rebuttal. It proves that it is possible, provided we get off the beaten path of democratic practice and do away with artificial imports, to invent an authentic democracy that reflects local realities.

Secondly, the FDD is not just inquisitorial or a « call-to-action». It turns out that its organisation goes beyond its name. It is not just a « Questioning » exercise but also a proposal, a contribution. It is clearly stated that the guests are also expected to read their « contributions ». Far from being a game of massacre or a surly, vindictive form of democracy, the FDD is intended to be a constructive process. It is important to understand, therefore, that it does not consist solely of accountability, but can willingly take the form of proposals for improving the quality of democracy. The exercise then reveals another of its dimensions. It transcends the opposition between governor and governed. It stems from a deliberative vision of democracy and encourages us to think of it in terms of duties, rather than just rights, contrary to what its name might suggest. Democracy is no longer simply an objective for which official institutions are debtors and citizens implacable creditors.. It is relived in the mode of the agora and exchange.

One final remark can be made. Democracy as reflected in the FDD does not end with a face-to-face meeting. Extending the constructive dimension just mentioned, this moment of demand for answers speaks to a plurality of people, it has addressees who are not just the two protagonists; the questioner and the questioned. The wide circle of guests reveals that the FDD is not just about highlighting the pathological nature of democracy, but also its holistic dimension in a country. It reminds us that at the banquet of democracy, all the guests are at least virtual actors, and not just spectators. It therefore induces a form of "empowerment".

What is more, the FDD is open to the world, so to speak, which is certainly a novelty. Indeed, we have seen that the Honorary Jury of the FDD could - indeed should - also be made up of "foreign personalities" and that the Mediator of the French Republic was free to choose "Key witnesses" from amongst the guests. This international hallmark of a national democratic practice is also rich in meaning. Symbolically, the FDD is a friendly and generous institution. By welcoming "strangers" by not confining them to a merely ceremonial role but entrusting them with an active role, the FDD gives rise to an international dimension, a kind of cross-border claim, but a claim confined to discretion and tact. As mentioned above, the event took place on 10 December, the anniversary of the adoption of the Universal Declaration of Human Rights, a universally symbolic legal instrument. The FDD is thus a message for the world. Therein lies another aspect of its novelty. It combines rootedness with openness, the promotion of national traditions with the acceptance of universal values.

The more "technical" analysis of the contentious nature of the questioning itself is also instructive. First, there are conditions of admissibility of questions. They must be drafted in an official language, observe the rules of democratic etiquette, be of individual or collective interest, and challenge an administration of the State, local authorities, public establishments or anybody entrusted with a public service role. In terms of content, the complaints must relate to acts that infringe on human rights, such as an infringement of the right to life, liberty, or physical integrity etc. They may also concern a case of injustice (discriminatory or inequitable treatment) or even administrative shortcomings (failure to uphold the principles of legality or good governance, for example).

As a result, the range of grievances likely to be raised in the context of the FDD is broad. Such liberalism is a credit to democracy. Indeed, one might have imagined that the exercise would be confined to cases of maladministration, in keeping with the vocation of the Mediator of the Republic, the FDD's leading agent. Let us agree that the range of grievances admitted is likely to cover almost all the actions about which citizens, in a democracy and a State governed by law, are accustomed to complaining. The text regulating the FDD provides for only two exceptions: cases pending before the courts - which is easy to understand, from a purely logical point of view - and claims of a political nature, a dismissal that calls for some explanation, particularly from our perspective, which is to link the FDD to democracy.

Does such an exclusion mean that the FDD is outside the realm of politics, and is therefore democratic in name only? In our view, nothing could be further from the truth. It is important to understand the meaning of the prohibition. It is not a question of denying the political nature of the questioning exercise, but rather to avoid opening the floodgates to too "general" petitions, which fall within the discretionary power of political expediency, which can only be exercised precisely by an authority of a political nature. What is at stake here is not so much the limitation of the rights of individuals in a democracy as the very possibility of finding solutions to the claims expressed. A question relating to national security policy in general, or the definition of a voting system for a particular election, for example, would probably be considered to be of a political nature. These are issues where the very practicability of solutions poses a problem. As a realist, the FDD only wants to consider issues that are within human capabilities, i.e., that are likely to be resolved more or less immediately. Excluding issues of a political nature is therefore, not against the grain of the "democratic" exercise.

At least three other considerations can be highlighted to underscore the democratic importance of the FDD. Firstly, it is not subject to the usual limitations of formal judicial procedures. There are no "time limits for appeal", and the debates are not, far from it, conducted in purely legal terms, even though the presence of lawyers is envisaged in the composition of the FDD's bodies. The focus is on "cases of injustice", equity is present – perhaps even predominant - in the assessment of the facts in question. The FDD is therefore not a court of law, in the sense that it would be provided with reference standards of a legal nature. And while it does refer to an " interest to act", this is conceived in very open terms: not only can the interest be: individual, but it can also be collective. Popular action is therefore possible and involves the right of any person to submit a petition. Finally, the FDD is not simply a ceremonial parade, a festive and ceremonious display whose work is forgotten as soon as it is finished. In fact, it culminates in "recommendations ", the outcome of a consideration of the petitions, and which "are periodically monitored and evaluated" through meetings organised by the Permanent Secretariat, which comprises the bodies and individuals who took part in preparing towards the exercise. It should be added that the respondents, who were able to publicly discuss their concerns with the highest-ranking public officials on the day of the event, are informed of the action taken in response to their requests, and always have the option of resubmitting their grievances to the FDD.

This institution is undoubtedly a work of democracy, in the sense that for a moment it re-establishes "communication" between governor and governed, at a time when the alienation of political power is one of the indictments on democracy. It provides an organised forum for dialogue, whereas in some parts of the world such a "confrontation", institutionally impossible, is readily reduced to improvised, caricatured or even violent forms. One only needs look at scenes in countries with established democratic traditions where, out of a sense of despair or powerlessness, citizens resolve to impromptu appeals to passing government officials...

The FDD is also unique in the powerful symbols it carries. A symbol of tradition and modernity, of being true to oneself and caring for others. A national exercise in democracy, it is resolutely open to the international community, and to this end it adapts its symbols to those of the international community. Intended to provide concrete responses to individual or group concerns, it is nonetheless a point of democratic synchronicity, since it invites almost all those who hold or embody power to reflect and act, reviving the collective and deliberative dimension that is the very source and principle of democracy.

In the debate on the crisis of democracy, which we like to portray from every angle, we would undoubtedly benefit from rediscovering the two African practices of the national conference and the FDD. While some aspects of these two processes are open to criticism in some respects, and certainly capable of improvement, these two processes have nonetheless exuded a freshness that reveals, perhaps, if not that the disease is not incurable, at least that at some point in their history, African political societies have invented democratic forms that are definitely innovative and endowed, at least potentially, with a paradigmatic vocation, in the strongest sense of the term.

CHAPTER 10

THE RIGHT OF INTERVENTION OF THE AFRICAN UNION

We must then combine justice and might, and for this end make what is just strong, or what is strong just

Blaise Pascal, *Pensées.*

Under Article 4 (h) of the Constitutive Act of the African Union, adopted in 2000, the organisation has the right " to intervene in a Member State pursuant to a decision of the Assembly in respect of grave circumstances, namely: war crimes, genocide and crimes against humanity; "[352]. Everything in this statement is, of course, about what is meant by " intervene". But it very quickly became apparent that such " intervention" should be seen as a genuine replacement for a State found wanting, or even, if it is proven that the State is itself responsible for violations of the rights in question, a "punitive expedition" against it. In any case, this provision, which has no equivalent in the Constitutive Act of the Organisation of African Unity (OAU) – predecessor of the AU - constitutes a veritable subversion of the rules of international law in that it attacks the sovereignty of a State head-on, thereby breaking with the discreet circumlocutions of the breaches that may have been

[352] In 2003, as we shall see below, a Protocol amending the Constitutive Act of the AU was adopted, adding another instance of humanitarian intervention: that of: « restoring peace and stability » in a Member State.

opened in that sovereignty, under the vulgate of a "right to intervene" that was given its baptismal font in the 90s.

The option thus adopted by the pan-African organisation is certainly revolutionary. It is unusual in two respects. Firstly, from the point of view of general international law, the rule laid down in Article 4 h) of the Constitutive Act is somewhat dissident, or at least it should be noted that it does not reflect the state of international law today (I). From a point of view that is both more contemporary and more comparative, the African States are also distancing themselves from a United Nations Organisation that has been able, for almost three decades now, to push back the limits of State sovereignty. The UN has partly succeeded in this undermining by promoting a " right to intervene" now a " duty to protect" which, as we shall see, amounts to challenging the all-powerful State within its national borders (II).

I. A BREAK FROM THE CELEBRATION OF STATE SOVEREIGNTY

Behind its innocuous wording, the rule laid down by the Constitutive Act of the AU remains heretical. The organisation's right to intervene does indeed refer to military and coercive action. Faced with a risk or a reality of egregious crimes; war crimes, genocide, crimes against humanity, that trilogy which informs the repressive consensus of the international community, the AU must take the place of a State when the latter fails to put an end to the atrocities, or impose itself on it, when the state is responsible for such crimes.

The eminently political and coercive nature of such an operation result from two other factors. On the one hand, it is established that the exercise of such a power falls to the "supreme" and political body par excellence, the Conference of Heads of State and Government. On the other hand, the implementation of article 4 (h) requires the mobilisation of the Peace and Security Council, the secular arm of the organisation, whose founding protocol states that it shall "perform functions" in the areas of "peace support operations and interventions, in pursuant to article 4 h and j) of the Constitutive Act"[353]. It is also provided that " jointly with the President of the Commission, the PSC (...) approve the modalities of intervention of the Union in a Member State, following a decision of the Assembly, in accordance with article 4 j) of the constitutive act" of the AU [354]. Finally, it is the PSC which "recommends intervention where it believes that the conditions set out in article 4 are met"[355]. In short, the action envisaged by the pan-African organisation could deliberately disregard the will of the State. Such a radical approach is the antithesis of both classic rules of international law (A) and of those of regional organisations secreting legal orders that are particularly sensitive to the issue of collective intervention against a Member State. (B).

A. On General International Law

The "right to intervene" against a State has never really been looked on favourably in contemporary international law. A symbol of an unequal order, and as a marker of a world dominated by the imperialism of the superpowers, it is the perfect illustration of gunboat diplomacy the decline of which coincides withthe rise of the doctrine prohibiting the use of force in international relations. And indeed, the mention of a right to intervene in a historical context not only dominated by the subjugation of certain peoples but in which the use of force is not being restricted, arouses suspicion.

It was this right, the use of force, cloaked in the trappings of morality that Antoine Rougier was talking about when he justified

---

[353] Article 6 of the Durban Protocol on the Security Council of the AU adopted 9 July 2002.

[354] Article 7 of the Protocol Durban Protocol.

[355] Ibid.

it at the beginning of the twentieth century under the banner of " humanitarian intervention". He wrote that "the theory of humanitarian intervention is properly that which recognises as a right the exercise of international control by one State over the acts of internal sovereignty of another State that violate the "laws of humanity" and which claims to organise its operation legally. According to this doctrine, whenever the human rights of a people are disregarded by its rulers, one or more States may intervene on behalf of the League of Nations, either to demand the annulment of questionable acts of government, or to prevent the recurrence of such acts in the future, or to make up for the government's inaction by taking urgent precautionary measures, and temporarily substituting their sovereignty for that of the controlled State (…). The justification for intervention must be a violation of human rights and not simply a violation of substantive national law"[356] In the same vein, P. Guggenheim wrote in the 1950s that customary law confers on other States the right to put an end to the exclusive jurisdiction of the State which subjects its nationals to treatment below the minimum standard of the law of nations. In such a case, humanitarian intervention would be justified"[357].

Such opinions were very quickly challenged and criticised on the grounds that they failed to take account of the requirements of State sovereignty. The theory of humanitarian intervention was promptly discarded and the precedents cited in its defence were considered irrelevant, in the light of settled international law. The International Court of Justice repudiated this theory when it had the opportunity to do so, in the Corfu Channel case, decided in 1949. It did so in the following terms: The Court can only regard the alleged right of intervention as the manifestation of a policy of force, such as has, in the past, given rise to most serious abuses and

---

[356] Rougier A., « L'intervention d'humanité », *Revue générale de droit international public*, 1910.

[357] Guggenheim P., *Traité de droit international public*, Georg, 1953, p. 289.

such as cannot, whatever be the present defects in international organization, find a place in international law (...) Between independent States, respect for territorial sovereignty is an essential foundation of international relations"[358]

Not only does State sovereignty remain, to a large extent, the unassailable horizon of international law, but the guarantees of disinterest on the part of the intervening State or States are ignored by the theory of humanitarian intervention as we have just described it. It is not enough to be moved, even justifiably, by the intolerable fate that a State may inflict on its citizens; interference in the State's internal affairs must be perceived as a concern devoid of any political or strategic ulterior motive, or any hegemonic motive.

Things have undoubtedly changed in recent years and there have been breaches in the bastion of state sovereignty, as we shall see below. But in an international order that remains committed to the principles expressed by the ICJ in the terms outlined above, the right of intervention as codified within the AU cannot escape our notice. In view of the classic and still largely enshrined rules of international law, it is somewhat extraordinary for an international organisation to envisage, without embellishment or other diplomatic precautions repressing a State or taking its place when crimes are likely to be committed on a large scale. Admittedly, at the United Nations itself, this idea is readily whispered, but within a legal framework that is not as permissive as that of the pan-African organisation. Article 4 h) of the Constitutive Act of the AU puts the theory of humanitarian intervention back in the saddle, in a different guise from the one advocated by its proponents in past centuries, but from the same perspective, resolutely contrary to the absolute sovereignty of the State. From the point of view of the well-established dogmas of international law and its tradition, the option taken by the African states therefore constitutes a break with

---

[358] ICJ, *LR*, 1949, p. 35.

the past. It is also a break with the law of regional organisations, another place where the question of collective intervention against a member state has been addressed.

B. On Regional law

Article 4 h) is first and foremost a departure from the history of the pan-African organisation itself. Under the OAU, such a right of collective intervention was unthinkable. Admittedly, in 1963, it was not possible to foresee the legal developments in this area, and it is certainly not the international organisation's fault. But what needs to be emphasised is that the whole philosophy of the Addis Ababa Charter is the antithesis of interventionism. What emerges from this founding treaty of the OAU is a very rigorous conception of the sovereignty of States, and its corollary, the principle of non-interference in domestic affairs. The scholars are therefore right to emphasise that "the enshrinement of this right of intervention in the AU's legislative arsenal is certainly surprising, given the traditional philosophy of the pan-African organisation"[359].

Among the first three "Principles" that appear on the frontispiece of the OAU are rules that converge on the rejection of any external intervention. At no time is the possibility of such interference mentioned. In fact, Article III refers to the following principles:

> **1.** Sovereign equality of Member States.
>
> **2.** Non-interference in the domestic affairs of States.
>
> **3.** Respect for the sovereignty and territorial integrity of each State and its inalienable right to an independent existence (...).

---

[359] Soma Kabore V.E., « Le droit d'intervention de l'Union africaine », *Revue du CAMES*, 2017-1, p. 134.

Driven by the "temptation to exist", the new African states of the 1960s were keen to assert their independence and were not prepared to accept that their sovereignty should be called into question. In addition to the fact that intervention was not in vogue anywhere in the world, these new States were not psychologically inclined to make sacrifices in terms of sovereignty.

Things did not change fundamentally and immediately on this point. When, in particular, the OAU Member States set up a Mechanism for Conflict Prevention, Management and Resolution in 1993, a mechanism designed to respond to crises, there was no mention of collective intervention for humanitarian purposes, and the "fundamentals" of the pan-African organisation were not called into question. On the contrary, one needs only read the Statement of the Assembly of Heads of State and Government on the Mechanism. It states that: the Mechanism shall be based on the objectives and principles of the OAU Charter, in particular the sovereign equality of Member States, non-interference in the internal affairs of States, respect for the sovereignty and territorial integrity of Member States and their inalienable right to an independent existence (…)"[360]. It is true that the hypothesis of a conflict requiring "collective international intervention" is envisaged, but apart from the fact that it must be conducted under the banner of the United Nations, it should, according to the Statement itself, be conceived in the form of a "peace-keeping operation"[361].

A comparison with the Organisation of American States (OAS) leads to similar conclusions, i.e., the irreducibility of the AU's right of intervention to mechanisms existing in that international organisation. First, the same celebration of state sovereignty can be found there. Articles 15, 16 and 17 prove that the 1948 Bogotá

---

[360] Doc AGH/Decl.3 (XXIX), §14.

[361] Doc cited above, §15.

Charter, which established the organisation, was firmly intended to ward off the spectre of external interventionism, of which the American continent has regularly been the stage. It stipulates that "No State or group of States has the right to intervene, directly or indirectly, for any reason whatever, in the internal or external affairs of any other State. The foregoing principle prohibits not only armed force but also any other form of interference or attempted threat against the personality of the State or against its political, economic, and cultural elements"[362]. Moreover, « No State may use or encourage the use of coercive measures of an economic or political character in order to force the sovereign will of another State and obtain from it, advantages of any kind"[363]. Finally, it is specified that "The territory of a State is inviolable; it may not be the object, even temporarily, of military occupation or of other measures of force taken by another State, directly or indirectly, on any grounds whatever (…)"[364].

The phenomenon observed about the OAU can also be seen here. Over time, the OAS will be led to relax its doctrine on intervention, but very quickly, the organisation will return to a more "conventional" stance that is more in line with the spirit of the provisions just mentioned. The debates that took place within the Pan-American organisation revealed the extent to which States can insist that their sovereign prerogatives are never compromised, even in the case of humanitarian intervention. The Santiago Convention, adopted in June 1991 within the framework of the OAS, stipulated that member states should impose economic sanctions against any government that came to power through a coup d'état and endangered people's lives by exacting violence on them. A sort of "right to interfere in the interest of democracy" in

---

[362] Article 15 of the founding Charter of the OAS.

[363] Article 16 of the Bogota Charter.

[364] Article 17 of the Bogota Charter.

the words of the representative of Mexico. However, the meeting held in Managua in June 1993 put a stop to this emerging right to intervene, by enshrining a more traditional interpretation of the principle of non-interference. In short, the Pan-American organisation remained reluctant to enshrine a right of external intervention based on humanitarian considerations.

With regard to the European continent, apart from the fact that its integration has been marked by a kind of difficulty in gaining access to a military form, a prerequisite for humanitarian intervention as we understand it here, the "Common Foreign and Security Policy" (CFSP) that it has had difficulty constructing does not seem to make any room for an operation of the kind envisaged in Article 4 h) of the Constitutive Act of the AU. To be convinced of this, one need only look at Articles 42 et seq. of the Treaty on European Union, the "missions" envisaged under the "Common Security and Defence Policy" never clearly referring to the possibility of a coercive operation for humanitarian purposes.

All in all, it appears that the African version of the right of intervention has no real equivalent in other regional organisations. However, the original nature of the African approach to humanitarian intervention in its updated version is more apparent when compared with UN developments on the issue. In recent years, these have been marked by the development of the concept of the "responsibility to protect", which has replaced the controversial concept of the right or duty to intervene. A comparative reading of the two concepts of collective intervention reveals major differences between the UN and the AU. In other words, the AU's right to intervene is not only characterised by its departure from the rules of general international law, but also original in the light of recent challenges to the principle of sovereignty within the United Nations.

II. A SHIFT IN THE CONTEMPORARY CHALLENGES TO STATE SOVEREIGNTY

Two levels of divergence can be noted when attempting to compare the AU's right to intervene and the responsibility to protect conceived by the United Nations. On the one hand, it appears that the world body, while admitting that its intervention may clash with sovereignty, is much more cautious, much more respectful of the independence of the State. The African approach places much less emphasis on the principle of State sovereignty. On the question of what might be called the premise of sovereignty, the AU's right to intervene is peculiar, in a sense (A).

But there is something else. While the right to intervene could be seen as a moral breakthrough in international relations, reflecting what the ICJ terms fundamental considerations of humanity, the perpetration of crimes in the cold, formal world of states is a requirement of universal conscience - the fact remains that it is in the UN, rather than the African context, that this right to intervene is still heavily fraught with « Realpolitik ». In other words, the moralising podium on which it stands is undermined by the need to consider the interests of all sides, i.e. the major powers, who wield the real power within the organisation. Such political servitude, characterised by the practice of the responsibility to protect does not exist in the AU. This is not because states do not have special interests to safeguard, as they do at the United Nations, but simply because the structure of power within the African organisation and the way in which the right to intervene is handled are not such that they are immediately and clearly contingent on the interests and alliances of states. This fact is also evident in the various recent attempts within the UN to 'decouple' the implementation of the responsibility to protect from the discretionary use of the power of prevention available to the major powers through the 'right of veto' (B).

A. Sovereignty and its Presuppositions

The International Commission on Intervention and State Sovereignty (ICISS) introduced the responsibility to protect in a report published in December 2001. The 2005 World Summit endorsed the concept, incorporating it into its Outcome Document. The aim is to affirm the right of the international community - the UN - to ensure the protection of populations that are victims of mass crimes that may be classified as crimes against humanity, war crimes, genocide, and ethnic cleansing. It is then up to the Security Council, acting under Chapter VII of the Charter, to implement this collective responsibility.

However, one fundamental principle must be borne in mind, and it governs the implementation of such an extraordinary jurisdiction. This is the subsidiary nature of international protection, whereby the primary responsibility to protect lies with the State concerned. This is what is referred to here as the presupposition of sovereignty. As a tribute to this sovereignty, it is regularly pointed out that it is in principle the responsibility of the State, and not the United Nations, to protect the population from crimes that may be committed. The report of the International Commission on Intervention and Sovereignty underscores this point:

> The Commission believes that responsibility to protect resides first and foremost with the state whose people are directly affected. This fact reflects not only international law and the modern state system, but also the practical realities of who is best placed to make a positive difference. [365].

---

[365] International Commission on Intervention and State Sovereignty, *The Responsibility to Protect,* December 2001, p. 8.

It is hardly surprising, then, that the report describes UN action as subsidiary or even residual.[366] Following the principle of subsidiarity of UN intervention, the report specifies that the decision to intervene should be considered « only in extreme cases »[367].

Better still, it seems that the responsibility to protect can be expressed in non-military actions, such as simple humanitarian assistance. The report is also precise on this point: « In extreme and exceptional cases, the responsibility to act may mean the need to take military action.[368] There is, therefore, a first limit to coercive action, or a first requirement for it, which is the seriousness of the danger. There is a second limit, which relates to its relevance or the probability of its success. In other words, the responsibility to protect can only take an armed form if it is likely to be successful. In addition to the objective conditions linked to the extreme nature of the situation is its strategic relevance and the assessment of the chances of success. It is important to understand that these conditions are cumulative. In other words, there may be circumstances, such as a rising tide of danger, that make a military intervention perfectly defensible, but it may not be carried out because its success is compromised. "Military action can only be justified if it has a reasonable chance of succeeding, i.e., putting an end to the atrocities or suffering that warranted the intervention. Military intervention is not justified if it does not effectively provide the desired protection, or if it leads to worse consequences than the consequences of inaction", the ICISS report further argues[369].

The balloon then somewhat deflates. This clarification of the responsibility to protect alters the militaristic prejudice, the idea

---

366 Ibid.

367 Report cited earlier, p. 35.

368 Ibid.

369 Report cited earlier, p.42

that this intervention, which is an infringement on state sovereignty, would invariably take the form of armed coercion. In so doing, the concept fulfils its calming function, which is why it has replaced the notion of the right or duty to interfere. It brings things back to their proper dimensions, so to speak. The responsibility to protect is not a monstrous transgression of state sovereignty. It is not condemned either to be exercised automatically or to take on a coercive and militaristic form. On the contrary, it could be achieved in more flexible, "softer", consensual, and circumscribed ways. The militant fervour that presided its birth would then be dampened, and the revolutionary mystique that engulfs it would be dealt a blow. If the responsibility to protect is to consist of a simple humanitarian assistance operation, as the report suggests, it must be admitted that it could fit perfectly into existing UN mechanisms, and does not then necessarily need to be presented in the guise of a novelty.

This unsuspected conservatism of the concept is not specific to it. This unsuspected "conservatism" of the concept is not specific to it. The idea that the primary responsibility for protecting populations lies with the State is not defended solely in the context of the responsibility to protect. It runs through the entire UN normative framework for humanitarian intervention in general. Two important resolutions in this regard were adopted by the General Assembly: resolution 43/131 (December 1988 () on humanitarian assistance to victims of natural disasters and similar emergencies, and resolution 45/100 (14 December 1990) with the same title. Both resolutions emphasise the need for the consent of the State concerned, and therefore the non-coercive nature of the operation. The first resolution reaffirms "the sovereignty, territorial integrity and national unity of States and (recognises) that each State has the primary responsibility for caring for victims of natural disasters and similar emergencies occurring on its territory"[370]. The second resolution, which establishes humanitarian corridors, similarly suggests that "States near areas affected by natural disasters and similar emergencies (...) to participate closely in *international cooperation efforts with the affected countries,* with a view to facilitating, as far as possible, the transit of humanitarian assistance".

UN humanitarian operations are therefore essentially assistance in the true sense of the word. They are carried out in a spirit of cooperation with the affected State and must therefore be devoid of any ulterior motive that runs counter to the prerogatives deriving from the sovereignty of States. Humanitarian assistance makes up for the shortcomings of the affected State. Seen from this angle, it is not so much interference as an adjunct, an act of cooperation rather than substitution. It is therefore only when the State is unable to provide the care of any kind required by the situation that the international community must act. Our two resolutions set out this principle of subsidiarity in identical terms. Each also "reaffirms the sovereignty of affected States and their primary role in the initiation, coordination and implementation of humanitarian assistance on their respective territories"[371].

To sum up: these highly prescriptive resolutions of the UN General Assembly refer to humanitarian assistance, and not to the responsibility to protect as such, as this concept would be defined years later, but there are some tangential points between the two, some intersections, to use the mathematical language of set theory. There are two such points of intersection. On the one hand, from a practical point of view, they can merge, as in the case where the responsibility to protect consists precisely in humanitarian assistance, a scenario envisaged by the 2001 report, as we saw

---

[370] § 2 of the la resolution.

[371] § 14 and 16, respectively.

earlier. Secondly and more importantly, from a theoretical point of view, these two forms of intervention are governed by a principle of subsidiarity, in that the competence of the State in question is always established in principle, and external intervention should therefore be systematically supplementary. This is what is referred to here as the premise of sovereignty.

This theoretical bias is a constant in UN doctrine. It is clearly applied when the Security Council implements the responsibility to protect in its resolution 1970 on the situation in Libya, adopted on 26 February 2011. After literally linking its approach to this concept, the Council stated that "the Libyan authorities have the responsibility to protect the Libyan people", and that it remained committed "to the sovereignty, independence, territorial integrity and national unity of the Libyan Arab Jamahiriya". Admittedly, the practical significance of these statements remains largely open to question, since the same resolution already commits to a punitive process, but the reminder of the State's primary responsibility is not neutral. It adds flesh to the sovereigntist principle.

It is on this precise point that the responsibility to protect differs somewhat from the AU's right to intervene. In the - admittedly very laconic - African formulation of the latter, subsidiarity plays a lesser role, and the principle of sovereignty is almost ignored. The coercive coloration is therefore more marked in the African approach. Scholars agree that in the minds of AU member states, intervention is not only not posed in terms of a subsidiary option but may well take place without the consent of the state. Hence, it is a somewhat heretical and truly revolutionary character in the international order. It has not escaped the scrutiny of authors who have studied this right to intervene that "the only way to justify such a provision in relation to international law is to assume that the member states of the organisation have initiated a process of transferring their sovereignty to the Union"[372]. It has also been noted that:

> Even if the consent of the State on whose territory the AU intervenes would give greater legitimacy to this intervention, it is not theoretically necessary (...). Making the AU's right to intervene subject to the prior consent of the Member State concerned would distort it and transform its exercise into a conventional peacekeeping operation. It would even neutralise the scope, purpose, and object of the right.[373].

But we must be clear, because the opposition that has just been highlighted must be put into perspective. The downside is that the implementation of the responsibility to protect can, as in the African system, undermine State sovereignty. From the 1990s to the 2000s, there was an evolution in UN law and doctrine. Whereas the resolutions adopted nearly thirty years ago emphasised the neutrality and consensual nature of humanitarian interventions - just think of peacekeeping operations, which have the same characteristics - the responsibility to protect marginally but deliberately opens a crack in State sovereignty. The 2001 report is replete with formulations that suggest that, as is the case with the AU's right to intervene, the responsibility to protect could ignore sovereignty and be imposed on the State. There is, therefore, a degree of convergence between the global system and the regional system.

Many extracts from the ICISS report attest to this. They show that the State may either be a perpetrator or a party to the crimes in question or may be a kind of objective accomplice by failing to put an end to them. It goes without saying that in such cases, the

---

[372] Caligiuri A., « Le droit d'intervention de l'Union africaine et l'interdiction de l'usage de la force en droit international », *Paper,* June 2004.

[373] Soma Kabore V.E., op cit., p.149.

responsibility to protect can only be invoked *against* the State, and not with it. The means that the operation is carried out when the "State in question is unable or *unwilling* to put an end to this danger *or is the very perpetrator*"[374]. The report goes on to state that "in the Commission's view, military intervention for humanitarian protection purposes is justified in two broad categories of circumstances, namely when there is a need to halt or avert considerable actual or anticipated loss of life, with or without genocidal intent, resulting either from the *deliberate action of the State,* or from its negligence or inability to act, or from a *failure for which it is responsible* (...)"[375]. Finally, the report is careful to specify that the type of intervention in question may refer to "the measures taken *against a State or its leaders, without their consent,* for purposes presented as humanitarian or protective"[376].

These assumptions of the involvement of the State for crimes committed on its soil brings the responsibility to protect close to the right of intervention applied in Africa. It must be said once again that the opposition is not absolute, and lines of convergence can be drawn.

Nonetheless, certain differences remain undeniable. By glossing over the issue of sovereignty and establishing the coercive nature of its intervention as a principle, the AU departs from the UN approach. We must therefore agree on the innovative scope of the African concept of collective intervention in the face of the risk of crimes being committed on a large scale.

At this stage, the originality or uniqueness of this concept can be highlighted in at least two respects. As we have seen, it has a long history. In terms of substantive law alone, the possibility of external intervention in the face of the likelihood of mass atrocities was

---

374 Report cited above, p.16. Italics mine.

375 Report cited above, p.37. Italics mine.

376 Report cited above, p.18. Italics mine.

legally enshrined in Africa in the year 2000, and did not acquire this dignity within the United Nations until 2005 – when it was included in the World Summit Outcome Document, if such a reception can be regarded as equivalent to legal consecration - and was not put into practice until six years later (2011 resolution on Libya). Secondly, and on the substance, if we may say so, the African approach is less cautious regarding sovereignty, it is less permeated by the sovereigntist principle and, as a result, is more satisfactory for the advocates of "moralising" international relations, a moralisation which would consist precisely in making intervention less dependent on the will of states and their coldly calculated interests.

There is, however, another aspect in which the AU's right of intervention stands out. This is the democratic added value it brings with its revision by the Protocol of 3 February 2003 amending the Constitutive Act of the AU. This amendment adds a few words to Article 4(h). It is no longer only international crimes that justify intervention. The restoration of legitimate authority can also lead the pan-African organisation to act. The provision now reads as follows:

> The right of the African Union, by decision of the Assembly, to intervene in a member state in certain serious circumstances, namely: war crimes, genocide and crimes against humanity, as well as a serious threat to law and order, with a view to restoring peace and stability in the member state of the Union, on the recommendation of the Peace and Security Council.

It is clear from this new wording that the AU's right to intervene will no longer be limited to the conspiracy to commit mass crimes but will extend to situations in which peace and stability in the Member State could be disrupted. It should be emphasised from the outset that this revision does seem to be aimed at the overthrow or attempted overthrow of an established government, and that such a subversive undertaking could be carried out at home or abroad. This reform inspires several reflections.

The first point to note is that it seems to mark a sort of retreat from the ethical concern that has been highlighted. Whereas in the initial version of the text it was only crimes that shocked the conscience of humanity that were targeted, now the restoration of the authority of the State, a kind of shoddy legitimism, has been added to the list of justifications for intervention. Such a case of openness exudes a conservative flavour, marking a kind of more forceful return of the political factor in an organisation in which the Conference of Heads of State, the decision-making body, has been described as a "club" of persons with common interests, "sticking as thick as thieves" for mutual protection. The 2003 revision could thus be seen as symbolising the revenge of Realpolitik and State cynicism. If this were the case, the thesis developed in these lines would have to be strongly put into perspective, and the African distinctiveness, in relation to the UN's responsibility to protect in particular, would have to be tempered.

There are, however, two points to be made in the debate, which suggest that the politicisation of the right to intervene should not be taken for granted. On the one hand, such political abuse of the right to intervene has yet to be established, and there is no precedent for it. We will therefore have to wait and see how the new Article 4 (h) is used. On the other hand, the introduction of the new requirement of restoring peace and stability is not necessarily contrary to an intervention based solely on humanitarian grounds. In other words, the risk of crimes being committed can be part of a context of subversion of a state and its institutions, making it necessary to restore social peace and stability. Experience even shows that such a "cocktail" is common, because when a criminal scheme takes on certain dimensions and is carried out on a certain scale, it is often made possible by an absence of authority and a certain failure of institutions. Under such conditions, the 2003 revision could simply be a clarification of the context of the AU's intervention, and not the denial of a humanist philosophy. It would reflect a certain continuity, not discontinuity. In any case, all these questions will be answered in the future.

However, the revision of Article 4 h) widens the gap of difference, so to speak, with the responsibility to protect. The latter clearly excludes the situation covered by the 2003 revision. The ICISS set out its views on this issue in its report: it has, according to the report, "resisted the temptation to consider as grounds for military intervention human rights violations which, albeit serious, do not amount to outright murder or ethnic cleansing (...). The Commission adopted a similar position regarding situations where a population that has clearly voted in favour of a democratic regime is deprived of its democratic rights by a military coup d'état "[377].

By limiting the responsibility to protect to cases of harm to human life and collective distress, to breaches of the law of a vital nature, the UN is clearly demonstrating realism: it is easier to justify an intervention by the existence of a risk to life than by a – "simple", one would say, breakdown in a democratic process, human life being worth more than the absence of democracy. On the contrary, by including this as one of the reasons for its intervention, the AU is demonstrating a certain audacity, but runs the risk of being accused of a form of unrealism and of making a mockery of the sovereignty of States, of being accused of having gone too far. It is true that there has been at least one case on the African continent where external intervention re-established a legitimate government that had been ousted; the ECOWAS intervention force, ECOMOG,deployed in Sierra Leone in 1996, in the context of an unconstitutional change of government. But two caveats must be issued about the AU's right to intervene. Firstly, it was not a continental but a sub-regional initiative, within a legal and

---

[377] Report cited above, pp.38-39.

operational framework which the AU does not yet have, and the label of intervention was that of a peace-keeping operation, which turned into a coercive operation. It was not a formally binding intervention as is the case with the intervention referred to in Article 4h).

There is another point on which the right to intervene and the responsibility to protect differ. To date, the AU mechanism has not really worked and has never been tested, which has of course insulated it from political manipulation. There is no guarantee that such a "virginity", capable of sustaining the ideal of the moralisation of international law, will survive the test of its implementation, but the fact is that it exists. On the other hand, experiments or attempts to experiment with the responsibility to protect have exposed the political conditioning of this principle, to the extent that many attempts to depoliticise it have been made within the United Nations.

B. On the Attempt to Moralise the Practice of Protection

The responsibility to protect, an attempt to moralise international life and a manifestation of a form of community of international values, is struggling, in practice, to free itself from the shackles of the political and strategic interests of States, particularly the major powers within the UN Security Council. The imperative of protection responds to a moral imperative, but its application is not the same. It clearly comes up against the forces of alliance and power. In short, the practice of the international community tends to demystify the new institution, reminding us of the permanence of State logic and power play.

The resurgence of Realpolitik has not really affected the AU's right to intervene, but it could of course put a strain on it. The fact is, however, that it has hampered the implementation of the responsibility to protect. If only provisionally, it must therefore be noted that the definite infection of the right to protect by political considerations distinguishes it to date from the AU's right to intervene, which still retains the virginity of institutions that have not yet been tested. Of course, a word will be said about the challenges to which the African option will have to respond, but for the moment it suffices to point out that the political resistance observed within the UN is so serious and somewhat discouraging that it has given rise to reform proposals aimed precisely at circumventing it.

In concrete terms, this desire to spare the responsibility to protect from any political conditioning has resulted in a restriction on the right of veto of the five permanent members of the Council. Several initiatives of this type can be mentioned here.

The first is the report of the International Commission on Intervention and State Sovereignty. Suspecting that an institution as revolutionary as the responsibility to protect could not easily be implemented, the document's drafters made the following recommendation on the appropriate authority to authorise military intervention:

> The five permanent members of the Security Council should agree to waive their right to veto decisions in which their vital interests are not at stake, so as not to obstruct the adoption of resolutions authorising military intervention to ensure human protection, which would otherwise receive many votes.[378].

The second is a group initiative. It was formulated in the "Code of Conduct regarding the Security Council action against genocide, crimes against humanity, and war crimes", proposed on 24 September 2015 by twenty-five States meeting within the "Accountability, Coherence and Transparency" group. Point 1 of this draft reform reads as follows: the States " pledge to support

---

378 Report cited above, p.4.

timely and decisive action by the Security Council aimed at ending the commission of genocide, crimes against humanity or war crimes". Point 2 states that the permanent members of the Security Council "Pledge to not vote against a credible draft resolution submitted to a vote of the Security Council on timely and decisive action to halt or prevent the commission of genocide, crimes against humanity or war crimes".

At the seventieth session of the UN General Assembly itself, a "Political Declaration on the suspension of veto powers in the event of mass atrocities "was drafted. Presented by France and Mexico and open for signature by UN member states, this draft declaration states that "situations of mass atrocities, where genocide, crimes against humanity or war crimes are committed on a large scale, are of such a nature as to constitute a threat to international peace and security and require action by the international community (...). Consequently, the Security Council should not be prevented, by a veto, from acting to prevent or put an end to situations involving mass atrocities. We emphasise that the veto is not a privilege but an international responsibility."[379]

Finally, a permanent member of the Council, France, has consistently defended the idea of freezing the veto power in the event of the commission or risk of commission of international crimes. As we have already seen, France, together with Mexico, drew up the afore-mentioned Political Declaration. When it was open for signature, this initiative received the support of one hundred and five Member States in 2020. At the same session of the General Assembly, President François Hollande declared that " France wants the permanent members of the Security Council to no longer be able to exercise their veto in the event of mass atrocities... I pledge here that France will never use its veto when there are mass atrocities". The reform initiated by France would

[379] Political declaration on the suspension..., directly accessible on the Internet.

give the UN Secretary-General an important role, in line with Article 99 of the Charter, which gives him the right to draw the attention of the Security Council to any situation that may threaten international peace and security. The alert could also be triggered by a proposal from the Office of the High Commissioner for Human Rights or even a Member State[380].

The relatively high number of proposals to reform the Security Council's action in cases involving the responsibility to protect shows that this is still largely dependent on political considerations. This was cruelly illustrated once again by the handling of the Syrian issue. Faced with the worsening civil war following the challenge to Bashar Al Assad's regime, the United Nations was condemned to impotence precisely because of the opposition of the Council's permanent member states that are allies of Syria. There is no doubt that the objective conditions for implementing the responsibility to protect had been met, but the United Nations got bogged down in petty political considerations, far removed from the ethics of international relations that the responsibility to protect seems to recommend.

This stalemate shows the limits of the UN's right to intervene, even without the consent of the State, in a context where large-scale crimes are being committed. This politicisation of the responsibility to protect, as we have said, is not yet as clear-cut as it is for the AU's right to intervene. It is, of course, too early to say, but it can be said that because of the way it is implemented, the AU's right to intervene does not leave room for *institutionalisation* of the defence of special interests, as the power structure of the UN allows. If only from this very cautious but by no means naïve viewpoint, it is possible to assert that the right to intervene holds some uniqueness

---

[380] On the French proposal, see Pomes E., « Les projets d'abandon du droit de véto : les réalistes contre les idéalistes », https://hal.archives-ouvertes.fr/hal-02895176 submitted on 2 June 2021, as well as the site of the French Foreign Ministry, France diplomatie, « Politique étrangère de la France. La France et les Nations Unies ».

and that as such, deserves a place amongst the African legal singularities.

In short, the AU's right to intervene would not only be revolutionary in terms of the established principles of international law. From the point of view of the more recent movement to question State sovereignty in the face of the risk of mass crimes, a movement that can be observed particularly within the UN, the African originality remains. It remains, both from a theoretical point of view and from a practical perspective.

In theory, the African approach to intervention is less won over, less obsessed by the sovereigntist presupposition. The language precautions, the mantra of sovereignty in principle and the iterative reminder of the conditional nature of external intervention, all modest contortions that go to make up the responsibility to protect, do not exist at the AU.

In practice, simply because its implementation, or its implementation procedure, is not necessarily conducive to highlighting the clash of interests and the deadlocks arising from it, the AU's right of intervention seems less dependent on political considerations. So as not to be accused of romanticism, one may say that the AU system «veils» the bitterness of political opposition more than the UN system. In this way, its "ethical" dimension is more apparent than that of the responsibility to protect, which is still subject to political strictures.

Finally, it should be added that on this question of intervention for humanitarian reasons, the African system could claim a slight, very slight, precedence over that of the UN. If we look solely at substantive law, it is the Constitutive Act of the AU, adopted in 2000, which enshrines the AU's right to intervene, whereas the responsibility to protect, formulated in theory in 2001 and, "accepted" in 2005 in the Final Document of the 2005 Global Summit, was not applied in practice by the Security Council until 2011, with Resolution 1970 on the situation in Libya.

The AU's right to intervene deserves to be studied because its features are quite original in the current state of international law. It goes without saying, as we have seen, that the choice made by the African states is not the simplest one. The daunting challenges posed by such a bold approach are borne out by the very experience of AU interventions, and it is revealing that to date this provision has never been fully implemented. The pan-African organisation's military operations are more akin to peace-keeping operations, possibly with a coercive dimension. This just goes to show that the task is harder than expected. On the international landscape, there are institutions that are overtaken by the reality principle. Think of the initial version of the rule of universal jurisdiction, as originally devised by States such as Belgium and Spain. These countries quickly had to make realistic adjustments, given the impracticality of their original arrangements. Will this be the case for the AU's right of intervention? Only time will tell. But for the time being, Article 4 (h) of the Constitutive Act of the African organisation deserves attention for at least two reasons. The first is that it represents a breakthrough that it would not be an exaggeration to describe as unprecedented in international law, on account of the offence committed against state sovereignty. The second, subject to the observations made earlier, is that it reconciles law and, dare we say, morality, justice, and force, as has been dreamt of since, perhaps, the very origins of international law. It is a fact that this right has never been exercised, a fact that could be laughed at by diehard realists and the harshest critics of international law, but its status as a substantive norm cannot be disputed, and its accession to the legal world is not insignificant, given how difficult it can be to establish norms in an order where the clash of interests is so fierce.

Structures éditoriales du groupe L'Harmattan

L'Harmattan Italie
Via degli Artisti, 15
10124 Torino
harmattan.italia@gmail.com

L'Harmattan Hongrie
Kossuth l. u. 14-16.
1053 Budapest
harmattan@harmattan.hu

L'Harmattan Sénégal
10 VDN en face Mermoz
BP 45034 Dakar-Fann
senharmattan@gmail.com

L'Harmattan Cameroun
TSINGA/FECAFOOT
BP 11486 Yaoundé
inkoukam@gmail.com

L'Harmattan Burkina Faso
Achille Somé – tengnule@hotmail.fr

L'Harmattan Guinée
Almamya, rue KA 028 OKB Agency
BP 3470 Conakry
harmattanguinee@yahoo.fr

L'Harmattan RDC
185, avenue Nyangwe
Commune de Lingwala – Kinshasa
matangilamusadila@yahoo.fr

L'Harmattan Congo
67, boulevard Denis-Sassou-N'Guesso
BP 2874 Brazzaville
harmattan.congo@yahoo.fr

L'Harmattan Mali
ACI 2000 - Immeuble Mgr Jean Marie Cisse
Bureau 10
BP 145 Bamako-Mali
mali@harmattan.fr

L'Harmattan Togo
Djidjole – Lomé
Maison Amela
face EPP BATOME
ddamela@aol.com

L'Harmattan Côte d'Ivoire
Résidence Karl – Cité des Arts
Abidjan-Cocody
03 BP 1588 Abidjan
espace_harmattan.ci@hotmail.fr

Nos librairies en France

Librairie internationale
16, rue des Écoles
75005 Paris
librairie.internationale@harmattan.fr
01 40 46 79 11
www.librairieharmattan.com

Librairie des savoirs
21, rue des Écoles
75005 Paris
librairie.sh@harmattan.fr
01 46 34 13 71
www.librairieharmattansh.com

Librairie Le Lucernaire
53, rue Notre-Dame-des-Champs
75006 Paris
librairie@lucernaire.fr
01 42 22 67 13

www.ingramcontent.com/pod-product-compliance
Lightning Source LLC
LaVergne TN
LVHW011459061026
849535LV00004BA/1144
* 9 7 8 2 3 3 6 5 0 3 8 8 2 *